Graphics Programming with Perl

T0130694

Graphics
Programming
with Perl

MARTIEN VERBRUGGEN

MANNING

Greenwich
(74° w. long.)

For online information and ordering of this and other Manning books, go to www.manning.com. The publisher offers discounts on this book when ordered in quantity. For more information, please contact:

Special Sales Department
Manning Publications Co.
209 Bruce Park Avenue   Fax: (203) 661-9018
Greenwich, CT 06830   email: orders@manning.com

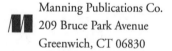

Manning Publications Co.   Copyeditor: Sharon Mullins
209 Bruce Park Avenue   Typesetter: Syd Brown
Greenwich, CT 06830   Cover designer: Leslie Haimes

ISBN 1-930110-02-2

Printed in the United States of America

To Margaret, because she thought that "Advanced RenderMan"
should be the name of a Super Hero

To Maxine, for being excited about appearing in this book

contents

preface

Welcome to *Graphics Programming with Perl*. When Manning Publications contacted me to assess my interest in writing a book about graphics programming for the Perl language, I was a bit skeptical at first. I didn't think there would be enough coherent material to write such a book, and I wasn't entirely certain there would be much room for one.

However, after doing some research I noticed that, in fact, there was a gap in the published material. The only book I could find that combined graphics programming and Perl was too general, and was largely a collection of recipes on how to use tools, many of which had no relation to Perl [1]. There were not enough references that described and explained how to achieve concrete graphics tasks in Perl.

So I accepted the challenge and started working, with the goal of providing a book that would sum up the ways to work with graphics from within Perl, and to offer sufficient background information to improve the understanding of graphics programming and graphics in general. This work seeks to provide a programmer with enough fundamental knowledge and pointers to achieve the most common graphics programming tasks. I hope those goals have been realized.

ABOUT THIS BOOK

The objective of the book is to show how graphical programming projects may be accomplished.

When commencing work on a program, you have probably formulated an idea of your goal, but you might not necessarily know how to reach it. In most cases all that is needed is a pointer to the right modules, tools, commands or techniques. This book aims at providing this sort of reference for graphics manipulation using the Perl programming language.

The content includes a wide range of topics related to manipulation and production of graphics with Perl, including the creation, editing and combining of images, the development of libraries, interfaces and modules for graphics creation, massaging of text for graphics, the building of charts, as well as working with single pixels in images. This book is not meant as a reference work for the modules available for graphics programming.[1] For that you are encouraged to read the documentation that comes with the modules, which in most cases is satisfactory. This book is also not intended to be an exhaustive introduction to graphics in general, or a detailed explanation of graphics algorithms, although where appropriate, some graphics theory and algorithm description will be touched on.

The reader is expected to have a basic knowledge of Perl. The programs and code fragments will be explained in terms of what they do and how they operate, and only occasionally in terms of what the Perl statements mean. The documentation that comes with Perl and the Camel [2] does a much better job of accurately describing Perl, and other books [3],[4] provide a useful introduction to programming with Perl. Where necessary, general programming techniques and their implementation in Perl will be explained when this is pertinent to graphics programming (as in chapter 10, "Writing your own graphics modules").

There are many tasks you can accomplish with graphics, and there is a plethora of questions you might ask when confronted with a graphics programming job. When thinking about how this book should be arranged, several highly structured possibilities for organizing the content sprang to mind. However, trying to fit various bits and pieces into this organization turned out to be not that simple. Many tasks in graphics programming defy neat categorization.

For that reason you might find that, even though the book is divided into chapters, some of the sections in those chapters might also apply to other chapters. The book is structured such that it may be read from beginning to end, but it is also arranged to facilitate access to specific information relevant to the actual tasks in which you are engaged.

WHO SHOULD READ THIS BOOK?

If you're a programmer who has done some work with Perl, but has almost never worked with graphics, this is the book for you. If you have worked with graphics, but want to have a look around to see what else is available in this area, this is the place to look. If you're just curious about what is available in graphics manipulation for Perl, you should be able to find it here.

If you're a programmer who has been only marginally exposed to Perl, and you need to dive into graphics programming and Perl at the same time, this book could be a fit for you, but I'd advise first learning the Perl language (see reference list [3],[4]). If you plan to learn Perl from this book, you will be disappointed.

This book concentrates mainly on how to accomplish tasks with the tools available, and within the boundaries of the Perl programming language. Since those boundaries are fairly flexible, this includes the use of a large number of modules, some of which work with external programs, some implement algorithms, others involve

---

[1] There is one exception to this: the *Image::Magick* module is used extensively in the book, but lacks well developed documentation of its own, so a reference is included in appendix A.

web work, and many other bits and pieces. If you want to know how to use the graphics modules available for Perl to write your programs, read this book. If you want to know for which graphics programming tasks Perl is suited, and for which ones it is less so, read this book. If you want some minimal introduction to graphics theory—just enough to get you to work—read this book. If you are looking for a reference for *Image::Magick* you will find this book useful. If you need to know how to generally combine graphics and HTML in your CGI applications, read this book. If you find yourself repeatedly doing the same graphics tasks in an interactive program, read this book.

On the other hand, if you are seeking a book that teaches you to build graphical user interfaces, this isn't it: there is no PerlTk discussion in this book. The programs presented all use a command-line interface, if they accept input at all.

If you want to learn about graphics theory and computer graphics algorithms, you will find some rudimentary introductions in this book, but a more elaborate discussion of these issues is available elsewhere.

CODING PRACTICES

The code in this book has been written to be as portable as possible between the different operating systems on which Perl runs. You might find a slight bias toward Unix[2] operating systems, since that is what I work on most of the time. Pathnames are always separated by a slash (/), which works on Unix and Microsoft-based operating systems, but not, for example, on older operating systems for the Macintosh. If you are on a system that doesn't support the slash as a directory separator, you might need to do some work before the example code will run for you. Really portable code of course uses *File::Spec*, but, for the sake of clarity I decided not to do that.

When writing code to create graphical output, which is often binary data, it is imperative to remember the use of `binmode()` on the file handles that are used to read and write image files. Failing to do this commonly leads to the creation of bugs that are difficult to track on platforms in which there is a distinction between text and binary files. On platforms where there is no such distinction, using `binmode()` has no effect; however, that is no excuse to leave it out. Portable code always calls `binmode()` on a file handle that is to be used for binary data. Apart from portability issues, using `binmode()`, even when you know it has no effect, is a good way to document that the data stream is of a binary nature.

Coding standards are always up for debate, and mine are not always consistent with the guidelines from the `perlstyle` documentation, although they come very close. I'll highlight some points that regularly crop up as a subject of disagreement, and some that I find important.

---

[2] ... and BSD and Linux and others. When I refer to Unix, I mean all Unix-like operating systems, not just the ones licensed by X/Open.

- In accordance with `perlstyle`, code should run under `-w`. The strict pragma is also a very good idea in programs and modules. Both help prevent a large number of otherwise hard-to-find bugs.

- Code blocks are indented in the BSD style: the start and end of a block have the curly brackets on a line of their own, both lined up with the keyword that starts the block. Many people, including Larry Wall, prefer to have the opening curly bracket on the same line as the keyword, but I find that style too cluttered and difficult to read. This is purely a matter of preference.

- Indenting code by one or two spaces is not clear enough. Three is not a power of two so it cannot be used. Using a full tab stop of eight spaces to indent code is just wasteful. The logical conclusion is that four spaces should be used to indent code.

- Operators have whitespace on both sides.

- Variable names are in all lowercase, with underscores to separate words. File handles are in all capitals.

- Whenever appropriate, I break these rules.

These points are valid for the complete listings, but might not be applicable to the short code fragments in the text. Sometimes clarity is more important than correctness, and fragments are just that: little parts of a larger whole.

The code in this book has been written for, and tested on, Perl 5.6.1 on a Linux system. Most of the code will probably work fine under Perl 5.005, and some might even work under 5.004, but there are no guarantees. Constructions that would stop code from working on Perl 5.005 have been avoided as much as possible, but might still have crept in here or there.

SOURCE CODE DOWNLOADS

The source code and the color versions of the figures presented in this book, as well as the inevitable list of errata, are available from the book's web page at www.manning.com/verbruggen.

author online

Purchase of *Graphics Programming with Perl* includes free access to a private web forum run by Manning Publications where you can make comments about the book, ask technical questions, and receive help from the author and from other users. To access the forum and subscribe to it, point your web browser to www.manning.com/verbruggen. This page provides information on how to get on the forum once you are registered, what kind of help is available, and the rules of conduct on the forum.

Manning's commitment to our readers is to provide a venue where a meaningful dialog between individual readers and between readers and the author can take place. It is not a commitment to any specific amount of participation on the part of the author, whose contribution to the AO remains voluntary (and unpaid). We suggest you try asking the author some challenging questions lest his interest stray!

The Author Online forum and the archives of previous discussions will be accessible from the publisher's web site as long as the book is in print.

acknowledgments

Thanks to Maxine, my daughter, for modeling for photographs that could be used for this book, and to my wife for being patient with me.

Thanks to Larry Wall for creating Perl, and to all the developers (you know who you are) who spent so much of their time working on the Perl language and distribution. Thanks to all the hackers and developers who have created the software used in this book, and made it available to the larger community of programmers.

The image map in the PGPLOT example (figure 5.9 on page 84) is based on data from an image of the M51 system, obtained by Dr. Patrick Seitner from the University of Michigan, who has graciously allowed me to use it.

The original of the image of the watch in figure 8.3 on page 150 was obtained from an excellent resource of free images at http://www.freeimages.co.uk/.

The images in section 9.2, "RenderMan," on page 164 were rendered with the Blue Moon Rendering Tools (BMRT), provided by Larry Gritz and Exluna Incorporated.

The Google search engine at http://www.google.com has been a tremendously useful and amazingly accurate tool in the research for this book.

Many thanks to Ron Savage for a thorough technical review of the final manuscript, and to John Cristy for taking time to look specifically at the ImageMagick parts, and to revert some of the changes that were made to the API to fit better with the code in this book. Special thanks to the many reviewers who took time out of their busy schedules to read the manuscript in its various stages of development and offer their suggestions for improvement. They are Bob Friesenhahn, Craig Berry, Dave Zempel, Greg London, Jonathan Stowe, Kai Jendrian, Matthias Neeracher, Phillip Whettlock, Rudi Farkas, and Theo Petersen.

And finally, many thanks to the people at Manning Publications for giving me a chance to write this book, and for being incredibly patient while I tried to balance my life and job with getting this text in an acceptable state. The people that have helped me most by prodding me regularly and providing invaluable advice are Marjan Bace, Syd Brown, Ted Kennedy, Mary Piergies, and Lianna Wlasiuk.

about the cover illustration

The figure on the cover of *Graphics Programming with Perl* is from a Spanish compendium of regional dress customs first published in Madrid in 1799. In the book, the figure is identified with two words: "Cartara Klamuka." Translating these words took us farther afield than usual. No Spanish dictionary and none of our usual sources were able to recognize, let alone define, either of them. We were even unsure which word represented the noun and which was the descriptor.

Searching on Google for the word Cartara led to dead ends, with links to real estate offerings in Porta Cartara in Italy or to the mythical city of Cartara in a role-playing game—definitely not what we needed.

After a few unsatisfactory tries with Klamuka and Klamuk, Google finally asked us, "Could you mean Kalmuk?" In languages whose orthography has not yet been formalized, such permutations are common. We immediately knew we were on the right track. Following the links, we learned that Kalmuk was a region in today's Russia near Mongolia. Kalmuk is also the name of its people. It comes from the Turkish word Kalmak, which in turn means "the people who stayed behind." Now our confidence rose: other figures clustered in the same part of the compendium were from the same general geographical region, with one pair identified as Cartara Mongolesa (female) and Cartaro Mongoles (male). So we at least knew with some assurance the origin and the gender of the figure.

But the word Cartara remained a mystery and still does as the book goes to press. That there are a number of other figures in the Spanish compendium with similar identifiers, for example, Cartara Eunguta or Cartaro Bukariano, indicates to us that this was a common Spanish word at the time—another reminder of how much the world has changed. Words that were understandable only 200 years ago have disappeared both from the spoken language and from contemporary dictionaries. (The closest word we could find is "cartero" which means postman, but this is clearly off the track.) We would welcome any suggestions from our readers. Please post them on the Author Online forum for this book.

The Spanish compendium's title page states:

Coleccion general de los Trages que usan actualmente todas las Nacio-nas del Mundo desubierto, dibujados y grabados con la mayor exacti-tud por R.M.V.A.R. Obra muy util y en special para los que tienen la del viajero universal

which we translate, as literally as possible, thus:

General collection of costumes currently used in the nations of the known world, designed and printed with great exactitude by R.M.V.A.R This work is very useful especially for those who hold themselves to be universal travelers

Although nothing is known of the designers, engravers, and workers who colored this illustration by hand, the "exactitude" of their execution is evident in this draw-ing. The "Cartara Klamuka" is just one of many figures in this colorful collection. Their diversity speaks vividly of the uniqueness and individuality of the world's towns and regions just 200 years ago. This was a time when the dress codes of two regions separated by a few dozen miles identified people uniquely as belonging to one or the other.

We at Manning celebrate the inventiveness, the initiative and the fun of the com-puter business with book covers based on the rich diversity of regional life of two cen-turies ago brought back to life by the pictures from this collection.

PART 1

Foundations

Part 1 contains a basic discussion of the foundations on which rest the other chapters in this book. It is not an exhaustive discussion of everything there is to know about Perl and graphics programming in general, because there is not enough room for that, but it provides the necessary background information and references you need to follow the discussions and examples in the book.

Chapter 1 discusses concepts in graphics programming in general terms and places them in a Perl context.

Chapter 2 contains information on the various storage formats for graphics, how to deal with them, and which ones are appropriate for which tasks.

In chapter 3 we'll look at which tools and modules are used in the book, and where they are used.

Overview of graphics

With the introduction of the Web, the sheer volume of graphics being manipulated has increased enormously. Even without the Web the amount of image processing would have grown, simply due to the fact that computers are faster than they used to be and have more memory, which makes dealing with graphics more feasible. The advent of digital cameras and affordable frame capture hardware have also contributed to the increase in graphics manipulation. There are more and more photos and stills from videos to manipulate, scale, and index every single day.

Because computers have become more powerful, there are also more applications that create graphical output. This in turn has increased the expectancy that *your* application creates graphical output—either interactively, possibly through a graphical user interface, or noninteractively, as files or database records. Charts and graphs are created to visualize everything ranging from business throughput, stock prices, temperature fluctuations, population densities, and web site visits, to the average life expectancy of female fruit flies during the wet season on Bali, all in their subspecies incarnations.

Apart from increasing the amount of graphics needed as buttons and embellishments for web sites, the Web has had a major influence in areas of images created on the fly and mass manipulation of large sets of graphics files. Just think of all the images out there that are resized, optimized, dithered, thumbnailed and cropped for display as part of a web site—for example as a list of available stock items. Then there are the images that are created on the fly as the result of user input; for example, charts or parts of maps or street directories. No one of course knows the exact numbers, but they are vast.

Together with the outpouring of images processed, there has been an increase in the number of software packages and modules that make their creation and manipulation possible, as well as a boom in the development rate of packages that already existed before the web came along. This proliferation of tools can make it difficult to pick the right one for the job at hand, especially since some of the tools overlap in application areas. Sometimes there is no tool available that will satisfy all the requirements of the task, and you have to write your own. Even when you do write your own tools, you need to choose, or rather, can choose, between several libraries and modules available. Which library you decide to use depends, of course, on your needs and on your familiarity with the products.

Not all graphics tasks lend themselves to automation. There are, and always will be, many that can only be achieved by sitting down at the screen of a computer, firing up your favorite drawing or graphics manipulation program, and interactively using your eyes and mouse skills to achieve the desired effect. Writing code for graphics manipulation can be quite time-consuming, and you need to take that into account when making a decision about whether you want to automate a certain task or process.

Programs that manipulate or create graphics are in many ways similar to programs for other tasks. There are, however, aspects which apply to, or which are particularly relevant to, graphics programming specifically. In this chapter we will have a look at the various elements of graphics programming that are important to programmers.

1.1 PERL AND GRAPHICS

One caveat that should be understood about Perl is that it is not a language particularly suited to large amounts of number crunching, and image manipulation requires large amounts of number crunching. So why does this book exist?

Perl is a glue language, which is one of the reasons why it is often described as the duct tape of the Internet.[1] Perl is good at snipping and gluing pieces of data, particularly text, and sticking tools and libraries together. What's more, it allows you to do all this with ease and a minimum of development time. And this is why Perl can be very useful for graphics programming.

Because of Perl's gluing ability, there are several interfaces to graphics manipulation libraries and programs available in the form of modules. Other packages have been written that make use of these modules to create graphics at a higher level, for example to create charts. Together, the number of these tools has grown sufficiently to allow the tackling of many graphics programming tasks in Perl.

---

[1] This is generally attributed to Hassan Schroeder, Sun's first webmaster.

Apart from the reasons just mentioned, Perl is also an attractive language with which to program, because of its flexible grammar, the large number of built-in tools and the variety of syntactical constructions. Perl can be used as a tool to quickly hack together a program that parses sets of log files, and gives some nice summaries and graphs with which to create a report. It can also be used to write large software projects, maintained by several programmers and developed over the course of a year or more. Perl is duct tape, but it is very flexible duct tape.

As a side note to the number crunching: Moore's law states that every two years the average speed of electronic computers doubles. Even if you generalize that to all computing, as Ray Kurzweil does in *The Age of the Spiritual Machine* [5], this law holds remarkably well from all the way back in the nineteenth century to today. This means that while Perl might be too slow for many tasks in computer graphics manipulation on today's computers, this will probably not hold true on computers in the not too distant future. The demands on programs that manipulate computer graphics will probably flatten out at some point, once the resolution of what is created is higher than the resolution of the human eye. At the same time, the increase in computing power will continue. Even if you don't believe this, the other reasons already stated are more than enough to see Perl as a valid programming language in the computer graphics world, if not generally, then at least for some tasks.

Many modules for Perl that concern themselves with the manipulation of graphics are written in C or C++, and provide an interface to this functionality in the Perl language. Most of these modules were, in fact, born as C libraries or programs, and their original authors probably didn't have Perl in mind at all when they wrote them. All the number crunching, array manipulation and bit-shifting happens in compiled low level code, and therefore is much faster than could be achieved in pure Perl. This does not mean that you cannot, under any circumstance, use Perl to directly manipulate pixels in an image. Chapter 12 gives a few examples of how to do this in pure Perl, but be forewarned that it will not be blindingly fast. The same chapter also explains how to write parts of your program in C, by including the C code directly in your program. This allows you to escape Perl's slowness when you need to, without losing any of its advantages.

Summarizing: while Perl isn't particularly suitable for low-level computer graphics manipulation, there are many modules available that make the most common graphics manipulation and creation task available to a Perl programmer. In cases where the need is to jump down to a low level and do some computationally intensive programming, Perl provides access to lower-level languages without too much fuss. Of course, if the majority of a program consists of these tasks, a language other than Perl should probably be considered.

1.2 THE BITS AND PIECES IN GRAPHICS PROGRAMMING

Generally speaking, programming for computer graphics consists of working with a limited set of concepts: the drawing primitives.

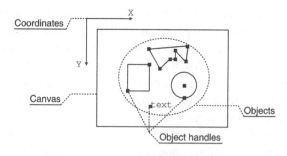

Figure 1.1
Some drawing primitives that can be created and manipulated with computer graphics programs and packages.

First of all there is the *canvas*, which is the medium that is being drawn on, or read from. In PostScript, for example, this is a page or part of a page, and for image manipulation packages such as *GD* this is a two-dimensional array of pixels. It is important to note that a canvas can be part of another canvas, and that certain images can be built up of multiple canvases, such as the layers and channels in a GIMP image.

A second element common to all graphics operations is a *frame of reference* expressed in coordinates. This indicates where on the canvas an object is located or an operation takes place. Most commonly these coordinates are Cartesian, with a horizontal and a vertical component, but sometimes it is easier to use polar coordinates (see, for example, section 10.1.1 "Coordinate transformation," on page 180).

Thirdly, there are the *objects* which are being drawn or manipulated, e.g., a rectangle, a circle, a polygon, a photo, a group of the previous, or a pixel array. Most of the time these objects will have one or more handles, which express their center or top left corner, and some dimensions.

The fourth element consists of the *tools* used for drawing. These can be a brush, a stamp, an eraser, a paint bucket or even a filter. These are normally found on icon bars in interactive drawing programs, but they also exist in noninteractive programming packages.

While the primitives of most graphics programming fall into one of the groups mentioned above, there is certainly not always a clear distinction. Something that is the canvas for one operation might be the brush or object to be drawn for another. And in fact, a lot of drawing software allows for use of part of one canvas as a brush for another. The whole graphic for one operation could be just a layer or a drawing object for another; think, for example of the object libraries of many drawing packages that predefine pictures of all kinds of common objects for use in a drawing.

Sometimes people consider the manipulation of single pixels in an image to be a separate class of actions. However, a pixel can be seen as a primitive object, and any action on a pixel is no different from any action on, for example, a circle. A pixel is simpler and has fewer parameters, but it is still an object.

Many graphics packages or graphics operations function at a higher level than described earlier, and you often won't need to deal with the lower level details directly. When you want to resize a set of images, you're not really concerned with what exactly happens in terms of canvas, coordinates, and objects. When you use one of the modules that creates a chart you are hardly interested in which low-level graphics operations it must execute to produce the picture.

In addition to the creation and handling of these drawing primitives, there are sets of operations that can be applied to the objects in a computer graphic. Some of these operations are stretching, rotating, skewing, or resizing of objects. Some others are filters that work directly on the contents of an object, the way that various convolution filters described in section 12.3 "Convolution," on page 215, work on the pixels in an image. There are also operations that let you combine graphical objects in various manners.

SEE ALSO We will see more about drawing primitives with the various modules that are available for Perl in chapter 4. More on the manipulation of images as a whole, and using images as objects to incorporate in other images, can be found in chapter 8. Chapter 10 contains more discussion on coordinate systems and frames of reference, and the manipulation of individual pixels is discussed in chapter 12.

1.3 COLOR SPACES AND PALETTES

One of the most important concepts in computer graphics is the storing and manipulation of color. The human eye is capable of distinguishing large numbers of colors, which ideally can all be represented in computer graphics terms. However, the more information needs to be represented, the more memory and CPU power is needed to work with that information. Apart from these considerations, the hardware used to present the colors also plays a major role in the conceptualization of a color model. This section provides a short overview of the color models most frequently used, and their relationship to each other.

All colors we see can be expressed as a composition of at least three other colors. This is because we use three different types of sensors on our retina to perceive color, each most sensitive to a different part of the visual spectrum. What exactly these three colors are isn't that important, since it turns out that it doesn't matter which three colors we pick to decompose colors into, as long as they are far enough away from each other. These colors are called primary colors, and every possible combination of three specific primary colors, taken together, makes up a color space. The coordinates into that space are the relative amounts of each primary color. As children we were taught that red, yellow and blue paint can be mixed in various combinations to make up virtually any other color of the rainbow. It turns out that it is possible to come up with several other useful color spaces. Let's look at some of them.

1.3.1 RGB

In computational graphics manipulation the most commonly used primary colors are red, green and blue, forming a color space referred to as RGB. The main reason that this color space is used is due to the fact that computer monitors perform their function with phosphorizing agents that emit those three colors. RGB is called an additive system, because each color can be expressed as a different sum of the three components, and adding more of one component adds intensity to the resulting color.

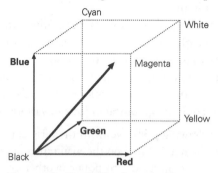

In color space coordinates, normally the three primary colors each can have a value between 0 and 1, which, for efficiency reasons, in most software applications is expressed as an integer value between 0 and 255. This means that visually, these colors can be mapped in a three-dimensional space; more precisely, to a cube. For the RGB color space this cube can be seen in figure 1.2

Figure 1.2   The RGB color cube illustrates the color space made up of the three colors red, green and blue. Each point inside the cube is a different valid color in RGB space.

Each color can be represented by a vector with coordinates (r,g,b) in that cube. Looking at this cube we see that yellow is represented by the coordinates (1,1,0), black by (0,0,0), white by (1,1,1) and a particularly irritating shade of blue-green by (0.5,0.7,0.7). The line that runs between the white and black corner represents all gray colors, and the coordinates for these points is (gr,gr,gr) where gr has a value between 0 (black) and 1 (white).

1.3.2   CMY and CMYK

Another color space made up of three primary colors is CMY, for cyan, magenta and yellow. CMY is often used for dyes and filters. These three primaries are the opposites, or more correctly, the complementaries of the RGB colors and form a so-called subtractive system, in which an increase in any color component causes a decrease in the intensity of the resulting color. In other words, the color seen when looking at a printed page is whatever is left over after the ink has absorbed part of the spectrum. If you have another look at the RGB cube in figure 1.2, you'll note that exactly opposite of the red, green and blue corners, are cyan, magenta and yellow. The relationship between RGB and CMY can be expressed as:

$$C = 1 - R$$
$$M = 1 - G$$
$$Y = 1 - B$$

Black in CMY color space is (1,1,1), white is (0,0,0), green is (1,0,1), and our irritating blue-green is (0.5,0.3,0,3). The gray colors are in exactly the same position, but their coordinates are reversed, i.e., white is given by (0,0,0) and black by (1,1,1).

In practice it is almost impossible to mix inks correctly and consistently, which is why printers normally work in a color space that has an added component—black. This color space is called CMYK. The largest possible value for the black K component is determined by taking the lowest of the CMY components, and subtracting that value from all three components. In effect, the maximum amount of black (gray) is subtracted from the color, and given its own coordinate. The relationship between RGB and CMYK is given by the following equations:

$$K \leq \min(1 - R, 1 - G, 1 - B)$$
$$C = (1 - R - K)$$
$$M = (1 - G - K)$$
$$Y = (1 - B - K)$$

$$R = 1 - (C + K)$$
$$G = 1 - (M + K)$$
$$B = 1 - (Y + K)$$

This, again, is an idealized representation of the way CMYK is used in the real world. Printers do not necessarily always subtract the largest amount of black from the individual colors, but they decide to use a value for K which better suits the inks they use. And even when the black component of a color is treated separately, the other inks are seldom clean or pure enough to be mixed in this ideal way. Instead, picking the correct mixing ratios is an art that printers practice for many years, and their experience will provide a much more solid foundation than the simplistic formula above.

1.3.3   HSV and HLS

Instead of using primary colors in certain combinations to identify a color, other attributes can be used. Some color spaces identify a color by its hue, which is basically the position on the rainbow, its saturation or pureness of the color, and its brightness (or value, or lightness). The two most common ones are HSV (for Hue, Saturation and Value) and HLS (Hue, Lightness and Saturation). Many people feel that a color is most naturally identified with these color spaces, because they closely reflect the way we perceive colors. When we see a color, typically we first observe its hue, i.e., whether it is green or purple or red. The next thing we notice is its saturation—whether it's a pastel tint or a pure color. And finally we take note of the brightness of the color.

Conversion from HSV or HLS to RGB is, unfortunately, not a linear process. Appendix B contains the algorithms for conversion to and from these color spaces. Before looking at those, it is probably important to understand how the HSV coordinates can be seen in terms of the RGB color cube.

Hue is normally expressed as a value from 0 to 360, which indicates a position on the color circle. The colors on the circle are arranged in the same order as they are on the rainbow, but in a circle, with pure red at an angle of 0 (and, of course, 360), green at 120 and blue at 240 degrees. All the colors with the same hue form a plane in the RGB color cube, as can be seen in figure 1.3.

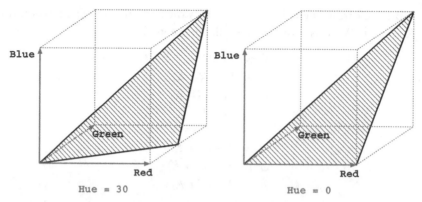

Hue = 30   Hue = 0

Figure 1.3   A set of colors with a constant hue forms a plane in the RGB color space. These planes form triangles inside the RGB color cube, where one of the sides is the diagonal from (0,0,0) to (1,1,1).

The saturation of a color expresses how pure the hue is, relative to white. A color with a saturation of 1 is pure, and a color with a saturation of 0 is gray. Pastel colors are colors with a low saturation, and the company colors picked by food chains and car dealerships normally have a high saturation. All the colors with the same saturation (but varying hue and value) fall on a cone in the RGB color cube, with the line between the white and black corners as its axis. See figure 1.4 for an illustration of this cone.

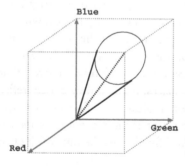

Figure 1.4   The cone of constant saturation in the RGB color cube. Note that the cube has been rotated 90 degrees around the blue axis, compared to figures 1.2 and 1.3.

The value for HSV and the lightness for HLS are both meant to express the amount of luminosity of the color. This is, however, not the same thing as the brightness of a color, which is often defined as the sum of the brightness of the individual colors. The lightness and value are slightly different quantities, and less directly mappable in the RGB space. The planes of constant lightness and value are difficult to draw, which is why I gave up trying and plotted them with gnuplot, using the subroutines in appendix B. An example of constant lightness can be seen in figure 1.5, and one of constant value in figure 1.6.

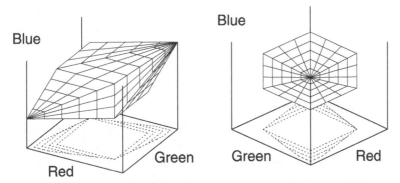

Figure 1.5   Constant HSL lightness (0.6) in the RGB color cube, seen from two angles. The three-dimensional figure becomes narrower when the lightness value decreases, and wider when it increases. The tips of the figure remain stationary.

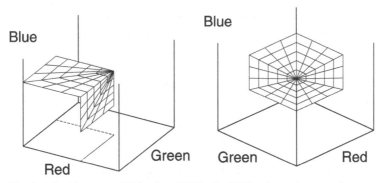

Figure 1.6   Constant HSV value (0.6) in the RGB color cube, seen from two angles. The figure grows smaller and closer to the origin when the value decreases, and larger and closer to the point (1,1,1) when the value increases.

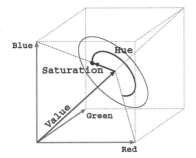

Figure 1.7   The HSV coordinates in the RGB color cube. Represented is a point that has a Hue of 240 degrees (and therefore points in the direction of the blue corner), a saturation of approximately 20 percent, and a value of 50 percent.

And finally, and then I'll stop talking about HSV, the coordinates of the HSV color system are depicted in figure 1.7.[2] The black dot in that figure represents a point in the HSV color space with a hue of approximately 240 degrees, a saturation of approximately 20 percent, and a value or lightness of 50 percent. This corresponds to a dark, dull blue or almost gray-blue, with RGB coordinates in the proximity of (0.4,0.4,0.5).

1.3.4 YUV, YIQ and YCbCr

One group of color spaces that is often used in video specifications expresses color as one component of luminance, and two of chrominance. This means that one of the three components expresses how bright the color is, and the other two determine its color. The most common of these are YUV, YIQ and YCbCr. YUV and YIQ are the color spaces used in the PAL (in use in Europe, among other places), and NTSC (used in the USA) video standards. Both of these are highly unportable, and it is unreliable to convert YUV or YIQ from or to RGB coordinates. The scale factors used in these color systems are just not appropriate outside their application domain. YCbCr is more appropriate. In fact, often when someone gives a formula to transform between RGB and YUV, what they have really given is the transformation from and to YCbCr.

The component that everything revolves around in these color spaces is the Luminance, Y. It can be calculated from the RGB coordinates with

$$Y = 0.299R + 0.587G + 0.114B$$

The meaning of the two chrominance components—with different scaling factors for the different color spaces—can be understood by loosely defining them as:

$$U, I, Cb = S1 \ (B - Y)$$
$$V, Q, Cr = S2 \ (R - Y)$$

wherein S1 and S2 are scaling factors that are defined by the respective standards.[3] These color spaces will not serve the purpose of this book, so I won't discuss them any further. Suffice it to say that they normally would be encountered only when working with video.

1.3.5 Grayscale

Finally, grayscale is an often used color space which really is only one dimensional, and therefore isn't much of a color space. It is capable only of expressing the relative brightness of pixels. Conversion from a real color space to grayscale is a one-way process, because the color information is lost along the way. There are several ways to

---

[2] It should be understood that this just is a schematic indication of the coordinates. The length of the various arrows is not directly related to the HSV coordinates. However, the drawing is useful for understanding the relationship between RGB and HSV.

[3] The exact magnitude of these scaling factors is not important for this discussion. See for example the reference entries [6],[7].

achieve this, some of which produce more natural results than others, depending on the nature of the original image. The most frequently used conversions are:

$$Luminance = 0.299\,R + 0.587G + 0.114B$$
$$Brightness = (R + G + B)/3$$
$$Lightness = [max(R, G, B) + min(R, G, B)]/2$$
$$Value = max(R, G, B)$$

Luminance is, of course, the Y component of the YUV or related color spaces (also see the color FAQ [7]). This generally renders the most natural result. Brightness is simply the average of the three color components, which tends to overemphasize any blue tints in an image. The eye is much less sensitive to blue than it is to red, and much less sensitive to red than it is to green. The scaling factors in the equation for luminance attempt to reflect this difference in sensitivity. The last two are the L component of the HSL color space and the V component of the HSV color space. Both are often easily implemented in software, because they require only a desaturation (setting the S component to 0) in the appropriate color space. However, the results of these conversions does not always meet expectations.

1.3.6   Color distance

One difference between the various color models is the way the distances in color space are calculated. The distance in a color space is defined in the same way that a distance in geometrical space is defined:

$$\|c_1 - c_2\| = \sqrt{\left(c_{1,\,x} - c_{2,\,x}\right)^2 + \left(c_{1,\,y} - c_{2,\,y}\right)^2 + \left(c_{1,\,z} - c_{2,\,z}\right)^2}$$

for a color space with three coordinates x, y and z. A different color space will yield a different distance between the same colors. This distance is used to calculate how similar two colors are, and picking a different color space can yield very different results. Some color spaces (such as YUV) provide distances that are more closely related to the way our perception of color works than the more standard RGB color space.

The color distance is most important when reducing the numbers of colors in an image. At some point this color reduction will require changing a pixel's color to one that is as close as possible to the original *and* part of the set of colors that are available after the reduction. Doing these operations in different color spaces can result in visibly different images.

1.3.7   Reducing the number of colors in an image

The main reason for wanting to reduce the number of colors in an image is to save it in an indexed image format. Indexed image formats store all available colors in a palette or color map. Each pixel in the image needs only to contain an index into that palette, instead of the three coordinates into the color space. This can result in remarkable savings in disk space, but it comes at the cost of losing some color resolution.

Currently, one of the best known color palettes is the web-safe palette, or the Netscape color palette (also see 6.2.1 "Web safe color palettes," on page 92). *Image::Magick* provides a built-in image type to convert images to that particular palette:

```
$map = Image::Magick->new();
$map->Read('netscape:');
$image = Image::Magick->new();
$image->Read('some_image.jpg');
$image->Map(image => $map, dither => 1);
$image->Write('some_image.gif');
```

You create an image, $map, that only contains the built-in `netscape` image type, which can then be used as a palette mapping image for *Image::Magick*'s `Map()` method. This method will remap the colors of the current image into the ones of the `image` argument.

1.4 SUMMARY

In this chapter we've discussed the basics of graphics programming in a general sense, with an emphasis on colors and color spaces. Chapter 4 has more practical information on how to work with graphics primitives. We haven't covered everything there is to know and have breezed over some of the details of the discussed matter; however, the introduction presented in this chapter should be sufficient to understand the rest of this book.

SEE ALSO   If you are interested in a more elaborate discussion of colors in computer graphics, I suggest you look at the color space FAQ and color FAQ listed in the references as [6] and [7], and pick up one of the books recommended there, if you wish.

Appendix B contains Perl code to convert from RGB to HSV or HLS and back.

CHAPTER 2

Overview of graphics file formats

One of the most common tasks in graphics programming is managing currently existing files. This can vary from obtaining information about a single image, to manipulation of large sets of images, to the storage and retrieval of graphics files.

As an example: your company is a publisher of content—all kinds of content. Apart from print publications, it provides a large amount of information on a web site. Part of the content is, of course, the images. These images come from a variety of sources. You have professional photographers who go out and take photographs of interesting subjects with expensive cameras, as well as sales representatives who visit your customers and make quick snapshots of their shops with digital cameras. You receive digital images by email from correspondents and clients. There is advertising artwork to be displayed.

All in all, thousands of pictures and images are generated for you every year. Most are not in a suitable format for display on your web site, so they'll need resizing, conversion, and possibly a little correction. The images will need to be stored somewhere for easy retrieval and indexing. Up until now, your company has employed several people who do this work manually, and they act as librarians as well as graphics editors.

The management, seeking to improve the bottom line, tells the technical staff to come up with an image manipulation and handling system that can do most of this work automatically. Given a set of business rules for a certain category of images, it should be able to accept a source image, store it somewhere, and manipulate it into a shape that is suitable for any of its assigned publication outlets. It should also provide an interface that makes it possible to find an image with relative ease.

Central to all of the above is the handling of graphics files and the information contained in them. This chapter will deal with some file formats in which graphics can be stored, and the ways in which you can retrieve information from them.

2.1 SOME GRAPHICS FORMATS

There exist a large number of formats for storing or transporting graphics information. These formats can be roughly divided into two groups: formats that store graphics as *vectors*, and formats that store graphics as *pixel maps*.[1]

Vector formats store their objects as mathematical descriptions and sets of coordinates. A circle is stored as the coordinates of the center and the radius; a rectangle as the coordinates of a corner and the height and width (and possibly rotation) of the rectangle. This allows for a good scalability of the image, but it requires the rendering engine to interpret and draw each object every time it needs to be displayed or used in any other way. Also, the calculations to switch display pixels on and off need to be performed each time.

Unfortunately, at present, there are very few Perl modules that work with formats such as these, at least in a native sense. Many modules can create vector graphics for output, and some can import them and translate them into an image format, but that is where it stops. Of course, when a vector graphic is stored in plain text, Perl can be easily used to create files of that type. Reading them back in is another matter, and requires a module or program with intimate knowledge of the format.

Image formats store graphics as a two-dimensional array of pixels, wherein each pixel represents one point of the image. These formats contain no information about whether sections are parts of a circle, rectangle, chair or clown face. Each pixel stands on its own, and is (largely) independent of the other pixels. Most commonly, each pixel contains a set of values that express the color, and sometimes transparency, of that particular pixel.

Some image formats allow you to store more than one image in a single file or data stream. Some will allow you to express a certain relationship between all of these images. One example of this is GIF animation, in which each image is a frame in a sequence, and there are extra data associated with each image that expresses how long it should be displayed and how it should be cleaned up after that time. Other examples

---

[1] Of course there are graphics formats and languages that allow both, but for the sake of simplicity we will just ignore that.

are the layers in a GIMP or Photoshop file. The ways in which these layers can relate to each other are too numerous to list. The main relationship between the layers is how they are combined with other layers below them in the stack.

Some file formats are not well suited for storing images for further processing because they are lossy, meaning that the image data is stored in a way that causes some information to get lost. A format such as JPEG uses some clever algorithmic techniques that can dramatically diminish the amount of data to be stored for photographic images. However, what gets stored is not a full representation of the original data; some information is lost. If you read this image later, manipulate it, and then save it again, you lose even more. A few of these repetitions can result in a considerable loss in quality.

Another way to lose information is by color reduction. Some image formats store colors not per pixel, but instead store a palette of colors, and each pixel points to one of the colors in the palette. For an RGB image in which each color component can have an integer value between 0 and 255, you need at least three bytes per pixel to store the image. However, if you allow a total of only 256 colors, you only need one byte per pixel, which is the index into the palette of 256 colors.

It is, therefore, important to always store the originals of your images in a lossless format, such as PNG or TIFF, and to convert to lossy formats, such as JPEG and GIF, only as the last step in the process.

There is a wealth of information available on the net covering the various graphics formats and their use and abuse [8,9,10,11,12,13]. I will only discuss a very small subset here, mainly the formats that are most usable for the Web. The main reason for this limitation is that the use of graphics on the Web is a mess. This is due to a lack of understanding regarding which format to use for which picture, as well as the limitation in usable formats (see also section 6.2, "Suitable image formats," on page 92).

2.1.1   GIF

The Graphics Interchange Format, GIF, was first designed by CompuServe in 1987 as version 87A, and later expanded upon with version 89A. The idea behind GIF was to facilitate the reduction of the size of bitmap files so that transport over modems would be faster.

The fact that the GIF format is so old shows in the limitation of 256 colors per data stream (or per image). However, the GIF format at the moment is the only widespread image format that supports animation of some sort.

The GIF format traditionally uses LZW (Lempel-Ziv & Welch) compression,[2] which is patented by Unisys. Unisys, after an extended period of allowing free use of the algorithm for nonprofit applications, decided recently to require a license for the use of LZW compression. There is much confusion about whether a license is also required for LZW decompression, although Unisys insists that a license is needed for

---

[2] LZW compression is not only used in the GIF format, but also, among others, in the TIFF format.

any use of the LZW algorithm. Unisys has changed its position a few times on who needs a license and who doesn't, and could change it again at any time.

In practice, if you use software that incorporates the LZW algorithm in any way, you or the vendor of the software are responsible for obtaining a license from Unisys. Even if your application is made available for free, you are currently required to obtain a license. An interesting detail is that a lot of commercial software, including many Microsoft products, have been licensed, but in such a way that the user of the software still has to obtain a license from Unisys.

> **SEE ALSO**   More information on the LZW license can be found at:
> http://www.unisys.com/unisys/lzw/ and http://burnallgifs.org/.

This license, and the fact that the folks at Unisys keep changing their minds about who should pay for one, has made it virtually impossible for many of the free products out in the Open Source community to continue supporting GIF. There is still a way to use GIF, since the GIF format does not *require* LZW compression. The libungif C library relies on that feature for creation of GIF images that are not subject to the patent. Of course, GIF images that don't use a compression algorithm are very large and virtually useless for the web, which is where GIF has its largest application domain.

This, taken together with the limitations of the GIF format itself, suggests that you should try to avoid using it, if at all possible. Use PNG images instead of GIF images. I can think of only two reasons to use the GIF format in favor of the PNG format: you need to create small and simple animations, or you need to support a user base that has obsolete software that doesn't read the PNG format. The first reason will disappear when the MNG and SVG formats become widely supported, since they can both be used for various kinds of animations. The second reason disappears when you no longer have to cater to obsolete software.

2.1.2   JPEG, JFIF

The image format which is normally called JPEG should really be called JFIF, which is short for JPEG File Interchange Format. JPEG stands for Joint Photographic Experts Group, the group that gave us the JFIF format and the compression techniques used in it. The compression technique itself is known as JPEG compression.

JPEG compression is at its best when the image is a photo (color or B&W), or any other image that resembles a real-world scene. It is not as good at images where most of the neighboring pixels have the same color. JPEG is a lossy format, meaning you cannot restore the original information from the compressed image. JFIF images work with a 24-bit color space (16 million colors).

2.1.3   PNG

The Portable Network Graphics format (see [14]) was designed with the web in mind, specifically to replace GIF and, to a lesser degree, TIFF. The advantages of PNG over GIF are that PNG has alpha channels, gamma correction, a better interlacing method, and generally slightly better compression. One feature of GIF that PNG sadly lacks is the popular animation or multiple-image format (see MNG).

PNG is a lossless image format, unlike GIF, which normally only stores up to 256 colors, and JFIF, which loses information due to its compression technique. Together with the 48-bit color (and 16-bit grayscale) support, this makes it a very suitable format for interchange between packages.

2.1.4 MNG

The Multi-Image Network Graphics format (see [15]) is strongly based on PNG, and was in fact designed by some of the same people. MNG is the answer to the desire of web designers to include animated images on their sites, and it promises a lot more, in better ways, than GIF animation is providing.

Unfortunately, the support for MNG is still limited, and the standard for the format has not yet been officially set down. For all practical purposes, at this time, animations will have to be provided with GIF streams.

2.1.5 SVG

The Scalable Vector Graphics format is a language used to describe graphics in XML. As the name suggests, it will allow vector graphics, but can also contain text and images. The language is a W3C recommendation, and therefore a web standard, and its specification can be found at http://www.w3.org/Graphics/SVG. SVG is clearly aimed at bringing more sane graphics to the Web by providing a standardized vector graphics format that is easy to parse and is transportable.

Support for the SVG format is still limited, but is growing fast. One Perl module that can import SVG graphics is *Image::Magick,* and other modules to work with SVG area appearing on CPAN. Support for this format in the major web browsers is also growing, and its acceptance promises that this well-designed and flexible format will be successful in solving many of the problems currently experienced with web graphics.

More information about SVG is available at the above-mentioned URL, and in the upcoming book *Definitive SVG* by Kelvin Lawrence, et al. [16].

2.1.6 TIFF

The Tag Image File Format (TIFF) is one of the most venerable of image formats. It has been around for a long time, and is supported by many pieces of software. The format allows for many image format features and compression schemes (including LZW compression). Originally, TIFF was defined by Adobe Systems Incorporated, but the format now is also defined by the Internet Engineering Task Force (IETF), and is described in RFC 2302.

The TIFF format is mainly intended for images originating from scanners and other imaging devices; hence the format is quite extensive in order to support all the various capabilities of these devices. The TIFF format specifies a baseline set of features that every compliant application should support. Apart from this baseline it also defines many extensions that applications can optionally implement.

The TIFF format allows multiple images per file, full color, grayscale and palette-based color data, as well as an alpha channel. This makes it a suitable format for storing images to use as a source, because it allows the storing of the complex information that image formats can contain, without loss, reasonably compressed, and portable between applications.

2.2   FINDING THE SIZE AND TYPE OF AN IMAGE

The first thing you do when you receive an image for further manipulation is to find out as much information about it as necessary. In the case of image files, that is, at the very least, the size and type of the image. Once you have such data, you can make decisions about which steps to take to get the image into the required format.

2.2.1   Image::Size

For most Perl applications, the fastest and easiest way to find the size of an image is to use the *Image::Size* module. It will handle the most commonly used image formats and it is easy to use. The imgsize() subroutine takes either a file name or an open file handle as its argument, and returns the width, height, and type of image.

```
use Image::Size qw(:all);
my $img_file = 'file.gif';
my ($width, $height, $id) = imgsize($img_file);

open(IN, $img_file) or die "Cannot open $img_file: $!";
($width, $height, $id) = imgsize(\*IN);
```

The last argument on the use Image::Size line is a directive to the standard Perl exporting mechanism. Many modules make some of their internal names optionally available for export.[3] *Image::Size* always exports imgsize() into the caller's name space, and optionally allows the import of the html_imgsize() and attr_imgsize() functions. The tag :all imports all three of them. In other words, if you only plan to use the imgsize() function, a simple use Image::Size; will suffice.

Alternatively, you can read the file yourself and pass a reference to the file contents to the imgsize() subroutine. This can also be handy if you get your image data from a source other than a file, such as a database or a pipe.

```
binmode(IN);
my $img_buf;
{
    local($/) = undef;
    $img_buf = <IN>;
}
close(IN);
($width, $height, $id) = imgsize(\$img_buf);
```

---

[3] For a full explanation, see the documentation of the standard Perl module *Exporter*.

Image::Size also offers two convenient methods, which can be used to generate HTML tags in a print statement:

```
use Image::Size qw(html_imgsize);
my $html_width_height = html_imgsize($img_file);
print qq(<IMG SRC="$img_file" $html_width_height>);
```

or to cooperate with the methods of the *CGI* module.

```
use CGI qw(:standard);
use Image::Size qw(attr_imgsize);
my @width_height_attributes = attr_imgsize($img_file);
print img {src => $img_file, @width_height_attributes};
```

or directly:

```
print img {src => $img_file, attr_imgsize($img_file)};
```

2.2.2 Image::Magick

If you have images in a format that *Image::Size* doesn't support, then you still have a few options. The simplest is to use a more powerful module, such as *Image::Magick*. *Image::Magick*'s Ping() method gives you the width and height of the images in a file of any of the formats it can read. As a bonus you also get the size (in bytes) and format of the image.[4]

```
use Image::Magick;
my $img_file = 'file.gif';
my ($width, $height, $size, $format) = Image::Magick->Ping($img_file)
    or die "Cannot get info for $img_file";
```

This works well if you are interested only in the dimensions of the image and don't plan to do anything else with it. If, however, you also need to read the image for manipulation with *Image::Magick*, it is probably better to do something such as:

```
my $img_file = 'file.gif';
my $im = Image::Magick->new();
my $rc = $im->Read($img_file);
die "Cannot read $img_file: $rc" if $rc;
my ($width, $height, $format) = $im->Get('width', 'height', 'magick');
```

Note that most *Image::Magick* methods return undef on success.[5] This means that you have to check whether the return value is *true* to detect an error, while most of the time, in Perl, you check whether a return value is false. This can be a bit counterintuitive.

Image::Magick is a fairly large and heavy module, which takes quite some CPU power to load. The reason for this is that *Image::Magick* is a very general purpose graphics manipulation module, and anything that is general purpose is bound to be

---

[4] In older versions of *Image::Magick*, the Ping() method returned a single string with comma-separated fields in the same order as in the example. A further explanation of this method appears on page 268.

[5] There are some exceptions to this rule; see appendix A, on page 241.

slower than something that has been written with only one specific task in mind. Newer versions have improved this situation by delaying the load phase of many components until they're needed. If you need to know some information on only one or two images, loading *Image::Magick* just for this might be too expensive.[6] If you plan to procure information on many images, the cost of loading is negligible.

2.2.3   Do it yourself

If you need something fast and lightweight that will work almost everywhere, especially when you know that you will only have to deal with one file format, writing your own subroutines can be the best option. As an illustration, we will do this for PNG and for XCF, the native format for the Gimp. The subroutines will return the same values as the imgsize() subroutine from *Image::Size*.

PNG

The PNG format[14] specifies a fixed header of 8 bytes, followed by a chunk of type IHDR. This chunk first contains a 4-byte integer, then a 4-byte identifier, and two 4-byte integers for the width and height. In PNG, all integers are stored in network byte order. If we translate this knowledge into Perl code, we get something like the following:

```
sub png_size
{
    my $file = shift or return;
    my $buf;
    local(*IMG);

    open(IMG, $file) or return;
    binmode(IMG);
    read(IMG, $buf, 24);            ● Read the first 8 + 4 + 4 + 4 + 4 bytes
    my ($hdr, $1, $ihdr, $w, $h) =
        unpack("a8 N a4 N N", $buf);
    return unless
        $hdr eq "\x89PNG\x0d\x0a\x1a\x0a" &&
        $ihdr eq 'IHDR';
    return ($w, $h, 'PNG');
}
```

You will notice the local(*IMG) and the absence of an explicit close(IMG). By localizing the file handle, we first make certain that we don't trample on any file handles in the rest of the program, and we assure that the file gets closed on exiting the block, i.e., when the subroutine returns. In more modern versions of Perl (post 5.6.0) you can also use a lexically scoped variable as a file handle, which has the same effect.

In this subroutine, unpack() is used to split up the binary information in the 24 header bytes into the parts in which we are interested. The translation of the unpack

---

[6] Generally, the newer your version of *Image::Magick*, the less this is a problem. For example, version 5.4.4 is about 20 percent faster than the previous version.

template can almost literally be found in the paragraph preceding the code. The second return value of the unpack() operation, which is the total length of the IHDR chunk, is captured, but not used, because it is not important to us. Next $hdr and $ihdr are checked to see if they are what they should be, and if they are not, a false value is returned. To round things off, the width, height and image type are returned.

The Gimp's XCF format

The documentation on XCF, the native format for the Gimp, is distributed with its source code, and is, in fact, the source code. So, to learn how to read this format, we have to get our hands on a source distribution of the GIMP.[7] In the file apps/xcf.c we find that there are currently (as of version 1.1.10) two versions of the file format, in comments called versions 0 and 1. The only difference for our purposes is the version number in the header of the file.

The first thing to be noted about the XCF format is that, like in the PNG format, integers are stored in network byte order. We read from the source code that the first 9 bytes contain a fixed header, and that the version number can be found, as a null terminated string, in the next 5 bytes. The width and height of the image are the next two 4-byte integers:

```
sub xcf_size
{
    my $file = shift or return;
    my $buf;
    local(*IMG);

    open(IMG, $file) or return;
    binmode(IMG);
    read(IMG, $buf, 22);        ●  Read the first 9 + 5 + 4 + 4 bytes
    my ($hdr, $v, $w, $h) =
        unpack("a9 Z5 N N", $buf);
    return unless ($hdr eq "gimp xcf ");
    SWITCH: {
        $v eq 'file' and $v = 'XCF0', last SWITCH;
        $v eq 'v001' and $v = 'XCF1', last SWITCH;
        # Unknown version. $w and $h may be unreliable
        return;
    }
    return ($w, $h, $v);
}
```

This code is very similar to png_size(), except that the type of the image is determined from the version number found in the file. The XCF version 0 format formerly had the first 13 bytes set to gimp xcf file, while the version 1 header contains gimp xcf v001. We capture the version as the last 4 bytes of this string, and rewrite it into something slightly more meaningful.

---

[7] Full sources for the GIMP are available from http://www.gimp.org/.

2.2.4 More on file size and information

This section should have given you enough of a beginning to read the basic information of any image format. If none of the modules can handle it, you can still find out by reading this yourself, if you know the image format specification. Of course, if you don't know that, you're on your own, but before despairing, have a look at the Wotsit site [13], to see if it has the specification of the format you're seeking.

2.3 CONVERSION OF GRAPHICS FORMATS

To convert graphics between formats it is best to use the *Image::Magick* module. This module can read and write a wide variety of image formats, sometimes with the help of external tools and libraries. Some of the formats that can be read by *Image::Magick* are listed in table 2.1.

Table 2.1 **A partial list of image formats recognized by *Image::Magick*. Some of these formats are parsed with the help of external modules or programs which require you to install these before compiling *Image::Magick*. See the documentation for a full list.**

Format	Description
BMP, BMP24	MS Windows bitmap image file
CGM	Computer Graphics Metafile
CMYK	Raw cyan, magenta, yellow, and black bytes
EPI, EPS, EPSF	Encapsulated PostScript Formats
GIF	CompuServe graphics interchange format
HTML	HTML with a client-side image map
JPEG	Joint Photographic Experts Group JFIF
MIFF	Magick image file format
MNG	Multiple-image Network Graphics
PBM, PGM, PNM, PPM	Portable Xmap format
PCD, PCDS	Photo CD
PICT	Apple Macintosh QuickDraw/PICT file
PNG	Portable Network Graphics
PSD	Adobe Photoshop bitmap file
TGA	Truevision Targa image file
TIFF	Tagged Image File Format
WMF	Windows Meta File
XBM, XPM	X Windows system bitmap/pixmap

For a complete list, see for example the ImageMagick web site [17] or the documentation for the command line tool *convert*. In addition to standard external image formats, *Image::Magick* has some built-in format specifiers, which are listed in table 2.2.

Table 2.2 **Some of the internal special image formats of** *Image::Magick*. **These formats are not really image formats, but are special instructions to the ImageMagick engine to create an image with certain characteristics.**

Specifiers	Description
GRADIENT	Gradual change from one shade to another
GRANITE	Granite texture
GRAY	Raw gray bytes
HISTOGRAM	Histogram of the image
LABEL	Create a text image
NETSCAPE	Netscape 6x6x6 color cube
PLASMA	plasma fractal image
VID	Visual Image Directory
XC	Filled with a single color

When reading a file, *Image::Magick* will usually be able to guess the file type by its signature.[8] In the rare cases in which that doesn't work, you may specify the file format in the file name you give to the `Read()` method. The `Write()` method can be used to save images to disk. It uses the extension of the file name specified to determine the format to save. If the file extension cannot be used, or you want to override it, you may specify a format explicitly (see the code examples below). If neither a file extension or explicit format are specified, the image attribute `magick` will be used to determine the format of the file to save. We will discuss some concrete examples after showing the code that you will find at the start of almost any Perl program using *Image::Magick*:

```
use Image::Magick;

my $rc;
my $img = Image::Magick->new();
```

We read in a GIF format file, and save it as a PNG format file.

```
$rc = $img->Read('file.gif');
warn $rc if $rc;
$rc = $img->Write('file.png');
warn $rc if $rc;
```

---

[8] Most, if not all, graphics file formats can be identified by looking at the first few bytes of the file. Each format has its own characteristic sequence of bytes, called the signature. See the definition of `png_size()` and `xcf_size()` in the previous section for examples of this.

Then we create a white tile of 70 by 70 pixels, and save it as a TIFF format file.

```
@$img = ();
$img->Set(size => '70x70');
$rc = $img->Read('xc:white');
warn $rc if $rc;
$rc = $img->Write('whiteTile.tiff');
warn $rc if $rc;
```

In the preceding code you might have noticed the @$img = (). That is the best way to remove all the images from the $img object, without actually destroying the object itself. If this were not done, subsequent reads would create a multi-image object (see also chapter 7).

To create an image with a gradient going from light to dark gray the following code can be used:

```
@$img = ();
$img->Set(size => '100x600');
$rc = $img->Read('gradient:#efefef-#3f3f3f');
warn $rc if $rc;
$img->Rotate(degrees => -90);
$rc = $img->Write('grayGradient.jpg');
warn $rc if $rc;
```

Image::Magick gradients always run from top to bottom, so to attain a gradient that changes horizontally, we rotate the created image by 90 degrees. The result can be seen in figure 2.1.

Figure 2.1 An illustration of *Image::Magick*'s built-in type gradient, rotated and converted to a JPEG image.

2.4 SUMMARY

In this chapter some image formats and methods to obtain information about the image size and format were discussed, and the conversion of one image format to another with the help of *Image::Magick* was demonstrated. This is hopefully sufficient to provide a solid base from which to work with image files and the various formats that are available.

SEE ALSO   The *Image::Magick* documentation and the reference in appendix A should be consulted for more information on the various *Image::Magick* methods discussed. The *Image::Size* module comes equipped with useful documentation which is recommended reading for anyone wishing to use the module.

C H A P T E R 3

Overview of tools and modules

If you had to write all graphics code yourself each time you needed some work done, and if you had to study all the relevant theory yourself every time, you wouldn't actually finish many programs. One of the strengths of Perl is that it provides a good interface for developers to create modules that can be reused by others. This is an excellent way to package knowledge about a certain protocol, technique or algorithm in some code, and to share it with the wider Perl community.

Many programmers have done this. They have spent time creating software libraries and modules, and have made them available for others to use. Apart from Perl modules, there are some programs that can be used to work with graphics from within Perl. This chapter provides a list of software tools and modules used in this book, with a short description for each. When necessary it has been noted where to find the tools and their documentation, and where in the book they are used (but also check the index to find other references).

Since most modules for Perl are available from CPAN, we'll first spend some time explaining what it is, and how to use it.

3.1 CPAN

The Comprehensive Perl Archive Network[1] (CPAN) is the best place to start looking for any modules for Perl, and all the modules used in this book are available there. The modules are distributed as gzipped tar archives. The distribution mechanism is, at this moment, quite Unix-oriented, and requires at least a working make tool. The modules that are interfaces to C libraries or contain C code, require a working C compiler as well.

For platforms where these tools are not as standard, there are other solutions. If you use MacPerl, you should probably start at http://www.macperl.com/, and follow the pointers from there. Alternatively, you can visit the MacPerl Module Porters page directly at http://pudge.net/cgi-bin/mmp.plx.

ActiveState distributes the *de facto* standard Perl for the 32-bit Microsoft Windows platforms, ActivePerl. The company also maintains an archive of prepackaged and precompiled modules in the (ActivePerl-specific) ppm format. ActivePerl comes bundled with a tool, also called ppm, that will automatically fetch and install modules from the archive. To get ActivePerl, and read more about it and its use, start at http://www.activestate.com/.

While these platform-specific archives are convenient, it also means that the only modules available there are the ones that have been prepackaged, ported, or otherwise prepared. Sometimes modules in these archives can grow severely out of date with respect to the latest versions on CPAN, and many CPAN modules never make it there. If the module you're interested in only uses Perl code, I suggest you use the CPAN distribution. If the module needs any form of byte code compilation, e.g., contains C code, you will have to either wait for it to become available, or you can opt to purchase for yourself a compiler that works with the ActiveState distribution, install it, and compile the module yourself.

Most of the modules can be found on CPAN (http://www.cpan.org) and can be installed with the well-known mantra:

```
$ perl Makefile.PL
$ make
$ make test
$ make install
```

or, alternatively, with the CPAN module, shipped with any standard Perl distribution.

The documentation for the modules from CPAN is normally contained in the module source code itself, and is installed together with the module. On Unix systems this documentation will also be extracted and made available as standard manual pages. On Unix and most other platforms, the documentation can be extracted and read with the help of the *perldoc* tool that is installed with Perl. To find out more about it, type *perldoc perldoc* at the prompt. The ActiveState ppm installation program will extract

---

[1] http://www.cpan.org/,http://www.perl.com/CPAN/ or http://www.perl.org/CPAN/

the documentation from a module and install it as HTML on the local machine. For MacPerl, a program called Shuck is available to read Perl documentation.

3.2 THE TOOLS

This section provides a list of modules and tools used throughout this book. Included is a short description of what each module does and where to find occurrences of its use in the book. Specific notes about where to obtain the module, how to install it, and what to be aware of are also provided here when necessary.

3.2.1 The Chart::* modules

These modules provide an object-oriented interface to create many different types of charts. The interface originally borrowed a lot of the ideas from *GIFgraph* but it has since gone its own way, and provides different sets of functionality. The modules were originally created by David Bonner, and are maintained by Peter Clark.

A full set of documentation comes with the modules, as a single manual page. Examples of the use of these modules can be found in section 5.2, "The Chart distribution," on page 74.

3.2.2 Gnuplot

Gnuplot is a program to create charts and graphs. It supports a wide variety of chart and data types, including three-dimensional surface plots. The program can be used interactively, and comes with a reasonable on-line help system. The documentation may be installed separately, or downloaded from the gnuplot web page (see [18]). Note that the gnu in gnuplot has nothing to do with the GNU Free Software Foundation. *Chart::GnuPlot* provides an interface to gnuplot, but is still in a very early stage, and not ready for production use. Section 5.4, "Interfacing with gnuplot," on page 85 shows some examples of the use of gnuplot from Perl. These examples have been tested with gnuplot version 3.7.

3.2.3 GD

GD is written and maintained by Lincoln Stein and provides an object-oriented interface to Thomas Boutell's C library libgd. It offers a simple, but reasonably powerful and fast, drawing interface for bitmaps. Recent versions of *GD* can work with PNG, JPEG, XBM, WBMP (Windows bitmap), and a native file format. Older versions (before 1.20) used to work with the GIF format, which explains why the internal GD image format has much in common with GIF.

You will find several references in this book to the shortcomings of *GD* where color is concerned; as such, *GD* only supports palettes of up to 256 colors. However, since it is an interface to libgd, and a new version of libgd that supports true color images currently is in beta, I suspect that the next major release of *GD* will do this as well. This new version most likely will be released with a version number of 2.0.

GD comes with an excellent manual page, and examples of its use can be found in many places in this book. The code there has been tested with *GD* version 1.33.

3.2.4   GD::Graph, GIFgraph and Chart::PNGgraph

These modules all use *GD* to create charts of various kinds and require the GDText-Utils to work. *GIFgraph* and *GD::Graph* were written and are maintained by the author. *Chart::PNGgraph* was created by Steve Bonds, based on the code base of *GIFgraph*, when GIF support was dropped from *GD*. Both *GIFgraph* and *Chart::PNGgraph* exist nowadays only to provide backward compatible name space wrappers around *GD::Graph* directly.

GD::Graph comes with a set of reasonably complete documentation, and examples of its use can be found in section 5.1, "GD::Graph and friends," on page 62, section 6.3, "CGI and dynamically generated graphics," on page 94 and 7.6, "Animated charts," on page 132. The code in this book has been tested with *GD::Graph* version 1.33.

3.2.5   GD::Text

The *GD::Text* module and its cousins *GD::Text::Align* and *GD::Text::Wrap* provide a generic interface to string handling and font management for the *GD* module. They were created during the writing of chapter 11 of this book by the author, and made available from CPAN under the name GDTextUtils. A full set of documentation is included in the modules.

Code that uses the *GD::Text* modules can be found in section 11.2.1, "Aligning text with GD," on page 194, and has been tested with *GD::Text* version 0.80.

3.2.6   The Gimp

The GNU Image Manipulation Program [19] has almost the same application domain as Adobe Photoshop,[2] almost the same capabilities, but a much more attractive price; it's free. The Gimp itself is an interactive program, but has a readily accessible extension interface, and tasks can be automated in the Gimp by using the *Gimp* and *Gimp::Fu* Perl modules. These modules can be used to write command line programs, as well as plug-in filters and programs for the Gimp. The *Gimp* Perl modules can be complex, and require a working knowledge of the program and the way it stores and manipulates images, layers and selections.

The Gimp is available from http://www.gimp.org/ and the distribution includes the Perl modules. The module is only sparsely used in this book, but the program is definitely a must for anyone serious about working with image files on Unix platforms.

3.2.7   Image::Magick

Image::Magick is an object-oriented interface to ImageMagick, which is an extremely versatile and powerful image manipulation tool that works with a wide range of

---

[2] Photoshop is generally better suited for images that are destined for print.

image formats and offers an extensive set of operations. ImageMagick and its companion Perl module are written and maintained by John Cristy with the assistance of other developers.

The module is available as part of the ImageMagick distribution under the name PerlMagick, as well as separately from CPAN. If you download the module from CPAN, be sure its version number matches the installation of the ImageMagick library. Binary distributions for several platforms (including Microsoft Windows) are available from the ImageMagick web pages (see [17]); however, if you can, compile it yourself. ImageMagick uses a multitude of external libraries and programs, and the more it is tuned to your system, the better.

Appendix A contains an introduction to and a reference for *Image::Magick*. Examples using the modules are presented throughout the book.

The code in this book should run with *Image::Magick* version 5.4.4. Older versions might lack some of the presented functionality, and some support for old methods or arguments might have been dropped or changed (see also section A.3 on page 245). Wherever possible, notes have been provided to warn the reader if this is the case. John Cristy is aware of this book, and has promised to keep new versions of *Image::Magick* as compatible with the presented code as possible.

3.2.8 Image::Size

This lightweight Perl module is intended mainly to be used in determining the size of image files. It will read various file formats, such as GIF, JPEG, XBM, XPM, PPM/PGM, PBM, PNG, TIFF, SWF, PSD and BMP. Its main subroutine, `imgsize()` returns the width, height, and image type as a list. You can pass it either a string containing a file name, a reference to a file handle, or a reference to a scalar containing the image data. The other two subroutines are merely convenience wrappers around `imgsize()`. The module is maintained by Randy Ray, and is based on code by Alex Knowles and Andrew Tong.

The module comes with a helpful documentation page, available through the `perldoc` command, and examples of its use can be found in section 2.2, "Finding the size and type of an image," on page 20. *Image::Size* version 2.93 was used to test this code.

3.2.9 Inline

The *Inline* modules allow a programmer to enclose non-Perl source code in a Perl program. The modules make sure that code gets compiled and loaded when needed. When the code is compiled, a cached copy of the object file is written to a (configurable) place, which means that it is compiled only once (unless you change the code). This helps to dramatically speed up subsequent executions. The most obvious place to use the *Inline* modules is wherever Perl's execution model is too slow to be useful.

The standard Inline distribution, written and maintained by Brian Ingerson, comes with the *Inline::C*, which lets you include C code in your Perl programs. CPAN also has Inline modules for C++, Python and CPR. According to the documentation, modules for Java, Fortran, Ruby and Bash are in the making.

An example of the use of *Inline::C* is available in section 12.4, "Alpha channels and transparency," on page 229. The code in this book was run with *Inline* version 0.43.

3.2.10 OpenGL

The *OpenGL* module is a Perl interface to the OpenGL programming interface, which in turn is a software interface to graphics hardware. OpenGL was developed by Silicon Graphics Inc. for their hardware and OS, but is now available for a wide range of platforms and is implemented on a large number of hardware graphics cards.

To use this module you must first have OpenGL installed on your system. Some operating systems come with the required libraries installed and available; with others you need to install them yourself. You can either buy a commercial implementation of the library, or download and install Mesa 3D (http://www.mesa3d.org/). This freely available, open source implementation of the OpenGL library is fully functional, and some unofficial support is even available from Silicon Graphics.

The *OpenGL* modules are available from CPAN. The latest version on CPAN is 0.5, which was placed there by Kenneth Albanowski, the original developer for the module. Ilya Zakharevich has added some portability code, fixed some problems and removed some bugs from this version; but these changes haven't made it to CPAN yet. At the time of this writing, the latest version of *OpenGL* is available from ftp://ftp.math.ohio-state.edu/pub/users/ilya/perl/modules. At some point in the not too distant future these updated versions will probably be made accessible by CPAN. (See the note on page 156.)

Examples of the use of *OpenGL* modules can be found in section 9.1, "OpenGL," on page 154. Version 0.54 of the OpenGL module was used to test this code, running on the Mesa 3D libraries, version 3.4.

3.2.11 PGPLOT

This module provides an interface to the PGPLOT graphics library, which is very popular with astronomers and many other scientists. It creates charts and plots for all kinds of data, but with a certain emphasis on data sets that would very likely be found on an astronomer's hard disk. The original PGPLOT library was written in FORTRAN by Tim Pearson but also comes with a C interface. The Perl module, written by Karl Glazebrook, is an almost direct mapping to this C interface, which in turn is an almost direct mapping to the FORTRAN library calls.

The documentation for the *PGPLOT* module from Perl explains only the calling conventions for all these functions, and refers the user to the original FORTRAN-based documentation available from the PGPLOT web pages (see [20]). In addition to the documentation, which is quite good, it is also advisable to browse through the examples that come with the PGPLOT library distribution and the *PGPLOT* module.

More information on and examples of the use of *PGPLOT* can be found in section 5.3, "PGPLOT," on page 76. The version used for these examples was 2.18, running on version 5.2 of the PGPLOT library.

3.2.12   RenderMan

The *RenderMan* module is an interface to Blue Moon Rendering Tools (http://www.bmrt.org), and can be used to directly interact with BMRT programs, or create RenderMan-compliant output files. The BMRT were originally written and developed by Larry Gritz, and development is now in the hands of Exluna.

The RenderMan API was developed by Pixar Animation Studios to provide a standard, portable communication layer between 3D modeling programs and rendering programs. The API doesn't concern itself with how the rendering is achieved, but only describes what gets rendered, and what its properties are. The rendering engine can choose any method it pleases to create computer graphics from the described scene.

To work with the output of this module, you will need a RenderMan-compliant renderer. The standard commercial one is Photorealistic RenderMan, Pixar's own engine. If you don't have a Hollywood-sized budget, the already mentioned BMRT is available for free for personal use, and for a small fee for commercial use.

The *RenderMan* module is further described in section 9.2 on page 164. The code in this section was tested against *RenderMan* 0.04 compiled with BMRT 2.5. The *RenderMan* module cannot be compiled against version 2.6 of BMRT without considerable work.

3.2.13   Term::Gnuplot

Term::Gnuplot provides a Perl interface to the output drivers that are part of the gnuplot program. It offers a set of drawing primitives useful for any drawing task, as long as this drawing task is simple. Changing the output format of a program simply becomes a matter of changing the output driver. The only downside is that the set of drawing commands is fairly limited, as it is geared toward providing the minimal functionality needed by the gnuplot program, hence it could require some work to get it do what you need it to. Some examples of how to use *Term::Gnuplot* are found in section 4.4, "Drawing with Term::Gnuplot," on page 55.

Term::Gnuplot was created and is maintained by Ilya Zakharevich, and is available from CPAN. Rudimentary documentation is available for both *Term::Gnuplot* and *Term::GnuplotTerminals*. The code in this book has been tested and run with *Term::Gnuplot* 0.5601 and 0.5703.

NOTE   When compiling version 0.5601 of *Term::Gnuplot*, I noticed that it expects your version of libgd to provide GIF output. Modern versions of libgd don't do that anymore, so if your make test fails with a message containing undefined symbol: gdImageGif, you might need to edit the Makefile.PL and gnuterm/Makefile.PL and comment out the references to libgd, or find an older version that still supports GIF.

3.3 A NOTE ON MODULE VERSIONS

In this section we've enumerated the versions of the various modules used to test the code in this book. When you start using newer versions than those mentioned here— and that time will come—there are no guarantees that the code will still perform identically, or even run. We are not seers, and cannot predict what the developers will do with their modules.

In general, most developers are careful not to change the interface to their modules drastically, so you shouldn't require too many changes to your code relevant to these modules. Normally, the version numbering schemes provide a hint on this. When minor numbers change, it usually means that the interface has not become incompatible with the older version.[3] However, it is likely that a module interface has changed when the major version number changes. So, if the version you have installed differs significantly from the one used in this book, make sure you read up on the changes to that module.

3.4 SUMMARY

In this chapter the modules and tools used in this book were described. Refer to this chapter whenever you need to install modules or programs used in the example code in this book, or when you want to know which particular versions of the software were used.

---

[3] This is not a rule set in stone, and specifically *Image::Magick* has been released with only minor version number changes, but with incompatibilities in the API.

## PART 2

Creating graphics

This part of the book covers the creation of graphics from within Perl, using various modules, tools and techniques. The subject matter ranges from the use of low-level drawing of squares, circles and lines, to a more high-level use of modules that create, for example, charts and graphs.

In chapter 4 we will look at how to create your own drawings, using the graphics primitives from the modules that are available.

Chapter 5 provides an introduction to the various ways you can create graphs and charts in your Perl program.

Chapter 6 offers methods to dynamically create and serve graphics on your web site, and chapter 7 discusses some techniques that can be used to create animations in Perl.

Chapter 8 shows various ways in which whole images can be manipulated and combined.

And finally, the creation of graphics from three-dimensional model data with the help of the *OpenGL* and *RenderMan* modules is discussed in chapter 9.

C H A P T E R   4

Drawing

Unless you already have all the graphics you will ever need, you have to create them; and if you already had everything you needed, you wouldn't be reading this book, so I assume that you do need to create some graphics yourself. This part of the book covers how to do this. Throughout the book you will find many ways in which to create graphics, such as charts, images for your web pages, or animations. In this particular chapter we'll have a look at the groundwork for most computer graphics generation: drawing.

In the most basic sense, drawing computer graphics consists of the manipulation of certain *drawing primitives*, such as circles, rectangles, lines and text. No matter which drawing package you use, you will find the same, or very similar, primitives, methods, and functions. All drawing packages also have in common a coordinate space in which to work, and the objects and primitives you work with are all expressed in terms of this coordinate space. For example, you draw a line from coordinates (12,12) to (30,0) or a circle with the center at (50,0) and a radius of 20. What these coordinates express depends on the drawing package: some use pixels, others points, centimeters, or inches. It is always possible to translate between these different coordinate systems, so it doesn't really matter what is used natively in a drawing package. When the result needs to be imported in another package, the relevant coordinate space transformations can be taken into account.

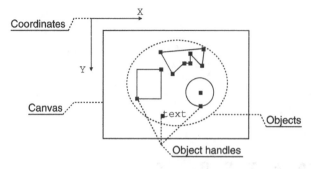

Figure 4.1
Some drawing primitives that can be created and manipulated with computer graphics programs and packages.

The drawing primitives for almost all graphics packages, Perl modules or otherwise, are limited to a fairly small set: lines, rectangles, circles, arcs, and polygons. One could argue that all that is really needed are a line and an arc, because all other primitives can be created from those. Nonetheless, the other primitives, such as the circle and rectangle, are sufficiently common to see them as primitives in their own right, especially when they need to be filled as well. Even though most drawing packages provide these primitives, each does it in a slightly different way.

One other previously mentioned primitive, which almost all packages define, is text. The handling of text is generally more complex than the other primitives, because it involves selections of fonts, calculations of bounding boxes and alignment concerns. These issues will be discussed in section 4.1.3 on page 43, section 4.2.4 on page 50, and in more detail in chapter 11.

The differences between drawing packages starts with the definition of a coordinate system. For some graphics applications, the coordinate origin is the bottom left of the canvas, and for others it's the top left. Some drawing packages work in real-life coordinates, such as inches or millimeters, and others work in pixels. I haven't seen any applications that have a coordinate system that is not Cartesian, but there is nothing that says it has to be, and in section 10.1.1, "Coordinate transformation," on page 180, we present a case in which a polar coordinate system is more convenient. Fortunately, the two main drawing packages for Perl, *GD* and *Image::Magick,* both use the same coordinate system: with the origin in the top left and the coordinates in pixels (see figure 4.1).

Many primitives can be specified in several ways. For example, the simple rectangle can be uniquely identified by providing the coordinates of one of its corners and the width and height of the rectangle. Alternatively, one can specify one of its corners and the corner on the other side of the diagonal. A circle can be specified as the coordinate of its center and a radius. It can also be specified as three points that are not on a straight line.[1] Another alternative is the coordinates of the center and the coordinates

---

[1] Euclidean geometry teaches us that a circle can always be drawn through any three points that are not on a straight line.

of one point on the circle itself. The only way to find out which of these specifications a drawing package uses, is to read its documentation.

In order to deal with all these ways of representing objects on a canvas, it helps if you are comfortable with geometric algebra, and can easily translate any of the specifications into something with which you are more comfortable.

In this chapter we'll look at how the various modules available for Perl deal with drawing primitives, what some of these primitives are, and how they can be used.

4.1 DRAWING WITH GD

GD provides a range of drawing primitives and some auxiliary methods, such as color allocation, color flood fill, and methods to set a brush. These methods are listed in table 4.1, and the text drawing methods are listed later in this chapter, in table 4.3 on page 45.

Table 4.1 The drawing primitives for the *GD* module which are available to the user of the module to create images. All of these methods should be called on a *GD::Image* object.

setPixel(x,y,color)	set the color of the pixel at the specified coordinates
line(x1,y1,x2,y2,color)	draw a solid line between the specified points
dashedLine(x1,y1,x2,y2,color)	draw a dashed line between the specified points
rectangle(x1,y1,x2,y2,color)	draw a rectangle with the specified corners
filledRectangle(x1,y1,x2,y2,color)	draw a filled rectangle with the specified corners
polygon(poly,color)	draw the polygon specified by poly, which is a polygon object created with GD::Polygon::new()
filledPolygon(poly,color)	draw the filled polygon specified by poly
arc(cx,cy,w,h,st,end,color)	draw an arc with the specified center, width and height, and start and end angle
fill(x,y,color)	flood-fill all pixels with the same color around the specified point
fillToBorder(x,y,bcolor,color)	flood-fill all pixels around the specified point, until a pixel with the specified bcolor is encountered
setBrush(brush)	Set the brush to be used to the specified brush, which is another *GD::Image* object
setStyle(color-list)	Set the line style to the specified color list. Each element of the list represents a single pixel on the line to be drawn.

Most drawing methods accept a color argument, which is either the index of a color previously allocated with one of the color allocation methods, or one of gdBrushed, gdStyled or gdStyledBrush. These three will cause the object to be drawn with the image's current brush, line style, or both.

Unfortunately, there is no filled form of the `arc()` drawing primitive, which can cause some hardship when trying to create filled partial circles or ellipses. There also is no variant of the arc primitive which allows you to specify a start and end point of the arc. Thus, it is almost impossible to reliably create a pie slice (or a pizza slice) that can be flood-filled. Because of little rounding errors it is possible that there are gaps between the arc that forms the outside bit of the slice, and the lines that form the wedge. When subsequently one of the fill methods is called, these little gaps will cause the flood-fill to leak out into the rest of your drawing. If there were an arc command that allowed one to specify start and end points, it would be possible to reliably close these gaps.

GD has its coordinate origin defined in the top left-hand corner of the canvas, at coordinate point (0,0). This means that all pixel coordinates are offset at 0, and the coordinates of the center point of a 100 by 100 pixel image are at (49,49).

In order to use colors in *GD* you first need to allocate them for your object. The total number of colors in a *GD::Image* object is limited to 256, which for most drawing purposes is fine (see also section 12.1, "GD and pixels," on page 211). You will find that you normally don't use more than about 10 colors anyway.

NOTE At the moment of writing, Thomas Boutell has a beta version of version 2 of libgd available for download. This new version supports true color images and a real alpha channel, and should become even more useful for all kinds of applications. Once this version of libgd stabilizes, I suspect that Lincoln Stein will release a new version of *GD*.

4.1.1 An example drawing

The best way to present how this works is to show some code:

```
use GD;

my $gd = GD::Image->new(400,300);          ● Create a new image

my $white  = $gd->colorAllocate(255, 255, 255);
my $black  = $gd->colorAllocate(  0,   0,   0);
my $red    = $gd->colorAllocate(255,   0,   0);     ● Allocate colors
my $green  = $gd->colorAllocate(  0, 255,   0);
my $blue   = $gd->colorAllocate(  0,   0, 255);
my $yellow = $gd->colorAllocate(255, 255,   0);

$gd->filledRectangle(0, 129, 199, 169, $blue);

my $poly = GD::Polygon->new();
$poly->addPt(199, 149);
$poly->addPt(399,  74);                    ❶ Create a polygon, and
$poly->addPt(324, 149);                       draw two copies
$poly->addPt(399, 224);
$gd->filledPolygon($poly, $yellow);
$gd->polygon       ($poly, $black);
```

```
$gd->arc(199, 149, 250, 250, 0, 360, $red);
$gd->arc(199, 149, 100, 200, 0, 360, $red);
$gd->fillToBorder(99, 149, $red, $green);

$gd->rectangle(0, 0, 399, 299, $red);
$gd->line(199, 0, 199, 299, $red);
$gd->line(0, 149, 399, 149, $red);
```

❷ **Create a circle, cut out an ellipse, and fill**

● **Frame with a red border, and draw a red cross**

The output of this program can be seen in figure 4.2.

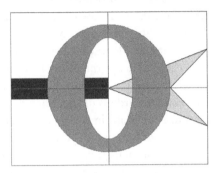

Figure 4.2
A simple drawing created with *GD*, demonstrating how to allocate color and use the `arc()`, `line()`, `rectangle()`, `filledRectangle()`, `filled-Polygon()`, and `fillToBorder()` drawing primitives and instructions.

A new image is created and a blue-filled rectangle is drawn around its horizontal center in the left half of the image.

❶ To draw a polygon, one first needs to create one with *GD::Polygon*'s `new()` method, and all the vertices need to be added to this polygon in order. In this case the polygon takes the shape of an arrowhead, pointing left, so we add the necessary points to the object. In general, it is not a bad idea to wrap this in a subroutine, one that possibly also takes a scaling parameter that can be used in the `map()` method which is provided for *GD::Polygon* objects. When all points have been added, the object can be used with the `polygon()` and `filledPolygon()` methods to actually draw it.

❷ The first call to the `arc()` method draws a red circle with a diameter of 250 pixels around the center of the image. Once that is done, an ellipse with a width of 100 pixels and a height of 200 pixels is drawn inside this circle. The circle and the ellipse now form the outlines of the big letter O that can be seen in figure 4.2. To fill the space between these two, a suitable point is picked in that area, and the `fillToBorder()` method is called, with the instruction to flood-fill until it encounters pixels that are red.

This example shows how to use most of the primitives provided by the *GD* module. The documentation that comes with *GD* is quite clear and extensive, and if you spend the minimum amount of time reading through it, you'll see how simple it is to use this module to create your drawings.

Real-life programs that need drawing capabilities will be only superficially more complex than the one presented here. The hardest job in graphics programming is defining what needs to be done, and subsequently mapping these requirements to the various primitives. In other words, the real complexity in graphics programming isn't writing the programs, but coming up with a clear way in which, with a limited set of tools, an objective can be reached.

4.1.2   Filling objects

It could prove useful to discuss filling of odd shapes, or even overlapping shapes, correctly with *GD*. The `fill()` method will color all the pixels that have the same color and that are adjacent to the target pixel. In other words, it will fill an area of uniform color that contains the target pixel. This works fine provided your drawing is not complex, and is relatively free of overlapping shapes. If however, the area that you want to fill isn't entirely uniform, but contains lines or edges in another color, this method cannot be used. Instead, you can use the `fillToBorder()` method.

The `fillToBorder()` method can be used to change the color of all adjacent pixels until another specified color is encountered. This last method can be used to create some interesting shapes, and fill them correctly, regardless of the other colors already present. But what if the image already has lines or blobs in the area that you need to fill, and these lines are of the identical color you wish to use for your border? You solve that problem by keeping one special color around, which you use only to create fill borders. Since colors in *GD* are always specified as an index, it doesn't even matter what RGB values you use for this.

Let's demonstrate this: suppose you need to add some more elements to the image from figure 4.2, with the same colors already present in the image. You decide to use the `colorResolve()` method to get at those colors, so that you don't accidentally run out of room in the palette. The element you want to add is a partial ellipse, and you want it to have a black border and a green inside.

You draw the partial ellipse and the boundary lines with the black color that you obtained from the `colorResolve()` method. Then you use `fillToBorder()` to fill the resulting figure with green, only to find out that the fill stops at the edges of the yellow polygon. You can solve this by creating a temporary color that you use as a boundary.

```
use GD;

my $gd = GD::Image->newFromPng('GDExample.png');

my $black  = $gd->colorResolve(  0,   0,   0);
my $green  = $gd->colorResolve(  0, 196,   0);

my $border = $gd->colorAllocate(0,   0,   0);

$gd->arc (199, 149, 300, 100, 0, 270, $border);
$gd->line(199, 149, 199,  99, $border);
$gd->line(199, 149, 349, 149, $border);
$gd->fillToBorder(149, 149, $border, $green);

$gd->arc (199, 149, 300, 100, 0, 270, $black);
$gd->line(199, 149, 199,  99, $black);
$gd->line(199, 149, 349, 149, $black);

$gd->colorDeallocate($border);
```

● **Allocate colors, and reuse ones that exist**

● **Allocate a color for the border**

● **Draw the arc's border, and fill**

❶ **Redraw in the wanted color**

❷ **Remove the border color**

The result of this code can be seen in figure 4.3. Note that the $border color is exactly the same color, by RGB value, as $black. However, since each color in *GD* is uniquely identified by a palette index, they are in effect different colors, their appearance notwithstanding. It matters little which RGB values you choose for the temporary border color.

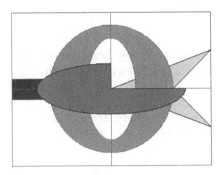

Figure 4.3
Adding a filled shape to an image with *GD*, using fillToBorder() with a temporary color for the border to make sure that the resulting filled shape is correct.

❶ After the flood fill has stopped, the color you used as a border color is still visible as a line around the object just filled. To resolve this, you can redraw the original shape, but this time in the desired color. For fully solid shapes, this would be the same color as the one used to fill the object.

❷ When the border color is no longer needed, it should be deallocated. This serves mainly to prevent repeated reads and writes of the same image, together with the operations discussed here, resulting in a palette which is filled with useless duplicate border colors. If this were not done, you would have to clean up the palette every time you detected that you were running out of index entries. (See section 12.1.2, "Removing duplicate color palette entries," on page 212, for a way to do this.)

Using this technique you can create shapes as complex as you wish. As long as these shapes can be limited on all sides by a unique color (and this should be a temporary color), you can fill the shape with any other color you want, after which you can redraw the boundaries in the colors you intended initially. In fact, it is not a bad idea to always use this method when you use fillToBorder(). It requires a few more lines of code, but is also much more portable and safe. If you ever move your code fragment that draws this complex shape into a subroutine, and start using that subroutine in all kinds of programs, you will benefit mightily from making certain that the border color you use will be unique in the whole image.

4.1.3 Drawing text with GD

The GD module has various ways to draw text. First, you can use one of the set of compiled-in fonts. These fonts are all of a fixed width and height, and are *GD::Font* objects. There are several methods available for these objects that allow the programmer to extract some information about them. The built-in fonts can only be drawn horizontally or vertically.

In later versions of GD, you can also use TrueType fonts. These can be scaled to virtually any size and drawn at any angle. The TrueType fonts in *GD* are not wrapped in an object, but enough information about the text to be drawn can be obtained through the use of the `stringTTF()` method.

4.1.4 GD's built-in fonts

The built-in font types in GD can be used by specifying their symbolic short name, or by invoking the *GD::Font* package method associated with them. The fonts and their character sizes in pixels are:

Table 4.2 The names of the built-in fonts in *GD* as aliases, and as fully specified *GD::Font* objects. Either of these names can be used anywhere a *GD::Image* method requires a font name.

short name	font object	size
gdTinyFont	GD::Font->Tiny	5 x 8
gdSmallFont	GD::Font->Small	6 x 13
gdMediumBoldFont	GD::Font->MediumBold	7 x 13
gdLargeFont	GD::Font->Large	8 x 16
gdGiantFont	GD::Font->Giant	9 x 15

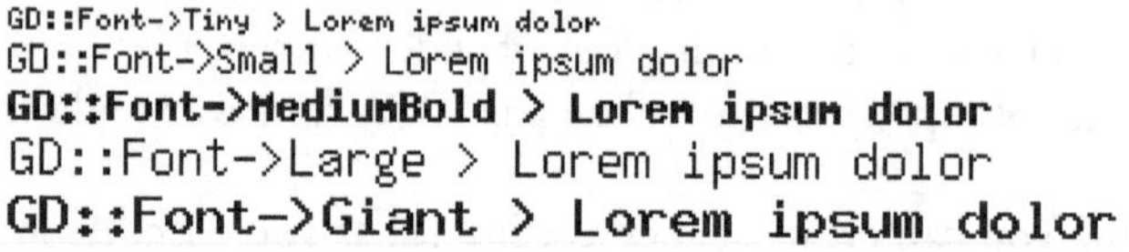

```
GD::Font->Tiny > Lorem ipsum dolor
GD::Font->Small > Lorem ipsum dolor
GD::Font->MediumBold > Lorem ipsum dolor
GD::Font->Large > Lorem ipsum dolor
GD::Font->Giant > Lorem ipsum dolor
```

Figure 4.4
The built-in fonts for *GD*.

These fonts are not pretty, but they do a reasonably good job for most low-resolution graphics, such as the ones you would display on a web page. Additionally, because they are compiled in and of a fixed size, they are really fast to use.

For the built-in fonts, you can use the `string()`, `stringUp()`, `char()` and `charUp()` object methods. The last two methods are an inheritance from the C interface of `libgd`; in Perl, of course, there is no formal distinction between characters and strings.

```
$im->string  (gdMediumBoldFont, 0, 0, 'Black Medium Bold', $black);
$im->stringUp(gdGiantFont,  0, 100, 'Red Giant', $red);
$im->char  (gdSmallFont, 50,  50, 'A', $black);
$im->charUp  (GD::Font->Tiny , 60,  50, 'B', $black);
```

This example uses both the short name and the full *GD::Font* object name as arguments to the methods; they are interchangeable. The coordinates that these functions expect denote the upper left corner for `string()` and `char()`, and the lower left corner for `stringUp()` and `charUp()`. Of course, from the string's perspective, these are both the upper left corner, and maybe that's a better way to look at it.

There are some methods available for the *GD::Font* objects that can be used to retrieve information.

```
$nchars = gdGiantFont->nchars;
$offset = GD::Font->Tiny->offset;
$width  = gdSmallFont->width;
$height = gdSmallFont->height;
```

The `nchars()` method tells us how many characters this font provides, and the `offset()` method gives us the ASCII value of the first character in the font. The `width()` and `height()` methods return the dimensions of a single character in the font, which is useful, since that means we don't have to hard-code font sizes in our programs.

Table 4.3   The text drawing primitives for *GD*. The top part of the table shows all methods that work on the built-in fonts, and the bottom part of the table shows the method that can be used for TrueType fonts. Note that the possibilities of drawing TrueType strings are more flexible and advanced than for built-in fonts.

string(font,x,y,string,color)	draw a horizontal string starting at the specified point
stringUp(font,x,y,string,color)	draw a vertical string starting at the specified point
char(font,x,y,char,color)	draw a single character starting at the specified point
charUp(font,x,y,char,color)	draw a vertical character starting at the specified point
stringTTF(color,font,size, angle,x,y,string)	draw a string with a TrueType font of the specified size starting at the specified point

4.1.5   TrueType fonts and GD

Versions of GD since 1.20 also support TrueType fonts, which can be drawn with the `stringTTF()` method. This method can be called as an object method (`$gd_object->stringTTF()`), in which case it draws the string on the calling object, or as a class method (`GD::Image->stringTTF()`), in which case it returns the bounding box of the text to be drawn, without actually drawing it. The list returned from this method consists of eight elements, denoting four coordinate pairs: the *x* and *y* coordinates of the lower left, lower right, upper right and upper left corner, in that order. The `stringTTF()` method draws the string aligned to the left side of the baseline of the font.

The following code first requests the bounding box for a string, and then adapts the coordinates by subtracting the horizontal and vertical offset from the baseline. This ensures that the string is aligned to the requested coordinates with its upper left corner.

```
$text     = 'String';
$font     = '/usr/share/fonts/ttfonts/arialbd.ttf';
$fontsize = 12;
$angle    = 0;
($x, $y)  = (20, 25);

@bb = GD::Image->stringTTF(0, $font, $fontsize, $angle, $x, $y, $text);
$x += $x - $bb[6];
$y += $y - $bb[7];
$im->stringTTF($black, $font, $fontsize, $angle, $x, $y, $text);
```

You might wonder why we bother recalculating the *x* coordinate as well as the *y* coordinate. That is because sometimes the bounding box returned by `stringTTF()` is slightly offset to the right; in other words, the baseline used to draw the string is not always exactly vertically aligned with the requested coordinates. If you don't need such precision, you can dispense with this check.

SEE ALSO   More manipulations of strings with the *GD* module can be found in chapter 11, as well as examples on how to align and position strings precisely.

4.2 DRAWING WITH IMAGE::MAGICK

Image::Magick possesses a wealth of methods, but few are actually designed to help create drawings. In fact, only one method is really useful, and that is the appropriately named `Draw()` method. There are quite a large number of options that can be passed to the method, and there are quite a number of primitives.

4.2.1 An example drawing

Let's see how the code would look in creating the same drawing as we did with *GD* in the previous section.

```
use Image::Magick;                                    ● Create a new empty
                                                         image object
my $im = Image::Magick->new(size => '400x300');

$im->Read('xc:white');                   ● Add a white image, and set
$im->Set(stroke => 'red');                  the default color

$im->Draw(primitive => 'rectangle',
          points     => '0,129 199,169',   ● Draw a rectangle
          fill       => 'blue',
          stroke     => 'blue');

$im->Draw(primitive => 'polygon',
          points     =>                    ● Draw a polygon
            '199,149 399,74 324,149 399,224',
          fill       => 'yellow',
          stroke     => 'black');

$im->Set(antialias => 0, fuzz => 15);   ❷ Tweak some parameters
```

```
$im->Draw(primitive => 'circle',
       strokewidth => 3,
          points     => '199,149 74,149');
$im->Draw(primitive => 'ellipse',
       strokewidth => 3,
          points     => '199,149 50,100 0,360');

$im->Draw(primitive    => 'color',
       method       => 'filltoborder',
       points       => '99,149',
       bordercolor  => 'red',
       fill         => 'green1');

$im->Draw(primitive => 'rectangle',
          points     => '0,0 399,299');
$im->Draw(primitive => 'line',
          points     => '199,0 199,299');
$im->Draw(primitive => 'line',
          points     => '0,149 399,149');
```

❶ Draw a circle and cut out an ellipse

❷ Flood-fill the gap

❸ Frame with a red border and cross

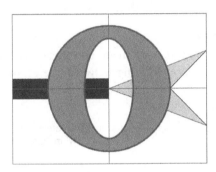

Figure 4.5
An example drawing created with *Image::Magick*, demonstrating the use of the `rectangle`, `polygon`, `circle`, `ellipse`, `filltoborder`, and `line` drawing instructions. The border lines need to be wide to avoid the fill color bleeding out of the circles, due to antialiasing.

As you can see, the code for *Image::Magick* is much more verbose than that for *GD*, even if we make use of a default drawing color. It is, however, not difficult to follow. To understand what the various parameters to the Draw() method mean, and how the points attribute changes its meaning for the various primitives, read the description of Draw() on page 257 in appendix A.

❶ The output of this example can be seen in figure 4.5. You immediately notice that the lines in this image are much wider than the lines in figure 4.2. You might have also noticed that these wide lines have been explicitly requested in the code. We will look at why, in this particular example, such wide lines were necessary.

4.2.2 Anti-alias and fuzz

❷ The use of the anti-alias and fuzz attributes warrants more explanation. By default, *Image::Magick* will anti-alias all objects it draws. However, since we want to use the red ellipses as boundaries to fill to, we need them to be of a reasonably uniform color, and anti-aliasing removes that uniformity. Even with anti-aliasing turned off, we still need fuzzy color matching, because of the way these algorithms work in *Image::Magick*. The fuzz attribute allows the color matching algorithms to match a color *near* the one we have specified, instead of matching only the exact color. The higher the value specified for fuzz, the more lenient the color matching will be.

Another solution could have been to draw the circle with an anti-aliased line width of 5, and to use a higher fuzziness. As it is, we already need to use a line width of 3 to prevent the fill color to bleed through. Either of the two methods can be used, and both are equally hard to get right. If at all possible, it is much better to stroke and fill in one go with *Image::Magick*.

NOTE   While playing with the anti-alias and fuzz attributes allows us to create shapes that we can successfully fill, it does require wide lines, and that is just not always desirable. Apart from that, it is not really possible to come up with a good set of rules that can be used to pick a decent value for the fuzz attribute. Instead, we have to rely on manually tweaking this value until the drawing looks as close to what we want as possible. We'll explore a few alternative ways of achieving our goal in the next sections.

4.2.3   Drawing by combining images

Another way to achieve the drawing we want is to create two images and combine them. In the code in the previous section, everything between the drawing of the polygon and the drawing of the red box can be replaced by the creation of a new image, on which the green O is drawn:

```
my $im2 = Image::Magick->new(size => '400x300');      ● Create a new
$im2->Read('xc:white');                                 white image

$im2->Draw(primitive => 'circle',
           stroke    => 'red',
           fill      => 'green1',
           points    => '199,149 74,149');
$im2->Draw(primitive => 'ellipse',
           stroke    => 'red',
           fill      => 'white',
           points    => '199,149 50,100 0,360');
                                               ● Make the background
$im2->Transparent(color => 'white');             transparent

$im->Composite(image   => $im2,      ● Combine with other image
               compose => 'Over');
```

The output of this code can be seen in figure 4.6. It is very similar to figure 4.5, except that the outlines of the O are thinner, and more smooth. However, the combination of the two images has introduced some slight artifacts where the O overlaps the polygon and the rectangle. This is due to the fact that *Image::Magick* has antialiased the edge of the circle it drew against the background of the secondary image, which was white. The call to the Transparent() method makes all white pixels in the image transparent, but the determination of which pixels are white is, once again, subject to the fuzzy matching that *Image::Magick* employs. The artifacts that show up are the pixels that weren't considered to be white.

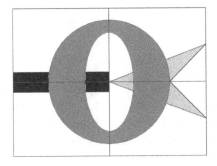

Figure 4.6
Creating a drawing with *Image::Magick* by overlaying several separate images which each represent part of the complete drawing.

The artifacts on the outside can be removed by starting with a transparent image, instead of a white one:

```
$im2->Read('xc:none');
```

This leaves the pixels on the inside of the O. Of course, we could simply increase the fuzziness of the matching algorithm before calling `Transparent()`. In this particular case that would probably work well, but it is not a universally workable solution. If we could fill the inner ellipse with a fully transparent color, there would be no artifacts; but unfortunately, setting the fill color to *none* or another color with full transparency (such as #000000ff) doesn't help, and the transparency will be silently ignored.[2]

There is one other solution that combines images, and that is to create a transparency mask for the secondary image:

```
my $im2 = Image::Magick->new(size => '400x300');
$im2->Read('xc:white');
$im2->Draw(primitive => 'circle',
           stroke    => 'red',
           fill      => 'green1',
           points    => '199,149 74,149');
$im2->Draw(primitive => 'ellipse',
           stroke    => 'red',
           fill      => 'white',
           points    => '199,149 50,100 0,360');

my $mask = Image::Magick->new(size => '400x300');
$mask->Read('xc:white');
$mask->Draw(primitive => 'circle',
            stroke    => 'black',
            fill      => 'black',
```

---

[2] It is anticipated that this will be fixed in a future release of *Image::Magick*

```
            points    => '199,149 74,149');
$mask->Draw(primitive => 'ellipse',
            stroke    => 'black',
            fill      => 'white',
            points    => '199,149 50,100 0,360');

$im2->Composite(image   => $mask,
                compose => 'ReplaceMatte');
$im ->Composite(image   => $im2,
                compose => 'Over');
```

Calls to `Transparent()` are eliminated because the transparency is created by the mask. The mask is created by repeating the drawing instructions on the new image, but with the colors set to either black or white, depending on what you want to be transparent and what opaque. A fully black pixel in the mask will result in an opaque pixel after the composition with the `ReplaceMatte` method, and a fully white pixel will result in a transparent pixel.

SEE ALSO   More discussion on how image composition works in *Image::Magick* can be found in section 8.2.2, "Combining Image::Magick images," on page 142, more on transparency and alpha masks in section 12.4, "Alpha channels and transparency," on page 229, and a description of the `Draw()` method and all its arguments in appendix A on page 257.

While the result of this method is reasonably acceptable, it is a lot to deal with, and the code to create images like these often becomes quite verbose. Overlaying images can be a very useful tool (see for example sections 8.2, "Combining Images," on page 140 and 12.4, "Alpha channels and transparency," on page 229), but it does not entirely provide us with the desired outcome for this particular task. Let's have a look at another method to achieve the drawing we want.

4.2.4   Drawing with paths

The two previous examples required several commands, and either some artful manipulation of fuzzy color matching or extra images to draw the filled O shape. There is a third way to draw this figure: recent versions of *Image::Magick* have introduced the *path* drawing primitive, based on the drawing paths in the Scalable Graphics Vector format.[3] These paths are formed by positioning a virtual pen and drawing strokes with this pen, based on a string of commands. The letters in the string define a drawing instruction, and the numbers following those letters are the arguments and coordinates for the command. Lowercase letters take relative coordinates to the current point, and uppercase letters take absolute coordinates; for example, a capital *M* means *move to* the coordinates that follow, and a lowercase *a* indicates an *arc* drawn relative to the current coordinates.

---

[3] For more information on the SVG format, see page 281. The *path* primitive is explained in more detail in appendix A.

With paths, all the work needed in the previous examples can be done with one single operation. The code to draw just the O shape is:

```
$im->Draw(
    primitive   => 'path',
    stroke      => 'black',
    fill        => 'green1',
    points      => 'M 74,149
                    a 125,125 0 0,1 250,0
                    a 125,125 0 0,1 -250,0
                    M 149,149
                    a 50,100 0 0,1 100,0
                    a 50,100 0 0,1 -100,0 z');
```

and the result of that code can be seen in figure 4.7. The remainder of the code stays exactly the same. As you can see, this avoids both the fat lines from the first example, as well as the introduced artifacts of the second example.

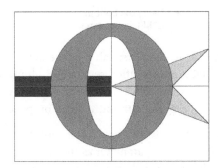

Figure 4.7
Drawing with *Image::Magick*'s path primitive, which allows complex filled shapes without artifacts.

The first line of the path specified in the example positions the pen at the coordinates (74,149). The arguments to the arc command *a* are the horizontal and vertical radius, the rotation of the arc, two flags that indicate the direction in which the arc will be drawn (see figure A.9 on page 283), and the second point through which to draw the arc. The coordinates of this second point are specified relative to the current position of the pen which is, of course, also the first point through which the arc runs. The path is closed by ending the command string with a *z*.

Which technique to use depends on your needs and the complexity of what you want to achieve. Most drawing tasks won't require the combining of images, but knowing that it can be done allows you to produce a drawing that most closely approximates what you intended to create.

4.2.5   Drawing text with Image::Magick

With *Image::Magick* you have a choice of several font specifications and sources (see also "Fonts," on page 278). You can use a qualified X11 font name such as -*-times-medium-r-*-*-12-*-*-*-p-*-*-*, a PostScript name like Helvetica, or a TrueType font from a file with @arialbd.

The following are possible ways in which we can draw text with *Image::Magick*:

```
$im->Read('xc:white')

$rc = $im->Annotate(
    x     => 10,
    y     => 20,
    text => 'Some String');          ❶ Using Annotate()
                                        to draw text
$rc = $im->Annotate(
    text      => 'Green Text',
    font      => '@timesbd.ttf',
    fill      => 'green',
    geometry  => '+20+30',
    pointsize => 8);

$rc = $im->Draw(
    primitive => 'Text',             ❷ Using Draw() with
    points    => '0,40 "Other String"');   the Text primitive

$rc = $im->Read('label:New Image');  ❸ Using the built in
                                        LABEL image type
```

❶ Annotate() is used in two ways in this code. The first call uses the default font and colors to draw a string, and the coordinates are specified separately. The second call customizes almost everything that can be customized, and uses the geometry attribute to specify the coordinates. Annotate() is described in more detail on page 252.

❷ As you can see, drawing text with Draw() is quite awkward. The coordinates and the contents of the string have to be passed as a single parameter as the value of the points attribute. This can easily cause your code to look ugly when the coordinates and the text are all variables, and the quotes and escaping of quotes become messy. Splitting up your string and concatenating it, or using the qq() operator instead of quotes can help to keep it all readable. The Draw() method is described in further detail on page 257.

❸ The last line demonstrates the use of Read() with the built-in LABEL image type, to create an image with text only. This can be used to approximately predict the size of the string to be drawn, before we actually draw it on an image. We will see more on this in section 11.1, "Determining text size," on page 191.

SEE ALSO *Image::Magick* is described in quite some detail in appendix A, and it would probably be a good idea to browse through it to familiarize yourself with its functionality. The Draw() method is discussed in the section, "Draw()," on page 257, and the path primitive in section A.7, "The path drawing primitive," on page 281. The global image options are discussed in section A.4, "Image attributes," on page 246, and acceptable color and font names are described in "Common method arguments," on page 276. More information on combining images with *Image::Magick* can be found in section 8.2.2, "Combining Image::Magick images," on page 142.

4.3 COMBINING *GD* AND *IMAGE::MAGICK*

There might be a time when you would like to use *GD* to draw some objects, then transport your image to *Image::Magick*, manipulate it a bit, maybe draw some more, and then transport it back. One good reason to do this is to make use of the many image filters and special effects that *Image::Magick* provides, while benefitting from the higher speed of drawing in *GD*. Also, it might be that you have all this legacy code lying around that uses *GD*, and now you need to do something that this module doesn't allow, but *Image::Magick* does. Instead of rewriting all your code, you can use the techniques presented in this section to allow you to keep using all your legacy code, at least until you find the time to fully rewrite it all.[4] Of course, there is a computational cost associated with transporting the image back and forth between the two modules, so you will have to take that into consideration before you decide to go this way.

One way of transporting the image data between the modules is to save the image to a file with one module, and read it with the other. However, this is terribly inefficient and unnecessary. Since version 1.30, the *GD::Image*'s new() method accepts more arguments, and it is now possible to pass in the raw data of the image file as a scalar. Together with the ImageToBlob() and BlobToImage() methods that *Image::Magick* provides, we have a perfect mechanism to transport images back and forth between the two modules. The following example code illustrates how to transport an image in both directions:

```
use GD;
use Image::Magick;

my $gd = GD::Image->new(400,100);
my $white  = $gd->colorAllocate(255, 255, 255);
my $red    = $gd->colorAllocate(255,   0,   0);
my $blue   = $gd->colorAllocate(  0,   0, 255);
my $yellow = $gd->colorAllocate(255, 255,   0);

$gd->filledRectangle(49, 2, 349, 97, $yellow);
$gd->rectangle      (49, 2, 349, 97, $blue);
$gd->stringTTF($red,
    '/usr/share/fonts/ttfonts/arialbd.ttf',
    30, 0, 74, 64, 'This is a flag');
```

```
my $rc;
my $im = Image::Magick->new();
$rc = $im->BlobToImage($gd->png);
die $rc if $rc;

$rc = $im->Wave(amplitude => 12);
warn $rc if $rc;
```

❶ Transport the image from GD to Image::Magick

● Make the rectangle look like a wavy flag

---

[4] As if *that* is ever going to happen...

```
$rc = $im->Quantize(colors => 256);
warn $rc if $rc;
$gd = GD::Image->new($im->ImageToBlob());

$red = $gd->colorClosest(255, 0, 0);
my ($w, $h) = $gd->getBounds();
$gd->rectangle(0, 0, $w - 1, $h - 1, $red);
```

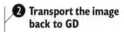

2 Transport the image
back to GD

3 Draw a rectangle
around the edge of the
image

Figure 4.8
An image created with a combination
of *GD* and *Image::Magick*. The flag
was drawn with *GD*, the wave effect
applied with *Image::Magick*, and the
border drawn again with *GD*.

In this case, the whole figure could have been created with the *Image::Magick* object directly. But the point is that there might be situations, as discussed earlier, in which you have good reason to do it this way.

1 To export the image from *GD* and import it into *Image::Magick*, the output from the png() method is directly fed into the BlobToImage() method. In real production code it might not be a bad idea to make this into two separate steps, and to verify in between that everything went as planned.

NOTE   While *Image::Magick* is designed to preserve as much as possible from any image that gets imported, this is certainly not true for *GD*. The latter is limited to working with a 256 color palette (but also see the note on page 40), of which only one can be marked as transparent. *Image::Magick* supports full RGB color as well as an 8-bit alpha channel for transparency; hence, if you export an image from *Image::Magick* to *GD*, you run the risk of losing some information. Whether that is acceptable depends on the image, and on what you are prepared to sacrifice.

2 *GD*'s limited palette is the reason the Quantize() method is called before exporting the image data back to *GD* from *Image::Magick*. We make certain that the number of colors introduced in the Wave() operation due to anti-aliasing doesn't exceed the 256 with which *GD* can comfortably deal. If you don't do this, the output of BlobToImage might be a truecolor PNG format, and *GD* doesn't deal with that very well. We hand the output of ImageToBlob() directly to *GD*'s new() method. This is doable, as the image type of the $im object will default to PNG, since that is also what it read in. Thus we know that *GD* will be able to read it.

3 Once the image is back in *GD* we get the closest color to a pure red, and draw a rectangular frame around the edges of the image. This is done mainly to show that it is actually possible. There is, of course, no guarantee that the color we will be using is actually pure red, since we use the colorClosest() call, but that is the price we pay for working with a small palette.

Once we're finished working with $gd, we can save the image, print it, or even pass it back to *Image::Magick* again. The point is that it is easy to do this, although it is also computationally slightly expensive. Use this only if you have an absolutely genuine need to do so.

4.4 DRAWING WITH TERM::GNUPLOT

The Perl module *Term::Gnuplot* provides an interface to the drawing routines and terminal drivers that are used internally by gnuplot (see section 5.4, "Interfacing with gnuplot," on page 85). Because these routines have been specifically designed and written for gnuplot, they are also strictly limited to the functionality required by this charting program, which means they are *very* limited. But even with the few primitives that *Term::Gnuplot* provides, one can do surprisingly nice things.

One feature that makes *Term::Gnuplot* worth looking at is the large number of output devices that it supports, many of which are vector based, making it feasible to create graphics with this module that scales a lot better than do images. As said, the main reason for these terminal drivers is to supply gnuplot internally with a drawing interface that is consistent for all output. However, paraphrasing an old saying: all output terminals are equal, but some are more equal than others; i.e., that, while all terminal drivers provide the identical interface, not all terminals have the same capabilities. The actual results cannot always be as finely controlled as one would like to see in a generic drawing package, as the interface is written to a lowest common denominator, and sometimes at a fairly abstract high level.

For example, not all terminals support color, so there is no direct way to manipulate the color of the line you're drawing. Instead there are generic line types (set with line_type()). How exactly a particular line type gets drawn is up to the driver, and the driver alone. Font support is another feature that differs markedly between the various terminals. Some, such as the PostScript one, support several built-in fonts, others support only a very small list.

In practice, unless you can make your drawing very generic, you shouldn't be using this module.

In part, to steer past some of the problems that a totally generic drawing interface introduces, each terminal device in *Term::Gnuplot* has its own characteristics and options that can be set with the set_options() function. What exactly those options do, and how they affect the outcome of the drawing, is up to the driver. All terminal drivers, and their options, are documented in the *Term::GnuplotTerminals* documentation, as well as in the internal help of the gnuplot program.

Let's write something that makes *Term::Gnuplot* do what it does best: a program that plots a function.[5] The skeleton of the program looks like this:

---

[5] This example borrows heavily from Ilya Zakharevich's example in the *Term::Gnuplot* documentation.

```
use Term::Gnuplot ':ALL';

plot_outfile_set('TermGnuplot.eps');
change_term('postscript');
set_options('eps', 'enhanced', '"Helvetica"', 24);
term_init();
term_start_plot();

draw_axes(-6, 6, -1, 1, 0.1);
plot_function(sub {sin $_[0]/2});
plot_function(sub {cos $_[0] * sin $_[0]});
plot_function(sub {-0.2 * $_[0]}, 2);

term_end_plot();
Term::Gnuplot::reset;
```

❶ Set up and initialize the terminal

Plot some functions

❷ And end the output

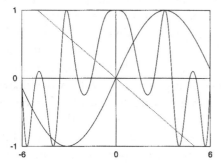

Figure 4.9
The drawing capabilities of
***Term::Gnuplot* lend themselves**
well for plotting functions, which is
not surprising, given that the mod-
ule is an interface to the drawing li-
brary of gnuplot.

❶ There are a few things that need to be set up before we can start writing the code that actually creates the drawing. First, we need to initiate and open an output device with `plot_outfile_set()`, `change_term()` and `set_options()`. These three lines are the only output-specific code in the program. For this particular example we'll create an EPS output file, and initiate the font to a 24-point Helvetica. Once that is done, the terminal can be initialized and the plot started.

❷ After all the drawing is completed, we need to call `term_end_plot()` to end our plot, and `Term::Gnuplot::reset()`[6] to free all resources that were allocated with `term_init()`. Calling `reset()` is optional if you are going to exit from the program anyway, but it's a good idea to get into the habit of making it part of your code.

We'll now have a look at the function that draws the axes of the plot, and sets up some variables needed for the plotting functions.

```
my ($h_offset, $v_offset);
my ($delta_x, $delta_y);
my ($xmin, $xmax, $ymin, $ymax);
```

❶ Some variables used by
draw_axes() and
plot_function()

---

[6] We use the fully qualified name of the subroutine here, because the name `reset()` is already taken by a Perl built-in function.

CHAPTER 4 DRAWING

```
sub draw_axes
{
    my ($margin);
    ($xmin, $xmax, $ymin, $ymax, $margin) = @_;
    my ($h_points, $v_points);

    $h_offset = $v_offset = 0;
    $h_points = scaled_xmax() - 1;
    $v_points = scaled_ymax() - 1;

    if ($margin)
    {
        $h_offset  = $margin * $h_points;
        $v_offset  = $margin * $v_points;
        $h_points -= 2 * $h_offset;
        $v_points -= 2 * $v_offset;
    }

    linetype -2;
    linewidth 2;
    move  ($h_offset,               $v_offset);
    vector($h_offset + $h_points, $v_offset);
    vector($h_offset + $h_points, $v_offset + $v_points);
    vector($h_offset            , $v_offset + $v_points);
    vector($h_offset            , $v_offset);

    justify_text(RIGHT);
    put_text($h_offset - h_char(), $v_offset, $ymin);
    put_text($h_offset - h_char(), $v_offset + $v_points, $ymax);
    justify_text(CENTRE);
    put_text($h_offset, $v_offset - v_char(), $xmin);
    put_text($h_offset + $h_points, $v_offset - v_char(), $xmax);

    $delta_x = ($xmax - $xmin)/$h_points;
    $delta_y = ($ymax - $ymin)/$v_points;

    if ($xmin < 0 && $xmax > 0)
    {
        my $h_zero = $h_offset - $xmin/$delta_x;
        move  ($h_zero, $v_offset);
        vector($h_zero, $v_offset + $v_points);
        justify_text(CENTRE);
        put_text($h_zero, $v_offset - v_char(), "0");
    }
    if ($ymin < 0 && $ymax > 0)
    {
        my $v_zero = $v_offset - $ymin/$delta_y;
        move  ($h_offset,               $v_zero);
        vector($h_offset + $h_points, $v_zero);
        justify_text(RIGHT);
        put_text($h_offset - h_char(), $v_zero, "0");
    }
}
```

❷ Set up the boundaries of the plot

❸ Draw the box

❹ Draw the axes

❶ The `draw_axes()` subroutine initializes the coordinates for the plot relative to the actual coordinates of the medium we're working with, and draws the axes. It accepts 5 arguments: The minimum and maximum *x* value to plot, the minimum and maximum *y* values to plot and the amount of space to leave open for margins. This last parameter is relative to the total size, i.e., a value of 0.1 will leave a 10 percent margin all around the plot.

❷ The subroutine starts off by asking the terminal it is going to write to how many horizontal and vertical points it has. The plotting code will use those numbers for the resolution with which the functions are going to be plotted.

❸ Once we have calculated the resolution of the plot, it is time to draw a box. We set the line type and width, and move the pen to the lower left corner of the box in which the plot will appear. We then draw the box with the four `vector()` calls. These calls are equivalent to a `lineto` statement in PostScript or SVG paths; they draw a straight line. To complete the box, we put the requested minimum and maximum values along the axes. If the *x* or *y* values to be plotted include 0, we also plot the zero point axes, and label them as such.

❹ The axes inside the plot are only drawn when necessary; if the zero point doesn't fall between the minimum and maximum axis on the value, we don't need to draw anything.

The subroutine that plots the functions is:

```
sub plot_function
{
    my $function   = shift;
    my $line_type  = shift || 0;
    my $line_width = shift || 4;

    linetype $line_type;
    my $moved = 0;

    for (my $x = $xmin; $x <= $xmax; $x += $delta_x)
    {
        my $y = $function->($x);
        next unless $y >= $ymin && $y <= $ymax;
        my $hor = $h_offset + ($x - $xmin)/$delta_x;
        my $ver = $v_offset + ($y - $ymin)/$delta_y;
        ($moved) &&
            vector($hor, $ver) ||
            move   ($hor, $ver), $moved = 1;
    }
}
```

The `plot_function()` subroutine is fairly simple. It accepts as its first argument a reference to a subroutine that can be used to calculate the *y* value, given an *x* value, and a line type and width as the optional second and third arguments. To determine the resolution and boundaries of the plot, it uses the values that were previously calculated and set by `draw_axes()`.

The output of this code can be seen in figure 4.9. As you can see, the result is surprisingly good-looking for a relatively simple program.

Using *Term::Gnuplot* can seem daunting at first, but once you have built yourself a few subroutines such as the ones just described, it becomes easier to deal with. All you need to do is write some wrapper functions that allow you to draw some circles, squares, and other shapes, and maybe some fill patterns. *Term::Gnuplot* will never take the place of *GD* or *Image::Magick*, but it does provide a low-level drawing library that is capable of creating various vector format graphics.

SEE ALSO The documentation for *Term::Gnuplot* is fairly minimal at this time; however, it provides enough information to work with the modules with sufficient study. The terminals and output devices that are supported by this module are documented in a separate manual page: *Term::GnuplotTerminals*.

4.5 *POSTSCRIPT AND SVG*

Most of this chapter has focused on creating image graphics with *GD* and *Image::Magick*. *Term::Gnuplot* offers drivers that allow you to create some vector formats, but its set of drawing primitives is rather limited. There are, however, other possibilities to create vector graphics.

Perl is a text processing language. Postscript and SVG, for example, are both text-based formats. Even better, SVG is based on XML. Thus you can easily create output files in these formats. Both PostScript and SVG are vector formats, or at least, both support vector graphics as part of their native format.

To describe the PostScript language or Scalable Vector Graphics format in this book is not really possible, since they both are quite large and extensive. However, if you want to bone up on PostScript, you could read the PostScript language reference [21], and for SVG I'd recommend the specifications on the Web Consortium website [22]. Additionally, take a look at the PostScript and SVG implementations of a module discussed in chapter 10, and which are listed in appendix C.

4.6 *SUMMARY*

In this chapter we've looked at the various modules that are available for Perl to create two-dimensional computer graphics. We've seen that *GD* is simple to use and reasonably featureful, but is limited in the number of colors it supports, and lacks some higher-level functionality. *Image::Magick* offers many more features, but is more difficult to use, and the code needed to create drawings can become quite verbose. However, it supports a wide variety of output formats and a good set of drawing commands. We've also seen that *GD* and *Image::Magick* can be combined to attain the best of both worlds.

If you need to produce graphics that are not bitmaps, Term::Gnuplot is a possibility, although its interface is limited. Alternatively, you can directly create PostScript or SVG files.

C H A P T E R 5

Creating charts

Wherever a business is running, there is a need to report on the results of the company, the size of the customer base, the number of business transactions, and their monetary value. Whenever scientific research is performed, the results of that research have to be communicated to the public and to peers. Services, particularly computer services, need to be monitored, and their use reported. Traffic flows, animal populations, rainfall, stock numbers, land values, disease patterns, temperatures, stock market indexes, conductivities, electricity usage, web site visits, and crime rates all are measured and monitored.

When sets of data need to be reported, the best way to do so is to represent them visually, and this is precisely what charts and graphs do.[1] They give a visual representation of the relationships between data in a single set, and between sets of data. In this way, they make the data much more accessible than it otherwise would have been. If you follow financial markets, you know that much of the information in that world is expressed in the form of charts. Stock values and oil and gold prices are invariably represented as a squiggly line, plotted as a function of the time. While these lines are

---

[1] The terms graph, chart and plot are all used to refer to the same thing, although chart is more often used for business graphics, and graph for scientific charts. In this chapter, all three terms are used interchangeably.

much less precise than a table with the values of these data, they do at a glance convey the important information contained in the data set, show the trends, and allow you to quickly relate all values to each other. If you were looking at numbers in a table, you would have to jump backward and forward, do a lot of mental arithmetic, and probably still not get the picture. Computers are good at working with tables of numbers, but humans are visual animals. This is why using the computer to translate tables into graphs is useful. We view the data in the way that makes the most sense to us, and the computer gets to do what it does best.

Often the relationship that needs to be shown is the change of a parameter over time: examples of this are charts showing the gold price, population figures of a city, or the quarterly results of a company, plotted over a period of time. Sometimes the relationship that needs to be expressed is of a different nature: the variation of the conductivity or viscosity of liquid helium as a function of the temperature, or the price of a product related to the number of items bought.

Other times the differences, similarities, or correlations between different data sets need to be visualized. An example of this could be a plot of the incidences of malaria in parts of the USA and the population sizes of the malaria mosquitoes *Anopheles freeborni* and *Anopheles quadrimaculatus*, plotted over a certain time interval. If the plots of these numbers show similar trends, there could be a correlation. Another example of this is a plot of the rainfall in parts of Australia and the Southern Oscillation Index against time (see section 5.1.7, "Mixed charts," on page 72).

Because all types of data have their own peculiarities and needs, there are different ways of plotting them. Business data and other time-related series are often shown with the help of bar and line charts. Results of physics research frequently include lines, points and error bars. When the relative amounts or contributions of the members of a data set need to be shown, pie charts are often used. Each of the mentioned types of charts has numerous variants, each with its own application domain. Professional groups have adopted their own standard set of graphs that they frequently use, and members of these groups can immediately read and interpret these charts.

There are several modules available for the creation of charts and graphs with Perl, and it isn't always easy to pick the right one. Some modules are strongly geared toward creating business graphics, while others are more oriented toward scientific users. Apart from these modules, which are directly available from within a Perl program, you can also choose to use an external plotting program. What you choose, and what works best, depend on your needs and preferences.

A general rule of thumb that you can use to select the tool you are going to work with is that if you want to create business graphics, such as bar and pie charts, you should either use *GD::Graph* or one of the *Chart* modules. If, however, you need to plot functions or scientific graphs, the *PGPLOT* module or the gnuplot program are likely to be better alternatives. Of course, you always have the option to create your own solution using *GD*, *Image::Magick*, *Term::Gnuplot* (see section 4.4, "Drawing with Term::Gnuplot," on page 55 for an example), or by directly writing Encapsulated PostScript files.

Another factor in the decision process should be the destination for your chart. Are you looking to create an image for inclusion on a web page, or are you preparing a graph for print? Do you require the same chart to be available in multiple formats? At this moment in time, the *GD::Graph* and *Chart::* modules all are based on *GD*, and therefore can only create images as output. In practical terms, if you are looking for a solution that can create pie or bar charts for print, you are mostly out of luck. Both *PGPLOT* and the gnuplot program come with a wide variety of drivers, some of which produce image files, and some of which produce vector graphics such as PostScript. If you need to create charts for a print publication, either of these can create output of the required quality. Unfortunately, neither of them can be used decently for the creation of business charts.

One of the areas in chart creation that has seen a tremendous growth over the last years is the creation of charts on the fly. This is, of course, largely due to the explosion of the World Wide Web, and the exposure of large amounts of data directly to the public. Much information is accessible nowadays via the Web, and a reasonable amount of that data is presented as charts, which often are dynamically generated based on input of the user. Any module or program that can generate GIF, JPEG or PNG output can be used for this task, since those are the three graphics formats that most browsers can display. Chapter 6 explains the issues related to creating graphics dynamically for display in a web browser, and contains an example of chart creation for the Web.

Let's have a look at the various methods we have at our disposal to actually create some graphs, instead of just talking abstractly about them.

5.1   GD::GRAPH AND FRIENDS

I started writing *GIFgraph* in early 1995 as a helper module for a redesigned version of getgraph,[2] and released it to CPAN in 1997. The rewritten version of getgraph was never released—it was never finished—but *GIFgraph* took on a life of its own when people started using it for all sorts of things for which it wasn't originally intended. While getgraph used gnuplot to create charts, *GIFgraph* implemented the drawing of charts itself, with the help of the *GD* module.

In 1999 Thomas Boutell removed support for the GIF format from libgd and instead supported the PNG format. Lincoln Stein followed (of course) by doing the same for the *GD* module, which is mostly an object-oriented Perl interface to the C library libgd. Since *GIFgraph* uses *GD* to draw its charts, it stopped working as soon as people installed these newer versions of *GD*. Because it is silly to have a module that is called *GIFgraph* but produces PNG files, I decided to instead take the code and create a new module *GD::Graph* which worked with *GD*, without worrying about what

---

[2]   One of the first programs that displayed web server log statistics graphically. It used getstats for its input and gnuplot and HTML for output.

particular file format it supports. *GIFgraph* became a wrapper around that, either directly producing GIF from an old version of *GD* or using *Image::Magick* to convert the PNG output of the newer versions.

Because of time restraints, it took me a little longer than expected, and many people kept knocking on my email box, asking me when I was going to finally release a new version. Luckily, one of those people, Steve Bonds, didn't just ask, but told me that he had adapted the code, and put it on CPAN as *Chart::PNGgraph*.[3]

GD::Graph supports different types of charts through subclasses, and is itself only a base class for all of the others. The classes that can actually be used are:

GD::Graph::bars	bar charts
GD::Graph::area	area charts
GD::Graph::lines	line charts
GD::Graph::points	points charts or scatter graphs
GD::Graph::linespoints	A combination of lines and points
GD::Graph::mixed	Mixed type chart (any of the above)
GD::Graph::pie	pie charts

The fact that *GIFgraph* was originally intended only to display log statistics explains why it is mainly suitable for business type charts, in which the horizontal axis is a label instead of a numerical value, or *X* data is equidistantly spaced. If you are looking for a module that allows you to draw scientific charts, this isn't it (yet).

5.1.1 Preparing your data sets for GD::Graph

Older versions of *GD::Graph* used to have a rather primitive interface for accepting data.[4] The plot method expected a reference to an array that contained references to other arrays for the *X* value list and *Y* value lists. Because of the troubles associated with manipulating this structure, the *GD::Graph::Data* class was created to hide the chaos. The documentation for this module at first seems overwhelming because there is so much text describing so many methods. But rest assured, you will probably only need about ten percent of it. The most important method, and the one that you will probably use most, is the `add_point()` method. Suppose you have a data file containing the quarterly income and expenditure numbers in cents for your squash club:

```
"Qtr 1"     723194      534934
"Qtr 2"     534530      619562
"Qtr 3"     296105      745690
"Qtr 4"     528170      264585
```

---

[3] *Chart::PNGgraph* is now, as of version 1.21, a wrapper class around *GD::Graph*, which has reconciled the code branches that existed for a while.

[4] ... and this interface is in fact still supported.

Once you recover from the fact that your club lost money, you decide to make a nice looking graph to soften the blow when you present these figures to the board. You decide to use *GD::Graph* and write the following code to read in the data:

```
use Text::ParseWords;
use GD::Graph::Data;

my $data = GD::Graph::Data->new();
while (<DATA>)
{
    chomp;
    my @d = quotewords('\s+', 0, $_);
    $data->add_point($d[0], $d[1]/100, $d[2]/100);
}
```

If you were more organized and already had your data in a database (which you would naturally access using the *DBI* interface), you would do something like the following:

```
use DBI;
use GD::Graph::Data;
# open database connection here

my $data = GD::Graph::Data->new();

$sth = $dbh->prepare("select quarter, in, out from wallet")
    or warn $dbh->errstr;
$sth->execute;
while (my @d = $sth->fetchrow_array)
{
    $data->add_point($d[0], $d[1]/100, $d[2]/100);
}
$sth->finish;
```

You can now feed this data object to any of the plot methods of the *GD::Graph* classes.

The old data structure is still supported and recognized, so if you're more comfortable manipulating nested arrays than calling methods on an object, you can still do so. In some situations, for example where the complete data set is known at the time you write your program, it might be easier to use the old data structures.[5] *GD::Graph::Data* provides a method to generate an object from such a structure at any time you want to make the switch.

```
@data = (
['X1', 'X2', 'X3', 'X4'],
[   1,   13,   12,   15],
[  10,    9,    8,    5]
);

# ... time passes ...

$data = GD::Graph::Data->new();
$data->copy_from(\@data);
```

---

[5] ... and in some examples in this section you will actually see this.

This method can be used to gently change your older *GD::Graph* programs over to *GD::Graph::Data* objects, instead of the arrays of array references.

SEE ALSO   The *GD::Graph::Data* module can do much more with your data set, and I suggest you have a look at its documentation. See the *DBI* documentation for a unified interface to all kinds of databases.

5.1.2   Controlling the look of your chart

Almost all the options and settings for *GD::Graph* objects are passed in through the set() method, and can be queried with the get() method. There are many options for the various *GD::Graph* modules, and I suggest you read through the documentation to find out about them. I'll illustrate a few key choices in the following sections, but I won't duplicate the complete explanation of each single option here. The text would probably grow stale faster than a piece of brie.

5.1.3   GD::Graph and fonts

There are several textual elements in a *GD::Graph* object. Each of these objects has a font associated with it, which can be accessed through the appropriate method. *GD::Graph* supports fonts through the use of *GD::Text::Align* objects (see section 11.3.1, "The GD::Text modules," on page 207) from the GDTextUtils package, which means that it will support whatever your current version of *GD* supports. The objects that can be set, and the corresponding methods, are shown in table 5.1.

Table 5.1   The font handling methods for *GD::Graph*.
All of these methods accept either a built-in *GD* font,
or the name of a TrueType font file.

Charts with axes	
title	set_title_font()
X axis label	set_x_label_font()
Y axis labels	set_y_label_font()
X axis values	set_x_axis_font()
Y axis values	set_y_axis_font()
legend text	set_legend_font()
Pie charts	
title	set_title_font()
label under the pie	set_label_font()
values on the pie	set_value_font()

Each of these methods accepts either a built-in GD font, or the name of a TrueType font file, and a size. If you want to use GD built-in fonts, you will have to import the *GD* module as well.

```
use GD;
$chart->set_title_font('/fonts/arial.ttf', 18);
$chart->set_legend_font(gdTinyFont);
$chart->set_y_label_font(GD::Font->Giant);
```

Since the *GD::Graph* font handling gets delegated to a *GD::Text::Align* object, you can use all the fancy features that come with that module. So, supposing you have set your FONT_PATH environment variable correctly to point to your TrueType font files, you can do something such as this:

```
$chart->set_title_font(['verdana', 'arial', gdMediumBoldFont], 14);
```

This will first look in your font path for the file verdana.ttf, and if it is not found, it will look for arial.ttf, and as a last resort it will fall back on a built-in *GD* font.[6] This allows you to write code that creates charts which come out looking as pleasing as possible, given the system on which the program runs.

For more information see section 11.3.1, "The GD::Text modules," on page 207, and the *GD::Text* documentation.

5.1.4   Saving your chart to a file

GD::Graph does not provide any method to save an image, or to get image data to save. The plot() method instead returns a reference to a *GD::Image* object and leaves it up to the user to save the image data to a file. Alternatively, the gd() method can be used to get that same reference, any time after plot() has been called. Once that is accomplished, the *GD::Image* png()[7] method can be called to save the image.

```
$chart->plot(\@data);
my $gd_object = $chart->gd;
# or directly:
# my $gd_object = $chart->plot(\@data);
open(IMAGE, '>image.png') or die "open >image.png: $!";
binmode IMAGE;
print IMAGE $gd_object->png;
close IMAGE;
```

In version 1.20, *GD* dropped support for GIF output, and started writing PNG instead. Thus, if you write code that needs to save output from these modules, you run the risk of ending up on a platform where the version of *GD* provides unanticipated output methods. Since this can result in unwelcome runtime error messages, it is better to try to prevent it from happening. One possible approach is to check which version is available, and exit if it's the wrong one. A more forgiving strategy is to always output something, using the correct calls. This strategy can be especially

---

[6] Of course the size parameter will not influence the size of the built-in font.

[7] ... or any one of the other methods that return image data: jpeg(), wbmp(), gd(), gd2(), or in the case of older versions, the gif() method. Which ones are available depends on your particular version of *GD*.

successful in CGI programs and other web applications, in which the client on the other end can likely display PNG, GIF and JPEG images.

```
if ($gd_object->can('gif'))
{
     # save image as GIF
     open(IMAGE, '>image.gif') or die "open >image.gif: $!";
     binmode IMAGE;
     print IMAGE $chart->gd->gif;
     close IMAGE;
}
else
{
     # save image as PNG
     open(IMAGE, '>image.png') or die "open >image.png: $!";
     binmode IMAGE;
     print IMAGE $chart->gd->png;
     close IMAGE;
}
```

This can be awkward. Fortunately, *GD::Graph* provides the export_format() method. This method will return the string png if the underlying *GD* library exports PNG data, and the string gif if it exports GIF format images. This string can be used both to dynamically determine what the extension of the saved file should be, as well as the name of the method to use to get at that data. Perl's dynamic nature allows you to do the following:

```
my $format = $chart->export_format;
open(IMAGE, ">image.$format")
     or die "open >image.$format: $!";
binmode IMAGE;
print IMAGE $chart->gd->$format();
close IMAGE;
```

which is as short as it gets.

The *GIFgraph* and *Chart::PNGgraph* modules are different: in the first place the plot method of both these modules does not return a *GD* object, but does return the image data directly. Secondly, both modules provide a convenient method to directly plot your image to a file. For GIFgraph:

```
my $img_data = $chart->plot(\@data);
open(IMAGE, '>file.gif') or die $!;
binmode IMAGE;
print IMAGE $img_data;
close IMAGE;

# or

$chart->plot_to_gif('file2.gif', \@data);
```

Chart::PNGgraph provides the same functionality, but of course for PNG, and the method is called plot_to_png().

5.1.5 Bar and area charts

Bar charts are often used in financial reports and statistical comparisons. Most commonly the *X* axis displays the labels for each of the bars, such as month names or species names, and the distance between the bars has little significance. But only rarely do you see bar charts used in a situation in which the *X* axis has a numerical value that is not equidistantly spaced.

GD::Graph can create bar charts for multiple data sets in one figure. If you have more than one set, you might choose to display the bars next to each other, in front of each other, or on top of each other. Displaying bars in front of each other is useful mainly to clearly offset a difference between one data set and another, when one is consistently smaller than the other. The visible part of the rear dataset shows the difference. Placing bars on top of each other can be used, for example in financial charts, where one wants to show the cumulative effect of multiple sources of income or expenditure.

An example of a simple bar chart can be seen in figure 5.1. This chart was produced with the code:[8]

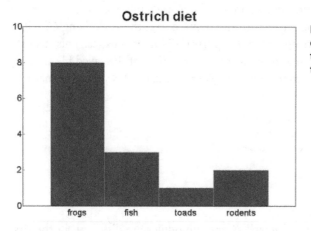

Figure 5.1 A simple bar chart, created with *GD::Graph*, illustrating the basic capabilities of the module.

```
use GD::Graph::bars;
my @data = (
    ['frogs','fish','toads','rodents'],
    [ 8,       3,      1,       2],
);

my $chart = GD::Graph::bars->new(700,500);
$chart->set(title => 'Ostrich diet');
$chart->set_title_font('arialbd', 24);
$chart->set_x_axis_font('arial', 16);
$chart->set_y_axis_font('arial', 16);
my $gd_object = $chart->plot(\@data);
```

---

[8] Note that the setting of the fonts is optional. It is done here purely for aesthetic considerations.

CHAPTER 5 CREATING CHARTS

Cumulative effects

Sometimes you'll want to show the cumulative effect of sets of data. For example, you have a log file from a web server and you filter out all the unimportant requests, such as images and the like. You are left with only requests which are important to you, and want to create a chart that expresses the total number of requests in each hour of the day. You are also interested in how these requests are divided between GET and POST requests, and how these are further split between the secure and nonsecure parts of your site.

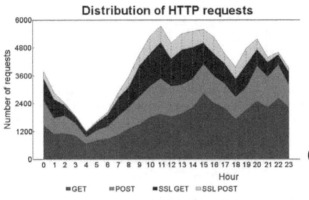

Figure 5.2
Two representations of one day of HTTP server log statistics, split up by the different types of requests. The data sets are cumulative, each band showing the respective contribution to the total of each type of request.

(a)

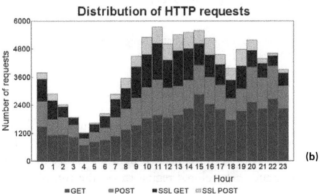

(b)

Of course you can create a few bar charts and some pie charts that show you all of the above. However, it is possible to do all of this in one figure, if you treat the data cumulatively as shown in figure 5.2. Suppose you have already created summary data for the number of requests per hour of the day, divided them into the relevant groups, and note that this data lives in a file with tab-separated fields of the following format:

```
# hour  GET     POST    SSL_GET    SSL_POST
0       1495    1057    955        278
1       1106    680     819        278
2       1120    757     455        94
# and more lines...
```

To prepare the data for use with *GD::Graph* you can use the following:

```
use strict;
use GD::Graph::area;
use GD::Graph::Data;

my $data = GD::Graph::Data->new();

open(IN, 'WWW.data') or die "Can't read WWW.data: $!";
while(<IN>)
{
    next if /^#/;
    chomp;
    my @d = map {$_ eq '' ? undef : $_} split /\t/;
    $data->add_point(@d);
}
close(IN);
```

This code creates a new *GD::Graph::Data* object, opens the data file, and processes it line by line. Lines that start with a hash are ignored, and all others are split on tab characters. The map() makes certain that empty fields are set to undef, meaning that *GD::Graph* will view this point as unavailable when creating the chart.

Now that you have your data in a *GD:Graph::Data* object, you can write the code to plot the chart:

```
my $chart = GD::Graph::area->new(800,500);
$chart->set_legend('GET', 'POST', 'SSL GET', 'SSL POST');
$chart->set(
    title      => 'Distribution of HTTP requests',
    y_label    => 'Number of requests',
    x_label    => 'Hour',
    cumulate   => 1,
);
```

The key option here is cumulate: when this is set to a true value, the data sets will be drawn on top of each other, i.e., cumulatively. Each data set point will use the sum of its predecessors as the baseline; in the created figures the tops of the areas signify the total of all data sets, and each colored region shows the contribution of a single data set.

The result of this code can be seen in figure 5.2a. The equivalent bar chart can be seen in figure 5.2b. Which one of these you use depends mainly on the sort of data you want to represent, as well as your personal preference. I tend to favor the area representation for cumulative charts with more than about 5 data points.

5.1.6 Lines, Points and LinesPoints charts

It is possible with *GD::Graph* to draw line charts, point charts—also referred to as scatter graphs—or a chart with both lines and points. One is hard pressed to proffer a general rule for when these types of charts are used, because they can be used for almost anything, even when a bar or area chart could have been more appropriate.

GD::Graph defines 8 different types of markers for the points, and each data set is tied to one of these types. The types are:

The numbered order is also the default order for the markers, i.e., the first (ninth, seventeenth, and so forth) dataset will have a filled square, the second an open square, the third a horizontal cross, and so on. You can set the choice and order of these markers with the `markers` attribute, and their size with the `markersize` attribute.

1	filled square
2	open square
3	horizontal cross
4	diagonal cross
5	filled diamond
6	open diamond
7	filled circle
8	open circle

There are four line types to choose from:

1	solid
2	dashed
3	dotted
4	alternating dots and dashes

You can set the order of these with the `line_types` attribute, and the width of the line with `line_width`. There is one further attribute that controls the visual appearance of lines, `line_type_scale`, which controls the length of the dashes in the lines. The higher the number, the longer the dashes. If you don't specify a `line_types` attribute, all data sets will use type 1, and will appear as a solid line.

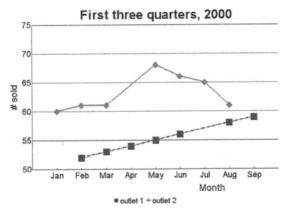

Figure 5.3
An example of a *GD::Graph* lines and points chart, showing the number of sold items per outlet for the first three quarters of the current year. For points where no data is available, no marker is drawn. This is indicated by an undefined value in the data set.

Figure 5.3 can be produced with the following code:

```
use GD::Graph::linespoints;

my @data = (
    [qw(Jan Feb Mar Apr May Jun Jul Aug Sep)],
    [undef, 52, 53, 54, 55, 56, undef, 58, 59],
    [60, 61, 61, undef, 68, 66, 65, 61, undef],
);

my $chart = new GD::Graph::linespoints(700,500);
```

```
$chart->set(
    x_label         => 'Month',
    y_label         => '# sold',
    title           => 'First three quarters, 2000',
    y_long_ticks    => 1,
    markers         => [1, 5],
    marker_size     => 8,
    line_types      => [4, 1],
    line_width      => 3,
);
$chart->set_legend('outlet 1', 'outlet 2');
```

5.1.7   Mixed charts

Sometimes, hopefully not often, you need to produce a chart that contains datasets in different formats. You might want to represent one data set with bars, and another one as a line or area; *GD::Graph* provides the *mixed* chart type for this.

Example

The Southern Oscillation Index (SOI) is a measure that expresses the difference in air pressure between Tahiti and Darwin and is commonly associated with El Niño. When the SOI is strongly positive, there is a higher probability of rain in Eastern and Northern Australia, and when it is strongly negative there is less chance of rain.[9] You will often see the SOI depicted as a line, and rainfall as bars. To present a graph that shows any relation between the two, it would be permissible to choose a mixed type, as shown in figure 5.4.

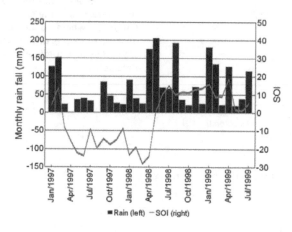

Figure 5.4
The Southern Oscillation Index and the rainfall per month for Sydney, Australia from January 1997 to July 1999. The rainfall is shown as bars, and the SOI as a line. From this picture, one could tentatively draw a cautious conclusion that a negative SOI could be related to a decrease in rainfall.

---

[9] Of course, the real story is more complicated, and depends on not just the value of the SOI, but also on how persistently positive or negative it is, and on some other variables.

CHAPTER 5   CREATING CHARTS

Suppose we have a database with the daily SOI values and rainfall in Sydney from January 1987 to December 1999. From this data we create a summary file that contains the monthly average SOI and total amount of rain. This file could have the following format:

```
# Month/Year    Rain    SOI
Jan/1987        49.8    -6.3
Feb/1987        35.2    -12.6
Mar/1987        154.0   -16.6
Apr/1987        36.6    -24.4

# more lines like this...

Oct/1999        149.4   9.1
Nov/1999                13.1
Dec/1999                13
```

with tab characters separating the values. We fill a *GD::Graph::Data* object with part of the data from this file (everything between a start and end date):

```perl
use strict;
use GD::Graph::mixed;
use DBI;

my ($start, $end) = qw(Jan/1997 Jul/1999);
my $data = GD::Graph::Data->new();

open(IN, 'SOI.data') or die "Can't read SOI.data:$!";
while(<IN>)
{
    next if /^#/;
    if (/^\Q$start/ .. /^\Q$end/)
    {
        chomp;
        my @d = map {$_ eq '' ? undef : $_} split /\t/;
        $data->add_point(@d);
    }
}
close(IN);
```

Note that in this example the start and end dates have been hard coded, but in a real world program they would most likely come from user input.

Once we have the data, a *GD::Graph::mixed* object is created and given a legend, so we can easily recognize which element in the resulting chart belongs to which data set.

```perl
my $chart = GD::Graph::mixed->new(700,500);
$chart->set_legend('Rain (left)', 'SOI (right)');
$chart->set(
    y1_label            => 'Monthly rain fall (mm)',
    y2_label            => 'SOI',
    types               => [qw(bars lines)],
    dclrs               => [qw(blue green)],
    line_width          => 5,
```

```
    two_axes           => 1,
    y_long_ticks       => 1,
    x_label_skip       => 3,
    x_labels_vertical  => 1,
    zero_axis          => 1,
    transparent        => 0,
);
```

The options for the chart are mostly self-explanatory, but I'll highlight a few: the option `two_axes` tells the chart object that the two data sets should be treated separately. The first one will have its values drawn on the left vertical axis, and the second on the right. This option is only valid when you have exactly two data sets. Because we have two Y axes, we can also label them separately, `y1_label` and `y2_label`. We set the `y_long_ticks` option to a true value for aesthetic reasons, and leave the `x_ticks` option at a false value to avoid vertical grid lines. It should also be noted that the `line_width` option only affects the width of the data lines, not of any of the axes.

GD::Graph summary

In this section we have seen how *GD::Graph* can be used to create a variety of charts, how it may be presented with the data you want plotted, and some specific examples. The module can do much more than has been shown here. The original distribution archive, available from CPAN, contains a set of examples, and the documentation is quite elaborate. More examples that use *GD::Graph* can be found in sections 6.3, "CGI and dynamically generated graphics," on page 94 and 7.7, "Animations with the Gimp," on page 134.

5.2 THE CHART DISTRIBUTION

The Chart distribution, originally by David Bonner, and now maintained by Peter Clark, is a collection of charting classes very much like *GD::Graph*. In fact, the documentation states that it originally borrowed most of its API from *GIFgraph*. The chart types that are supported are:

Chart::Points	points chart, or scatter graph
Chart::Lines	line chart
Chart::Bars	bar chart
Chart::LinesPoints	line and points chart
Chart::Composite	a composite of the above
Chart::Pareto	a sorted bar chart
Chart::StackedBars	bar chart with cumulative effect
Chart::Pie	pie chart

Most of these are comparable to the equivalents in the *GD::Graph* module, and their use is fairly similar as well. Since the Pareto chart is unique to this module, we'll have a look at an example that creates one.

5.2.1 Pareto charts

Charts of this type are named after the Italian economist Vilfredo Pareto (1848–1923), who noticed that 80 percent of wealth is owned by 20 percent of the people. The Pareto chart or diagram presents its data in a hierarchical order, which shows the most significant data first. This is a very useful tool in quality assurance and fault detection processes, because it allows one to quickly discern which of the data is the most significant, and would therefore be best to look at first. It is also often used in a more general sense to find out which factors are the largest contributors to a certain effect.

Pareto charts normally take the shape of a bar chart, with the bars representing the measured points. They will often contain a line, which denotes the cumulative contribution of all bars as a percentage. In most implementations, the least significant data points are grouped together in a category "other."

Suppose that you are a marine biologist, and your current task is to find out what exactly is causing the depletion of a certain nematode worm in Cat's Head Bay. To do so, you dive into the water, and start identifying species of underwater life that eat these worms. You count the number of individuals of all represented species, and multiply that by the mass of worms each individual needs on a daily basis, to get a biomass count.

You discover that there is a chemical factory in the vicinity, and you analyze the effluent coming from it. You notice that there is a component in this factory's effluent that causes nematode worms to die, and rather quickly. Luckily, you find data that relates the concentration of this chemical to death rates in nematode worms, so that you can calculate the number of worms dying per day in Cat's Head Bay as a result of this effluent.

Once you have identified all sources of nematode death, you write a report. Of course, you need to have a chart in your report showing a graphical representation of your findings, so you write the following program:[10]

```
use strict;
use Chart::Pareto;

my $chart = Chart::Pareto->new();
while (my @data = get_data())
{
    $chart->add_pt(@data);
}

$chart->gif("Pareto.gif");
```

---

[10] The get_data() method has been deliberately left out of this listing. It simply gets an *X* and *Y* value from some data store.

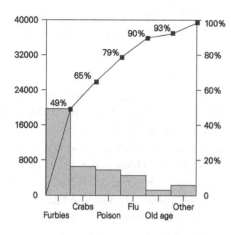

Figure 5.5 **Pareto chart of nematode worm mortality in Cat's Head Bay. This chart shows us that Furbies are the largest killers of nematode worms, and that the top 5 killers are responsible for 93% of the nematode deaths.**

It can be clearly seen from figure 5.5 that Furbies are the main cause of nematodic death in Cat's Head Bay.

5.3   PGPLOT

The *PGPLOT* module is the Perl interface to the PGPLOT graphics library. It used to be known as pgperl before Perl 5, but changed its name when modules became a possibility. PGPLOT is a high-level graphics package for plotting two-dimensional data sets, functions, histograms, contour maps and images. It is the *de facto* plotting package for astronomers around the world, and has many applications in other scientific areas. Unfortunately, it seems to be rarely used outside of academic institutes.

The PGPLOT library[20] was written by Tim Pearson of the Astronomy department of the California Institute of Technology. It has been in existence for a while and is very stable.[11] It is written in Fortran—which explains the short function names—but also comes with a C-callable interface, which is what the *PGPLOT* module uses. The Perl interface to the PGPLOT library is provided by Karl Glazebrook, who is also one of the driving forces behind the Perl Data Language (PDL).

The source distribution of the PGPLOT library comes with a wealth of examples, spread out over a number of Fortran demo programs. The *PGPLOT* module distribution also includes example code in the test files. The best way to become acquainted with the API is to read those example programs, while keeping an eye on the user's manual, which is available from the PGPLOT home page (see [20]).

5.3.1   PGPLOT devices

The pgopen() call takes one argument: the device to write to. A device specification is made up of two parts: optionally, the name of the device or file and the device type,

---

[11] Version 5.0.0 was released in December 1994, and the current version, 5.2.0, was released in June 1997.

preceded by a slash (/). If the device or file name contains slashes, it should be enclosed in double quotes:

```
my $device_id = pgopen('"/tmp/file.ps"/PS');
```

If the device or filename is left off, PGPLOT will use a default name. Which devices are available to you depends on how your local copy of the library has been compiled. The distribution ships with code for a large number of devices, some of which are shown in table 5.2.

Table 5.2 **The devices that can be used in *PGPLOT* programs, by specifying them as an argument to `pgopen()`. The device names starting with a V cause the output to be vertically oriented, the others have a horizontal orientation. For the devices that output to a file, a nondefault file name can be specified between double quotes before the slash.**

Type	Type specifications	Default device
GIF file	/GIF, /VGIF	pgplot.gif
HPGL plotters	/HPGL, /VHPGL	pgplot.hpgl
Portable pixel map	/PPM, /VPPM	pgplot.ppm
PostScript	/PS, /CPS, /VPS, /VCPS	pgplot.ps
X Windows	/XWINDOW, /XSERVE	default X display
Null device (no output)	/NULL	
LaTeX picture environment	/LATEX	pgplot.tex

The device names that start with a V plot their output in portrait (vertical) mode, the other ones plot in landscape mode. For example: to plot a GIF file in landscape mode, use /GIF. To plot in portrait mode, use /VGIF. The PostScript drivers with a C in the name will output color PostScript.

Each device can be controlled by setting environment variables which are described in the user manual. If you want to specify a different width, height or resolution than is the default for the driver, you would set the appropriate environment variables. For example, to set the width and height of a GIF output file, you would do something like:

```
$ENV{PGPLOT_GIF_WIDTH}  = 640;
$ENV{PGPLOT_GIF_HEIGHT} = 480;
pgopen('"/tmp/resized.gif"/GIF');
```

The user manual contains an appendix with a full description of each driver, including all the environment variables that affect the output for that driver. There are a number of device drivers available for specific printers, plotters, terminals and special applications, such as tcl/tk widgets.

5.3.2 Example: A simple *X-Y* plot

PGPLOT produces simple *X-Y* plots with a minimum of fuss, but there is a certain methodology that needs to be followed.

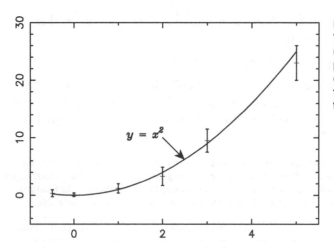

Figure 5.6
This graph illustrates how to use *PGPLOT* to plot data points with their respective error bars, a function to fit the data, and a visual label for this function's line.

Let's walk through the code that produced figure 5.6:

```
use PGPLOT;

my @x = (-0.5,    0,    1,    2,    3,   5);
my @y = (0.35, 0.1, 1.2, 3.3, 9.5, 23);
my @y_err = (0.6, 0.3, 0.8, 1.6, 2.0, 3);
my $num = @x;
```

First, the *PGPLOT* module is included, which exports all the functionality we need into the current name space, hence we can use the functions just as described in the PGPLOT user's manual. We then set up some data to plot. Most of the *PGPLOT* calls require an array of *X* values and an array of *Y* values of the same length. Since we want to draw error bars as well, we define an array containing the error in the measurements in both the upward and downward directions, i.e., the total error is twice as large as the elements of the array. These arrays will be used later in the program in calls to pgpt() and pgerry().

It's now time to open a device to write to, and set up the environment:

```
$ENV{PGPLOT_PS_WIDTH} = 4000;
$ENV{PGPLOT_PS_HEIGHT} = 3000;
my $dev_id = pgopen('pgplot1.eps/VPS');
die "Couldn't open plot" if $dev_id <= 0;
pgslw(2);
pgsch(1.5);
pgenv(-1, 5.5, -5, 30, 0, 0);
```

The pgopen() function is called to open a PostScript file for output. If this fails, pgopen() will return a false value, allowing us to check for success in the same way that we would with a regular open(). You will occasionally see a call to pgbeg() instead of pgopen(). This is a sign that you're looking at an older program, since pgbeg() is deprecated nowadays, and only available for compatibility with existing programs.

Next, we establish a line width, with `pgslw()`, and a character height with `pgsch()`. The line width is specified in units of 1/200 of an inch, and must be an integer between 1 and 201, inclusive. The character height defaults to 1.0, which normally corresponds to approximately 1/40 of the view size. Setting the character height also influences the length of tick marks.

The call to `pgenv()` sets up the graph and axes, and establishes the scaling for subsequent calls to the plotting functions. It is basically a wrapper around `pgswin()` and `pgbox()` (see user's manual). The first four arguments define how, in PGPLOT terminology, *world coordinates* will be translated into *viewport coordinates*. In other words, it defines the minimum and maximum values for your X and Y axis. In this example we set the X axis range from –1 to 5.5, and the Y axis range from –5 to 30. If the fifth argument is equal to 1, the X and Y axis scales will be equal; you almost never want this. The last argument is an integer that specifies how the axes will be formatted, and valid values for this argument can be found in the following table:

–2	no axes or labels
–1	axes as a box
0	box with coordinate labels
1	same as 0, with coordinate axes at X=0 and Y=0
2	same as 1, with grid lines at major increments
10	box with logarithmic X-axis
20	box with logarithmic Y-axis
30	box with both axes logarithmic

Now that we have set up our environment, it is time to draw the data we defined earlier:

```
pgpt($num, \@x, \@y, 2);        ❶ Draw the data points

my (@y_lo, @y_hi);
for my $i (0 .. $#y)
{
    $y_lo[$i] = $y[$i] - $y_err[$i];
    $y_hi[$i] = $y[$i] + $y_err[$i];                ❷ Calculate and draw
}                                                      the error bars
pgerry($num, \@x, \@y_lo, \@y_hi, 1.0);
```

❶ The first thing we do is draw the points that are defined by the arrays @x and @y with `pgpt()` or its alias `pgpoint()`. The first argument is the number of points that we want to draw,[12] and the second and third argument are *references* to arrays with the X and Y coordinates, respectively. The last argument is an integer that indicates which symbol should be used as a marker (see figure 5.7).

---

[12] Note that this is very unperlish, and shows that this module is an interface to a library written in a language where the size of arrays is not as easily obtainable as in Perl.

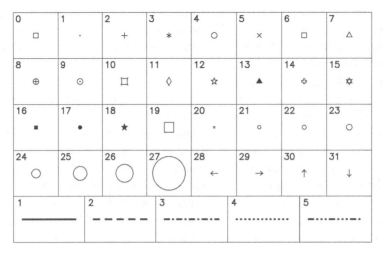

0	1	2	3	4	5	6	7
□	.	+	*	○	×	□	△
8	9	10	11	12	13	14	15
⊕	⊙	⊓	◇	☆	▲	✚	✿
16	17	18	19	20	21	22	23
■	•	★	□	∘	○	○	○
24	25	26	27	28	29	30	31
○	○	○	○	←	→	↑	↓

1	2	3	4	5
——	– – – –	·–··–··–	············	·–··–··–

Figure 5.7 The markers and line types for *PGPLOT*. The markers were drawn at a scaling of 1.75 (set with pgsch()), and the lines with a width of 4 (set with pgslw()).

❷ Next we draw the vertical error bars that go with the points, with the pgerry() function. It is also possible to draw horizontal error bars, with the appropriately named pgerrx() function. The first argument to pgerry() is, again, the number of points to draw, and the second argument is a reference to an array with X coordinates. The third and fourth arguments are references to arrays with the top and bottom Y coordinates of the error bar to draw. Since we have only an array with nominal errors per point, we calculate the top and bottom from the @y and @y_err arrays. The last argument is a number that expresses how long the terminals (crossbars) at each end of the error bar should be.

We want to compare the points we just plotted to a quadratic function, so we draw one:

```
sub square { $_[0]**2 }
pgfunx(\&square, 50, -0.5, 5, 1);
```

The pgfunx() can be used to draw an arbitrary function, $y = f(x)$. The first argument is a reference to a subroutine that defines the function, and the second argument is the number of sample points to take over the interval specified by the third and fourth argument. The last argument controls whether the function should be drawn on the current plot (1), or whether a new plot should be opened for it (0). There are also functions pgfuny() for functions of the form $x = f(y)$, and the parametric pgfunt() for functions of the form $x = f_x(t), y = f_y(t)$. Thus, in this particular example we are plotting the function $y = x^2$ in the range x = [−0.5, 5] with 50 samples, in the current plot. We then put a label in the plot, with an arrow pointing to the function that was just plotted:

```
pgarro(2, 10, 2.5, square(2.5));
pgptxt(2, 10, 0, 1, '\fiy = \fix\u2');

pgclos;
```

The pgarro() function draws an arrow from the point defined by the first two arguments to the point defined by the last two. Notice how we use the subroutine that we just defined to ensure that the arrow ends up touching the line. At the start of the arrow, we put some text expressing the function that has been plotted (see the user's manual for more on text formatting in PGPLOT).

To end the program, we close the output stream with pgclos(). Alternatively, this can be done by calling pgend(), which closes *all* open devices, and not just the current one.

5.3.3   Example: A contour plot

It is surprisingly easy to draw contour plots with PGPLOT, and only slightly harder to put labels in them.

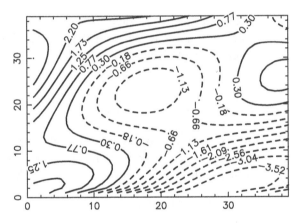

Figure 5.8
A contour plot of a trigono-metric function, created with *PGPLOT*. The solid lines show positive values, the dashed lines negative values.

Figure 5.8 was produced using the following code:

```
use PGPLOT;

my (@f, $fmin, $fmax);
for my $i (0 .. 39)
{
    for my $j (0 .. 39)
    {
        $f[$i][$j] =
            2 * cos(0.3 * sqrt($i * 2) - 0.4 * $j/3) *
            cos(0.4 * $i/3) + 3 * ($i - $j)/40;
        $fmin = min($f[$i][$j], $fmin);
        $fmax = max($f[$i][$j], $fmax);
    }
}
my @level =
    map { $fmin + $_ * ($fmax - $fmin)/15 } (0 .. 15);
```

● Set up the data

● Calculate which levels we want to contour

We start again by including the *PGPLOT* module, after which we declare and fill a two dimensional array `@f` with the values of a function that will give us a good picture. While filling the array, we keep track of the minimum and maximum values (the subroutines `min()` and `max()` are defined at the end of the program). We decide to draw 16 contour levels, and put the values of each contour into the array `@level`, in such a way that the first element in `@level` is equal to the minimum value in `@f`, the last element is equal to the maximum value in `@f`, and the intermediate elements are equidistantly spaced between these values.

We then open an output device and establish the environment.

```
$ENV{PGPLOT_PS_WIDTH} = 4000;
$ENV{PGPLOT_PS_HEIGHT} = 3000;
my $dev_id = pgopen('pgplot3.eps/VPS');
die "Couldn't open plot" if $dev_id <= 0;
pgslw(2);
pgsch(1.5);
pgenv(0, 39, 0, 39, 0, 0);
```

After setting the line width to 2 and the character height to 1.5, we call `pgenv()` to define the minimum and maximum *X* and *Y* axis values for the plot and the axis formatting. Next we draw the contours with a line width of 3:

```
my @tr = (0, 1, 0, 0, 0, 1);
pgslw(3);
pgcont(\@f, 40, 40, 1, 40, 1, 40, \@level, 16, \@tr);
```

The first item needing explanation is the `@tr` array. It contains six elements which are the coefficients in the equations defining the transformation between the indices into the two-dimensional array (*i* and *j*) and the *x* and *y* coordinates of the plot:

$$x = tr_1 + tr_2 i + tr_3 j$$
$$y = tr_4 + tr_5 i + tr_6 j$$

Normally you will see values in elements 1, 2, 4, and 6, and elements 3 and 5 will be zero, unless the coordinates really need to be rotated or sheared. In our example, there is a simple one-to-one mapping between the array coordinates and the graph coordinates, so we set the 2nd and 6th elements to 1, and the rest to 0.

Now that we have defined our mapping, we can plot the contours. We set the line width to 3 and call `pgcont()`, one of the five contour mapping functions of PGPLOT (see user's manual for the others). The first argument to `pgcont()` is a reference to the two-dimensional array `@f`. The next six arguments are the two dimensions of the array, and the first and last index of each of those two dimensions to be plotted.[13] The sixth

---

[13] Note that all indexes into arrays in PGPLOT are 1-based, *not* 0-based. This is most likely due to the fact that the underlying library was originally written in Fortran, where arrays are always 1-based.

argument is a reference to an array that contains the values at which a contour should be drawn, and the seventh argument is the number of elements in that array that you want to use. By default, pgcont() will draw contour levels with a positive value as solid lines, and those with negative values with dashed lines. You can override this behavior, and make pgcont() use the current line style, by specifying this seventh argument as a negative number. The last argument is a reference to the transformation array, @tr.

We'd like to have each contour labelled with the value it represents:

```
pgslw(2);
foreach my $level (@level)
{
    my $label = sprintf "%.2f", $level;
    pgconl(\@f, 40, 40, 1, 40, 1, 40, $level, \@tr,
        $label, 30, 20);
}
```

The pgconl() function places labels on a single contour. The first six arguments to this function are the same as the arguments to the pgcont() function. The seventh argument is the level of the contour that you want to label (this should be one of the values that you passed to pgcont() in the @level array). The eighth argument is the transformation array and the ninth argument is the label you want to put on the contour. The last two arguments control the spacing of the contours (see the user's manual for more information). To label each of the contours drawn in the previous step, we call pgconl() in a loop for each element of @level, setting the label to a rounded value of the current contour level.

All that is left to do is to close the output device and define a few subroutines that we used earlier in the program:

```
pgclos;

sub min
{
    return $_[0] unless defined $_[1];
    $_[0] < $_[1] ? $_[0] : $_[1];
}
sub max
{
    return $_[0] unless defined $_[1];
    $_[0] > $_[1] ? $_[0] : $_[1];
}
```

5.3.4   Example: Plotting a galaxy

It is also possible to display bitmaps with *PGPLOT* and accentuate certain features in them, a facility often used by astronomers to display parts of the night sky for publication.

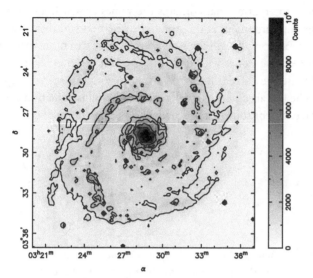

Figure 5.9
A *PGPLOT* graph, using a bitmap as background and data for a contour plot and a wedge to show the magnitude of the grayscale values. The data represents the M51 system, and was obtained by Dr. Patrick Seitner from the University of Michigan.

The program that produced figure 5.9 is short, so I'll present it as a whole:

```
use PGPLOT;

my $img;
open(IMG,"test.img") || die "Data file test.img not found";
read(IMG, $img, 128*128*2);      ❶ Read the image file
close(IMG);
my @image = unpack("n*", $img);

$ENV{PGPLOT_PS_WIDTH} = 4000;
$ENV{PGPLOT_PS_HEIGHT} = 3000;
pgopen('pgplot2.eps/VPS') or die "Couldn't open plot";

my @tr=(12000, 8, 0, 12000, 0, 8);        ❷ Set up a coordinate
pgwnad(12000, 13024, 13024, 12000);          transformation

pgslw(2);
pggray(\@image, 128, 128, 1, 128, 1, 128, 10000, 0, \@tr);  ❸ Display the
pglabel('\ga', '\gd', '');                                     image data
pgtbox('ZYHBCNST', 0, 0, 'ZYDBCNST', 0, 0);

pgwedg('R', 2, 5, 10000, 0, 'Counts');     ❹ Create a scaling wedge

my @levels = (1000, 2000, 3000, 5000, 7500);
pgcons(\@image, 128, 128, 1, 128, 1, 128, \@levels, 5, \@tr);

pgclos;
```

❶ The data for the image is located in a file with the name test.img, and is stored as a simple series of 128 rows of 128 2-byte network order integers. We read all those bytes into memory, and use the unpack() built in to transform them into an array of Perl numbers. This is followed by the customary setting up and opening of an output device.

❷ Next, a coordinate transformation matrix is created, as discussed on page 82, and a window is set up in which to plot the image.

❸ The pggray() function is used to display the image data from the array @image in this window. The second and third arguments to pggray() specify the number of rows and columns in the data set, and the fourth to seventh arguments specify which subset of those rows and columns to use. In this particular case, the image is 128 pixels wide and 128 high, and all pixels (1 to 128 inclusive) in both directions are used. If we wanted just part of the image, we could have specified something like:

```
# The left half
pggray(\@image, 128, 128, 1, 64, 1, 128, 10000, 0, \@tr);
# The top left quarter
pggray(\@image, 128, 128, 1, 64, 1, 64, 10000, 0, \@tr);
# The bottom half
pggray(\@image, 128, 128, 1, 128, 65, 128, 10000, 0, \@tr);
```

The eighth and ninth arguments to pggray() express how the values in the input array are to be translated to grayscale in the image. The eighth argument expresses the "white point" of the image, i.e., every pixel in the array with a value of 10000 and above will be displayed as white. The ninth argument expresses the "black point," and every pixel in the array equal to or lower than this value will be displayed as black. All other pixels will receive a grayscale value between 0 and 1. Thus, these numbers express the maximum and minimum values anyone is interested in distinguishing.

The axes are labelled with the Greek letters α and δ to indicate the inclination and declination of the pixels, and the box format is set up with pgtbox() (refer to the manual of PGPLOT for a full description), so that the coordinates are expressed in angular notation.

❹ Lastly, a wedge is created next to the window that shows a brightness scale for the image. To complete the picture, some contours are drawn on the picture with pgcons(), outlining areas of similar value on the image.

5.4   INTERFACING WITH GNUPLOT

Gnuplot[18] is not a Perl module and, in fact, has nothing to do with Perl at all.[14] It is, however, a very powerful charting program. It does many of the things that the previously mentioned Perl modules don't do (yet), and it is very easy to work with from within a Perl program. That alone should be enough reason to allow a few pages of discussion on it. Additionally, there are probably many people out there who are already using gnuplot, and are satisfied with its performance. Some of those might be happy to see that they don't have to abandon it.

---

[14] ... or with the GNU project. The similarity in the name is purely a coincidence.

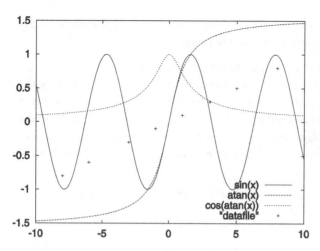

Figure 5.10
An example gnuplot chart showing several built-in functions and the data from a file in one plot. The line types and point markers were automatically chosen by the gnuplot program. The legend describes the lines and their corresponding functions.

Gnuplot is freely available for many platforms, and supports a great multitude of output formats. It has been in existence long enough to offer a very mature set of functionality. As input, it takes a set of commands that determine what sort of chart will be drawn and what it will look like. This set of commands is almost a language in its own right, albeit a very specialized language.

Among the Gnuplot possibilities are the plotting of 2D curves, lines, points, error bars, rudimentary bar charts, and 3D surfaces (or 2D projections of surfaces). You can create polar or parametric plots, scale your axes logarithmically, place arbitrary labels and arrows on your chart, and fit your data against mathematical functions in a variety of ways. I won't attempt to describe all the features of gnuplot, since they constitute enough for a whole book on their own. What I will do is show how to interface with gnuplot from Perl.

The easiest way to get your data and commands to gnuplot is simply by creating a string that contains the whole set of commands that you would normally feed to gnuplot, and piping it straight into gnuplot's standard input. The following code was used to create figure 5.10:

```
my $outputfile = 'gnuplot1.eps';

open(GNUPLOT, '| gnuplot') or die "open: $!";

print GNUPLOT <<EOF;
set terminal postscript eps 22
set output "$outputfile"
set key bottom
set samples 200
plot [-10:10] sin(x), atan(x), cos(atan(x)), "datafile"
EOF

close(GNUPLOT) or die "close: $!";
```

CHAPTER 5 CREATING CHARTS

If you have data points in a database, and wish to use gnuplot to display this, there are two options: you can save the data into a temporary file in a format readable by gnuplot (see the gnuplot documentation), or you can[15] inline the data in the commands that you feed to gnuplot. Suppose that you have written a function, get_data(), that returns a single data point from somewhere as an array with three elements: the X value, the Y value, and the possible size of the error in this measurement.

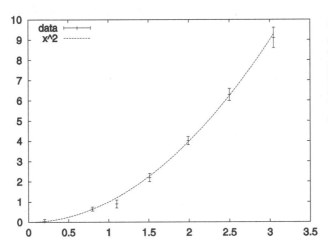

Figure 5.11
A gnuplot chart created with data generated by a Perl program and incorporated directly into the gnuplot program instead of through a data file. The data points also show an error bar.

The following code can be used to plot these points and to compare them to the function x^2 (see figure 5.11).

```
my $outputfile = 'gnuplot2.eps';

open(GNUPLOT, '| gnuplot') or die "open: $!";

print GNUPLOT <<EOF;
set terminal postscript eps 22
set output "$outputfile"
set key top left
set samples 200
plot [0:] [0:] \\
    '-' title "data" with errorbars, \\
    x**2 title "x^2" with lines
EOF

while (my @data = get_data())
{
    print GNUPLOT "@data\n";
}

print GNUPLOT "end\n";
close(GNUPLOT) or die "close: $!";
```

---

[15] ... as of version 3.7. If you still use an older one, I urge you to upgrade. There are many really useful improvements and additions made in 3.7.

In this piece of code the special filename ' - ' is used to indicate that the following lines of input contain data points to be plotted. Gnuplot will read these lines until the character 'e' is encountered on the first column of a line. We call our subroutine which returns the data points, and we print out each one to gnuplot. To indicate that we've finished specifying data points, we provide a character e in the first column by printing end, just to make it more readable.

The get_data() function and the data used to produce the figure are:

```
sub get_data
{
    my $line = <DATA>;
    return unless $line;
    chomp $line;
    return split ' ', $line;
}

__DATA__
0.2 0.04 0.1
0.8 0.65 0.1
1.1 0.9 0.2
1.51 2.20 0.2
1.99 4.02 0.2
2.5 6.29 0.3
3.05 9.1 0.5
```

Using inline data such as this means that we don't have to create temporary files. Thus we don't have to remember to clean them up, find a spot where we can actually create them, or worry about performance problems on saturated file systems.

If you are satisfied with limited functionality and the production of GIF output alone, you could have a look at the *Chart::GnuPlot* module, which is available from CPAN. The module is, at this time, still in a very early and immature stage, has been so for quite a while now (since November 1998), and doesn't look like it is actively being developed any longer.

SEE ALSO   Gnuplot doesn't really provide another API beside the interactive interface. If you need to get feedback from the gnuplot program in order to deal with errors and such, you will have to work out a way to get some bidirectional communication going. This would require using the (standard) *IPC::Open2* or *IPC::Open3* module, or maybe the Expect module from CPAN. That sort of interaction is well described in the `perlipc` documentation, which would be a good place to start.

5.5   SUMMARY

I hope this chapter has provided some glimpse into the many ways in which Perl can be used to create charts, graphs and plots. Each of these ways is different, has its unique strengths and weaknesses, and operates in a different application domain. If you need to create business types of graphics for inclusion in web pages, *GD::Graph* and the various *Chart::** modules are most appropriate. If you wish to plot scientific data, or have to create output that is of a higher quality than a bitmap, you will want to look at *PGPLOT* or gnuplot. If you want to create three-dimensional relief charts, gnuplot is most appropriate, and if your output is akin to figure 5.9, you need *PGPLOT*. Neither gnuplot nor *PGPLOT* can be used to create bar or pie charts, however. Unfortunately, there is no single module that as yet does everything, so your needs will dictate which of the solutions you use.

CHAPTER 6

Graphics and the Web

Perl has become increasingly popular for the dynamic delivery of World Wide Web content, and in doing so has put to good use the Common Gateway Interface (CGI), the standard interface to allow external programs to work with a web server. There are several reasons for Perl's success, the main one being that it gets the job done quickly and efficiently, which is due to its suitability for text processing and its large library of modules. The most important module for programming for the CGI is the appropriately named *CGI* module, written by Lincoln Stein. This module is part of the standard distribution of Perl.

Delivering dynamic content on the Web is becoming increasingly important in the world today where every business is expected to have an interface for its customers via the Web. Interfaces to product and other databases, shopping carts, customer information and documents are becoming more and more commonplace. Some of these interactive interfaces can benefit from having a graphical component that is also dynamic in nature.

In this chapter we'll see how to create and deliver dynamic graphics content for a World Wide Web interface, as well as ways to prepare static Web content with Perl.

6.1   THE COMMON GATEWAY INTERFACE

There is very little reason to write a CGI program in Perl that does not use the *CGI* module. The most frequently quoted reason is that it takes a considerable amount of CPU time to compile this module, or that a script is so trivial that using all the power of *CGI* is overkill. That might be true, but I have rarely seen a program that remains trivial for long. Sooner or later, more and more parts of the CGI interface need to be implemented, each step running the risk of introducing bugs—bugs that wouldn't exist if the *CGI* module had been used. If it's still felt that compiling the module for each invocation of a Perl program is too much load on the machine, use the Apache server and the `mod_perl` plug-in, or any server with FastCGI and the *CGI::Fast* module instead of *CGI*.

You could take a look at one of the smaller modules like *CGI::Lite*; however, one good reason to prefer the *CGI* module is that it's part of the standard Perl distribution. Anywhere a reasonably recent Perl is installed, this module will be available. Code that uses *CGI* is easily portable, unless other parts of the program make it hard to port.

Of course, writing your own code to work in the CGI environment will be as portable as you make it. If you still think that you do not want to use any of these modules, you can point your web browser to the documentation section at http://www.cgi-resources.com and read about the CGI interface.

6.1.1   HTTP and CGI

Something important to understand about HTTP is that each object that is fetched from the server is a separate request. Often HTTP and HTML are confused, and people only familiar with HTML believe, erroneously, that the HTTP protocol somehow magically knows what the contents of an HTML document are. This is not the case.

When an HTML document is being served to a browser, and this document contains 4 graphics files, then the browser will make 5 separate requests to the server.[1] To our human eye it might look like one single page, but as far as the HTTP server is concerned, there is no link between the 5 pieces of information it just served.

Consequently, your CGI programs need to deal with each of these requests separately. You can't write a program that at once delivers both the HTML document and the images referenced in that document. It will need to do so in multiple runs, the difference in output triggered by parameters, or you need to provide multiple programs. It is vitally important to understand this before attempting to write complex CGI programs.

---

[1]   This does not mean that it always needs to open a connection to the server 5 times. Nowadays, multiple HTTP requests can be sent in a single connection.

SEE ALSO The documentation for the *CGI* module and Lincoln Stein's web page on *CGI* at http://stein.cshl.org/WWW/CGI/ can tell you everything you want to know about the *CGI* module. The documentation section of http://www.cgi-resources.com is a useful resource to learn how the CGI works. The Apache Project web site at http://perl.apache.org/ contains information about setting up an Apache web server with `mod_perl` or `mod_fastcgi` to improve the performance of your Perl programs.

6.2 SUITABLE IMAGE FORMATS

The two most commonly used graphics formats on the web are GIF (Graphics Interchange Format) and JPEG. Normally, you will find the GIF format used in images that contain large areas of the same color, and the JPEG format for photographic, or real-world, images.

However, since the compression algorithm that makes GIF images so suitable for the web is patented, and requires a license from the patent holders, it is likely that GIF will slowly disappear. It is certain that there will be no freeware libraries or software available that will create compressed GIF images. Many will probably continue to import compressed GIF and write uncompressed GIF but in its uncompressed form the GIF format is nothing special, and is, in fact, a very bad choice.

There is a superior graphics file format that can take over most of the application area that GIF takes today: PNG. The most-used web browsers and graphics creation packages already support PNG images,[2] and we can expect more and better support for them in the future.

The only thing that GIF does, and PNG doesn't, is animation. For that we are still dependent on GIF. MNG, the Multi Image Network Graphics format that is being developed to fill that area, is based on PNG, and will allow much more sophisticated animations than GIF allows. The animations will also generally be smaller in size. Unfortunately, mainstream support for MNG is virtually non-existent thus far. Let's hope that changes quickly.

For the web, there are no other practical image formats widely supported by the mainstream web browsers. There are all kinds of plug-ins available that allow you to view almost any kind of image or graphic, but plug-ins are generally only available for a limited number of platforms. If possible, avoid anything that needs an external plug-in.

6.2.1 Web safe color palettes

Most computers now have graphics cards and drivers that allow them to display at least 16 million colors. There are, however, still a few out there that only support 256 colors (I often use an *X* terminal at work that only uses 256 colors). There are also some design houses and employers who insist on making all graphics that are to be displayed in a web page conform to the standard 216 color palette. Most graphic

---

[2] In fact, the GD module no longer creates GIF images, but PNG images instead.

designers have stopped worrying about this, and it won't take long until few will even remember why this particular palette was important. This section exists in part to insure that people won't forget about it, and won't automatically assume that all browsers and all platforms are equally capable.

The mainstream web browsers (Netscape Navigator and Microsoft IE) pre-allocate a certain set of colors which will be used to render pages. When running on a 256 color display, they will start dithering other colors to fit within this palette. This can produce surprisingly ugly results. For example: if a GIF image with 256 unique colors needs to be displayed in Netscape on a 256-color display, 40 colors will be dropped, and approximated with dithering techniques. If any of those dropped colors are widely used in the image, the end result can be far from the intended one.

To prevent dithering, a web designer can make certain that an image does not contain any colors but the ones that fall in the standard palette. This will guarantee that the image will be displayed correctly, and as intended, on the target browsers. The browsers mentioned earlier normally use a 6×6×6 color cube, which means that they use a palette with 216 colors with the red, green and blue components spread evenly.

Web safe colors with GD

The following subroutine allocates a color cube of size $n for a *GD::Image* object. The default $n is 6, which will allocate a web safe color palette:

```
sub allocate_web_palette
{
  my $gd    = shift;
  my $n     = shift || 6;

  my $step = 255/($n - 1);
  my @range = map
              { sprintf "%.0f", $_ * $step } 0 .. $n - 1;

  for my $r (@range)
  {
    for my $g (@range)
    {
      for my $b (@range)
      {
        $gd->colorAllocate($r, $g, $b);
      }
    }
  }
}
```

This loops over the red component of the desired color in steps that will allocate black (0,0,0) as the first color, and white (255,255,255) as the last. The colors are all more or less evenly spaced over the possible spectrum of colors in 8 bits per channel RGB. The steps used and the number of colors allocated are shown in table 6.1.

cube size	colors	step size
6 x 6 x 6	216	51
5 x 5 x 5	125	63.75
4 x 4 x 4	64	85
3 x 3 x 3	27	127.5

Notice that the step sizes aren't always even integral values—some colors in the palette will be slightly farther apart than others. To conform to the generally accepted color cubes with sides 5 and 3, the @range array in the subroutine is produced by rounding up the value to the nearest integer. If we didn't explicitly round it up ourselves, the floating values would be truncated to an integer, resulting in slightly different colors from the intended ones.

If you start drawing on this *GD::Image* object, use the colorClosest() method, so that you are guaranteed to use a color in the standard color map.

```
$gd = GD::Image->new(200,200);
allocate_web_palette($gd);
$greenish = $gd->colorClosest( 10, 127, 10);
$orange   = $gd->colorClosest(255, 165,  0);
```

Web safe colors with Image::Magick

Image::Magick provides a special built-in image type that contains the palette described previously. Together with the Map() method, any image can be converted to use that palette. Suppose that you have an *Image::Magick* object $image, you may convert it as follows:

```
$map = Image::Magick->new();
$map->Read('netscape:');
$image->Map(image => $map, dither => 1);
```

The Quantize() method allows you to reduce the colors in an image in other ways. You cannot specify which colors will be used, but the color reduction algorithms used by *Image::Magick* are very good at making certain the choice is optimal.

6.3 CGI AND DYNAMICALLY GENERATED GRAPHICS

Writing a CGI program that returns image data is very similar to writing one that returns HTML, text, or any other data. The main difference is the Content-type header that must be returned to the browser, and we are dealing with binary data instead of text. The programming logic remains the same.

There is one other difference, and that is the way in which these CGI programs are called. Since these programs return data that is typically embedded in an HTML page, they are called in an HTML IMG tag:

```
<IMG SRC="/cgi-bin/image_script.cgi?parameters">
```

Of course, the script is unaware whether it has been called from within an IMG tag or directly as a link, and the programmer does not need to take any extra measures or use any techniques that are different from any other CGI program.

As an example, we will write a CGI program that can be used to display a clock on an HTML page that shows the current time. We'll use the modules developed in chapter 10 for this. Since those modules already do all the hard work of creating a clock, all we are concerned with is the CGI specific code and the code that interfaces with the module.

```
#!/usr/bin/perl -wT
use strict;
use CGI qw(:standard);          ❶ Include the needed
use Canvas::Polar::GD;             modules
use Clock;

my $size    = param('size') || 90;   ❷ Get the size parameter

my $canvas = Canvas::Polar::GD->new(
    $size, $size, '#ffffff');        ❸ Create a Canvas::GD::Polar
my $clock = Clock->new(radius => $size/2);   object and draw a clock
$clock->draw($canvas, $size/2, $size/2);

binmode STDOUT;                      ❹ Write the image
print header(-type => 'image/png',      to the client
             -expires => '+1m');
print $canvas->gd->png;
```

This is a small, fairly standard CGI program for Perl. It runs with the -w and -T flags to Perl enabled, and uses the strict pragma. None of these three are absolutely necessary for the correct functioning of the program, but they can be valuable for debugging programs and for security in an environment in which user input needs to be tightly controlled. Furthermore, it uses the *CGI* module, which is the standard for any CGI work in Perl. It might be considered overkill for something as simple as this script, but I would still recommend the use of it (see also the introduction to this chapter).

❶ The two other modules that are included are *Canvas::Polar::GD* from section 10.1 "Interface design," on page 176, and the *Clock* module from section 10.2 "An OO implementation of a clock," on page 186. All you need to know about these modules right now is that they provide this program with the capability of drawing a clock on a *GD* canvas.

❷ The only parameter this example script will look for is size, which is the width and height of the clock. If no size parameter is given, a default of 90 pixels is assumed.

❸ A GD canvas is then created, and a clock object is created and drawn on the canvas. The dimensions used to create the GD object are the given size. The radius of the clock is half that, since the middle of the clock should be in the middle of the canvas.

❹ Once all the drawing work is done, we need to output the image to the client. First, we tell the browser that we are returning data of the type `image/png`, which is the MIME type for PNG data, and we add an expiration time of 1 minute from now.[3] We then prepare the file handle we are going to print to with `binmode()` and print the data.

We can now include a clock in an HTML page with something like:

```
<IMG SRC="/cgi-bin/clock.cgi?size=60" WIDTH="60" HEIGHT="60">
```

As you can see, there is nothing special about this sample script, compared to other programs that use the CGI. The handling of input parameters is the same as for any program that uses the *CGI* module, and nothing special needs to be done, apart from being aware that PNG data is binary, and therefore STDOUT should be prepared with `binmode()`.

6.4   FORMS AND ENCAPSULATED GRAPHICS

The example from the previous section is a minor one, because there is no interactive input to the program that creates the graphic. More often, there will be the requirement for some user input, and an HTML page as output with the graphic somewhere on it. As an example we will take the program that generates a chart of the Southern Oscillation index and rainfall from section 5.1.7 "Mixed charts," on page 72, and fashion that into an interactive Web application that combines a few select boxes and a display of a graph, as shown in figure 6.1. The only user input will be the start and end dates for the graph, which can be selected from 4 pop up menus at the top of the page. The output is the same form, with the pop-ups initialized to the selected values or to some default, if nothing was selected yet. If values have been submitted, then the HTML page will also contain a chart with the SOI and monthly rainfall plotted over the period indicated.

The program that provides this functionality is surprisingly simple, mainly thanks to the use of the *CGI* module. Let's have a look at how it works.

```perl
#!/usr/bin/perl -wT
use strict;
use CGI qw(:standard);
use CGI::Carp qw(fatalsToBrowser);        ❶ Include the needed
use GD::Graph::mixed;                         modules
use GD::Graph::Data;

use vars qw($data $start_date $end_date @months @years);
@months =
    qw(Jan Feb Mar Apr May Jun Jul Aug Sep Oct Nov Dec);
    @years  = (1987 .. 1999);
```

---

[3] The expiration time is here to make sure that well behaved browsers and proxies will refresh the image at least once every minute.

Jun/1993 to May/1997

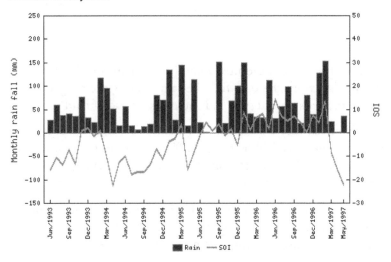

Figure 6.1 A screen shot of the Southern Oscillation Index CGI program in action. The interface allows the user to select a start and end date from a set of drop-down menus and, on submission of the request, the result of the query is shown in a chart.

❶ We start with the most common standard header for CGI scripts: the -w and -T flag for Perl, the strict pragma, and the *CGI* and *CGI::Carp* modules. The *CGI::Carp* module can help a CGI programmer quite a bit during development by routing any error messages from the program or Perl to the browser. Since the script must be able to create a chart, we include *GD::Graph::mixed*, and since we want to store our data somewhere, we'll use *GD::Graph::Data*. After that, we declare some variables that we want to be able to use globally, and which define the valid range of months and years used to populate the popup menus.

Next, we'll determine the input parameters, and read the relevant data from the data file:

```
if (param())      ❷ Only if parameters have
{                     been submitted
    $data = GD::Graph::Data->new();
    $start_date = param('start_month').'/'.param('start_year');
    $end_date = param('end_month').'/'.param('end_year');
    open(IN, '../Charts/SOI.data') or die "Can't read SOI.data:$!";
    while(<IN>)
    {
        next if /^#/;
```

```
        if (/^\Q$start_date/ .. /^\Q$end_date/)      ❸ Only read data in the
        {                                               wanted range
            chomp;
            my @d = map {$_ eq '' ? undef : $_} split /\t/;
            $data->add_point(@d);
        }
    }
    close(IN);
}
```

❷ The code in this block is executed only if any parameters have been submitted. It reads in the data from the data file, the same way as the program in section 5.1.7 does, but with user-supplied start and end dates instead of hard coded ones.

❸ This data is placed into the *GD::Graph::Data* object only when it falls between the start and end dates specified by the user. While storing the data, empty fields in the data file are mapped to undef values, since *GD::Graph* requires that non-existing data points be entered that way.

Note that in a real-life production script the input validation should probably be more sophisticated. Rather than merely checking for the presence of any parameters, the script should verify that the parameters it needs are present, and whether they have valid values.

The following step is taken to determine whether we want to generate an HTML form as output or a chart:

```
if (path_info() =~ /graph$/)
{
    make_graph();
}
else
{
    make_form();
}
```

For this example we distinguish between the two possible outputs by adding some path information at the end of the script. This is an often overlooked aspect of the CGI standard; the part of the path that comes after the script URL is passed to the program in the environment variable PATH_INFO, which we can access with the path_info() method from the *CGI* module. Suppose that the script is accessible as http://www.foo.com/weather/SOI.cgi, then the chart will be generated from the URL http://www.foo.com/weather/SOI.cgi/graph.

The code simply checks whether the return value of path_info() ends in the string graph. If so, the subroutine make_graph() is executed; if not, make_form() is executed.

Now let's see how the real work is done:

```
sub make_form
{
    print header(-type => 'text/html;charset = ISO-8859-1'),
        start_html(-title => 'SOI and Rainfall', -bgcolor => '#ffffff'),
        start_form,
        'From: ',
        popup_menu(-name => 'start_month',
            -values => \@months),
        popup_menu(-name => 'start_year',
            -values => \@years),
        'To: ',
        popup_menu(-name => 'end_month',
            -values => \@months),
        popup_menu(-name => 'end_year',
            -values => \@years),
        submit,
        hr;
    if (defined $data)
    {
        my $img_url = script_name() . '/graph?' . query_string();
        print
            h4("$start_date to $end_date"),
            p,
            img {src => $img_url};
    }
    print end_html;
}
```

4 **Populate the popup menus**

5 **If data was read in, embed a chart**

❹ This subroutine is responsible for returning the HTML to the browser that displays
the input form. It uses methods provided by the *CGI* module to generate HTML, and
to easily and conveniently create and populate the necessary form elements.

❺ It then checks whether $data is defined, which will be true only if the data file has
been read in by the code on page 98. If there is data, we construct a URL using the
extra path information /graph appended to the current script name, which will
instruct this script to generate an image instead of a form. We also append the current
parameters to the script as a query string. We then print a header and an IMG tag
with the constructed URL. When the browser loads this page, it will then hopefully
request the URL that prompts this script to generate a chart with the same parameters
that were submitted to this form processor. The subroutine that would carry out that
particular job is:

```
sub make_graph
{
    my $chart = new GD::Graph::mixed(500,300);
    $chart->set_legend(qw(Rain SOI));
    $chart->set(
        y1_label            => 'Monthly rain fall (mm)',
        y2_label            => 'SOI',
```

● **Create a chart object**

```
     types             => [qw(bars lines)],
     dclrs             => [qw(blue lgreen)],
     line_width        => 3,
     two_axes          => 1,
     x_label_skip      => 3,
     x_labels_vertical => 1,
     zero_axis         => 1,
 );

 binmode STDOUT;                                    ● Write chart
 print header(-type => 'image/png');                  to client
 print $chart->plot($data)->png;
}
```

First, a new *GD::Graph::mixed* object is created and given a legend and values for some attributes. The appropriate header is written to the client, STDOUT is prepared for use with binary data, and the chart is printed, using a shorthand version of

```
my $gd = $chart->plot($data);
print $gd->png;
```

That concludes the program. As you can see, a lot of the work of maintaining state (remembering which dates were selected between calls of the program) is performed by the *CGI* module. For graphics generating applications on the web, (which almost always need some transfer of state between the call to the script that generates the HTML page and the call that generates the actual image) this module really is a must.

SEE ALSO   The *CGI* module documentation and the *GD::Graph* documentation.

6.5   *IMAGE COLLECTIONS AND THUMBNAILING*

In the previous section we saw an example of a dynamic interface that responds to user input, displaying exactly the chart that was requested. Programs such as this can be quite a load on a web server, especially when they're requested frequently. There are several ways to decrease the demands on the CPU for this type data, the most effective one being to remove the interactivity totally, wherever that is possible. For example, financial company reports or log file statistics allow easy pregeneration of a set of charts and the HTML that goes with it.

Another example of data that lends itself well for automatic pregeneration of HTML and images is an image or photo directory. If you have a database of information about images and, of course, the images themselves, you can provide a useful interface to all this by writing an interactive application that queries the database and displays thumbnailed versions of those files in a browser. For a searching interface, this is a perfectly valid solution. For a browsing interface, in which a user just clicks on a set of links to reach a list of images, it is preferable to create the HTML and images in advance.

This section provides some alternative ways to present image directories or collections on the Web.

6.5.1   Thumbnails with *Image::Magick*

In this section we'll look at a small program that can be used to create thumbnails of a uniform size of a collection of images. It will create a directory (by default called `icons`) and put in thumbnail representations of all the images passed on the command line. You can call this program this way:

```
prompt> make_thumbnail -dir thumb *.gif *.jpg ../*.tiff
```

This will cause a new directory called `thumb` to be created in the current directory, and in it thumbnail images will be placed of all the GIF and JPEG images in the current directory, and all the TIFF images in the parent directory. The file names of the thumbnails will be the same as the image file names, but with `.png` appended.

```perl
#!/usr/local/bin/perl -w
use strict;
use Image::Magick;
use Getopt::Long;
use File::Basename;

my $out_dir = 'icons';            ● The default output
my $geometry = '120x120';           directory and
                                    thumbnail size
GetOptions(
    'geometry=s'  => \$geometry,
    'directory=s' => \$out_dir,
);
                                  ● Make sure the output
mkdir $out_dir, 0777 or             directory exists
    die "Cannot create $out_dir: $!" unless -d $out_dir;

foreach my $img (@ARGV)
{
    my $rc;
    my $im = Image::Magick->new();
    $rc = $im->Read($img);        ● Read the original image
    warn($rc), next if $rc;
    $rc = $im->Scale(geometry => $geometry);   ● Resize the image
    warn($rc), next if $rc;
    my $basename = basename $img;   ● Get the file name, and
    $basename =~ s/\.\w+$//;          remove the extension
    $rc = $im->Write("PNG:$out_dir/$basename.png");   ● Write the
    warn($rc) if $rc;                                   thumbnail
}
```

The program uses *Image::Magick* to manipulate the images and the standard Perl module *Getopt::Long* to process the command-line options. The options we look for are the geometry specification for the scaling (see "Geometry," on page 277 for a full explanation of possible values), and the directory into which the thumbnail images should go. If the directory does not yet exist, the program attempts to create it.

After processing the options, the program will loop over the remaining command-line arguments, treating each as a file name. It attempts to read these files, and if that fails (i.e., `$rc` has a true value) it prints a warning and continues with the next file.

If successful, it transforms the image according to the geometry specification, gets the basename of the file,[4] and saves the scaled image as a PNG file in the directory specified. Of course it is possible to make this program more flexible, for example, by allowing the file type of the saved thumbnails to be specified as an argument.

6.5.2 Thumbnails with *GD*

Even though *GD* doesn't directly provide any methods to resize an image, it can still be used to create thumbnails, thanks to its copyResized() method. Because of the limitations of *GD* compared to *Image::Magick*,[5] the program in this section will be less flexible, and the resulting thumbnails will generally be of a lower quality. However, since these are merely thumbnails, that might very well be acceptable. Since *GD* seems to be installed on a larger number of systems than *Image::Magick*, the following program is likely to be more widely usable than the one from the previous section:

```perl
#!/usr/local/bin/perl -w
use strict;
use GD;
use Getopt::Long;
use File::Basename;

my $out_dir = 'icons';                          ● The default output
my ($width, $height) = (120, 120);                directory and
                                                  thumbnail size
GetOptions(
    'width=i'     => \$width,
    'height=i'    => \$height,
    'directory=s' => \$out_dir,
);

mkdir $out_dir, 0777 or
    die "Cannot create $out_dir: $!" unless -d $out_dir;

foreach my $img (@ARGV)
{
    my $im = GD::Image->new($img) or            ❶ Read the original
        warn("Can't open $img"), next;            image and get its size
    my ($w, $h) = $im->getBounds();

    my ($w_scale, $h_scale) = ($width/$w, $height/$h);
    my $scale = $w_scale < $h_scale ? $w_scale : $h_scale;   ❷ Calculate the
    my ($w_out, $h_out) =                                       size for the
        map int, ($scale * $w, $scale * $h);                    thumbnail
                                                                and resize
    my $im_out = GD::Image->new($w_out, $h_out);
    $im_out->copyResized($im, 0, 0, 0, 0,
        $w_out, $h_out, $w, $h);
```

---

[4] In this case that is the full name of the file without any leading directory components and stripped of the file name extension.

[5] *GD* only works with 256 colors per image, it cannot deal with as many image formats as *Image::Magick* does, and it does not recognize the geometry specification.

```
    my $basename = basename $img;
    $basename =~ s/\.\w+$//;
    open(OUT, ">$out_dir/$basename.png") or
        warn("Can't open $out_dir/$basename.png: $!"), next;
    binmode OUT;
    print OUT $im_out->png;
    close OUT;
}
```

● Write
the
thumb
nail

The main difference between this program's interface and the previous one is that this one does not accept a geometry, but a width and height instead. These dimensions define the upper limits of the thumbnail's size, within which the aspect ratio of the original image will be preserved.

❶ The images specified on the command line are read in one by one, using the automatic detection of file formats in *GD* 1.30 and newer, and the size of the images is determined.

❷ We need to calculate the horizontal and vertical sizing scales separately, and we have to use the smallest of the two to resize the image. Once the dimensions of the thumbnail are known, a new image can be created according to those specifications, and copyResized() used to copy the original image on to the thumbnail-sized one. All that is left then is to save the image to a file.

6.5.3   Contact sheets with *Image::Magick*'s visual directory

Another way to provide a thumbnail view of a set of images is through contact sheets. A contact sheet is a single image which contains thumbnails of a set of other images. The name comes from the photography world, wherein it is customary to make a print of a set of negatives by placing them directly on photographic paper, and exposing that to light. Because the negatives are in contact with the photographic paper (which is not normally the case) this is known as a contact sheet.

Contact sheets can be handy if you need to send a set of samples or a directory of images directly to someone, for example by email. *Image::Magick* provides two ways to generate a contact sheet for a set of files.

If all your images are in a single directory and the highest quality is not required, then the visual directory input mode for *Image::Magick* might be sufficient.

```
use Image::Magick;

my $rc;
my $im = Image::Magick->new();
$im->Set(size => '45x45', label => '%f');
$rc = $im->Read('vid:*.{jpeg,jpg,png}');
die $rc if $rc;
$rc = $im->Write('contact.miff');
die $rc if $rc;
```

The built-in image type `vid` takes as its argument a shell wildcard expression (glob pattern), and creates as many contact sheets as necessary, with thumbnails of all the images matching the wildcard expression. Each of the thumbnails has the image name, pixel size and byte size printed below it. As of version 5.2.4, it is possible to control the size of the thumbnails with the `size` parameter, and the text printed under the images with the `label` attribute (see "String formatting," on page 280).

6.5.4 Contact sheets with Image::Magick::Montage

If you need more flexibility, look at the `Montage()` method. As well as greater control over the appearance of the output, this method also provides more and easier control in choosing which images to display. First, all the images you are interested in can be imported with the `Read()` or `BlobToImage()` methods, after which the `Montage()` method is called on the resulting object to create a new object that contains the sheets with thumbnail images.

```
use Image::Magick;

my $im = Image::Magick->new();
# Read all the images you want with the Read()
# or BlobToImage() methods into $im

my $montage = $im->Montage(
  geometry => '90x60+10+10', # tile size and border
  tile     => '4x3',
  frame    => '2x2',
  shadow   => 1,
  label    => '%f %wx%h',
);

$montage->Write('montage.miff');
```

The `Montage()` method takes a number of optional arguments, which are explained in the manual page of the montage command-line tool and enumerated on page 266. You can read in images in several ways. The `Read()` method accepts full glob patterns, so that you can do things such as `$im->Read('*.gif')` or `$im->Read('*.{gif,png})`. It also accepts a list of file names, so you can build your own list of names and pass it in, such as `$im->Read(@filename)` or even, if you prefer Perl's internal globbing, `$im->Read(<*.png>)`.

The `geometry` attribute controls the size of the tiles (width and height) and the borders (offsets) around the tiles (see also the explanation on page 277). In the above example code, the tiles will be 90 pixels wide, 60 pixels high, and there will be a vertical and horizontal 10 pixel gap between the tiles. If an image is smaller than the 90 by 60 pixels it will be scaled up. If you wish to avoid that, use a right angle bracket at the end of the geometry specification: `'90x60+10+10>'`.

You control the number of tiles per sheet with the `tile` attribute. For this example we request 4 columns of 3 tiles. In other words, we have a total of 12 tiles per sheet, 4 horizontal and 3 vertical. There are a few options that control the appearance of the tiles. The `frame` attribute puts each thumbnail in a frame, and the `shadow` attribute creates a drop shadow below each thumbnail.

The `label` attribute controls which text will be printed below each thumbnail. The string value of this attribute can contain escapes that each start with a percent sign. A full list of the possible escapes can be found in the manual page for the montage command-line tool, but I'll list a few of the more common ones here (also see page 266).

%b	file size (bytes)
%f	file name
%h	height in pixels
%w	width in pixels
%m	file type (magick)

If you want a tile to be empty, you can read in the special NULL file type, which is a special built-in *Image::Magick* file type:

```
$im->Read('NULL:');
```

Keep in mind when creating these contact sheets that their size (in bytes) can become unwieldy, causing users of your web site to sit and wait for some time before your images appear. A technique based on individual thumbnails is likely to be more appropriate and load faster. It also allows you to easily insert links to other pages, maybe with more description or other information. We will have a look at an application that does exactly that in the next section.

6.5.5   An example application: A web photo album

In this section we'll walk through an application that I wrote a while ago that creates a photo album, given a set of images and an XML file describing said images. I use it to keep my daughter's photo album on the web up to date, without having to actually do much HTML editing. I wanted an application that took some information from a database, together with the original scanned images, and would then generate a tree of HTML files and images that I could pack up and send to relatives, or deploy on a web server.

The photo album consists of a set of indexes, which allow one to group certain photos together. Each of the indexes displays a certain set of thumbnail images, which the user can click on to view a full-sized version of a photo (see figures 6.2 and 6.3).

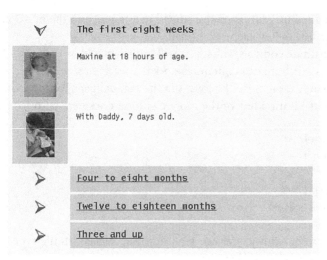

Figure 6.2
One of the index pages of a web photo album. The user can select any of the headers next to the little arrows to be taken to another index page, or they can select one of the thumbnail pictures to see the full-size photo with a longer description.

There is one master index with all the sections closed, and there is a single index page for each section. Selecting one of the arrows opens or closes the selected section by loading a different HTML document.

I had already created a set of HTML files with a prototype of this idea, which convinced me even more that I did not want to manually maintain this HTML. Each time I had to add a photo, or wanted to start a new series of photos, I had to resize and scale various images to the correct size, put them in the right location, and then edit several HTML documents, making certain to get all the names of these files correct.

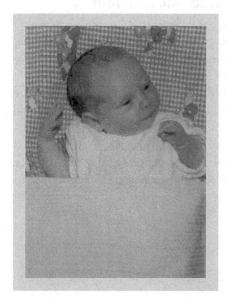

Figure 6.3
A single page of the web photo album, showing a full-size picture, plus an optional description of the picture.

Maxine's first
official
photo

CHAPTER 6 GRAPHICS AND THE WEB

6.5.6   **Designing the data**

The first decision to be made is how to maintain the data: which text goes with which image, and in which section does a picture appear. In this case, we'll use an XML file. This allows the combination of the data to be maintained together with processing instructions (I'll discuss that later), which is something that cannot be done as easily with a database-driven application. The XML file that drives the whole process looks like this:

```
<index title="Maxine's pictures">

<option name="source_dir" value="/spare/pictures" />
<option name="out_dir"    value="OUT" />

<list description="The first eight weeks">
  <picture name="newborn"
     label="Maxine at 18 hours of age.">
    <text>Maxine's first official photo.</text>
  </picture>
  <picture name="no_hand"
     label="With Daddy, 7 days old." />
</list>

<!-- More lists go here -->

</index>
```

The XML document's top node is the *index* node. This index consists of *list* nodes, and each list contains a set of *picture* nodes. Each *picture* node can contain text which will be displayed next to the full-sized version of the photo. Each of these elements can have several attributes set, which are fairly self-explanatory. The *index* has a title, which is used as the title of the HTML index pages. Each *list* can have a description, which is printed in the index as the section header (see figure 6.2). Each *picture* has a name and a label. The name is mandatory, and should be the first part of the name of the image you wish to include. The label is printed next to the thumbnail in the index pages.

In addition to the information pertaining to sections and pictures, the XML file can also contain *option* elements. These elements set various options in the program, and can appear anywhere in the document. For example, the source_dir option is set to a particular directory at the top of the document. This directory contains the original versions of the images you want to display, probably still in TIFF format, and at a much higher resolution than is appropriate for the web pages. If the next section has its source images somewhere else, a new *option* element can be included, and from then on the program will find its source images in that new directory.

Designing the application and data flow

Now that we have defined the data we need and how it is formatted, we can design a rough outline of an application and the data streams that go with it. Figure 6.4 contains a schematic drawing of the various elements of the application we need to build.

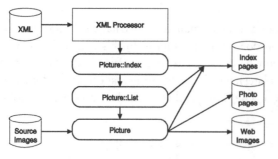

Figure 6.4
A high-level application diagram for the Web photo album generator, showing the inputs and outputs of the program and the main operative parts and data structures.

The main application reads the XML file, and constructs an in-memory representation of the indexes, lists, and pictures that need to be created, which will be represented by Perl classes. Each of these classes will create a part of the output needed for the photo album. The *Picture::Index* class is responsible for managing the lists and creating the output for the indexes, with the help of the other classes. The *Picture::List* class is responsible for managing the individual photos and their order. The *Picture* class represents a single picture with all its associated information, and is responsible for the creation of the HTML pages that display a single photo, as well as the creation of the web versions of the photos from the source images.

Parsing the XML

Let's have a look at the program that parses the XML data file, and that builds the relevant data structures.

```
#!/usr/local/bin/perl -w
use strict;
use Picture;
use XML::Parser;

my $DATABASE  = $ARGV[0] or    ❶
    die "Usage: $0 picture_data.xml\n";

my $xml = XML::Parser->new(
    Handlers => {
        Start   => \&xml_start,
        End     => \&xml_end,
        Char    => \&xml_char
    },
);

my $picture_index = Picture::Index->new();
$xml->parsefile($DATABASE);
$picture_index->generate_output;    ❷
```

Read the name of the XML database file ❶

And generate all HTML and images ❷

The program uses *XML::Parser*, since we don't want to do all the XML parsing ourselves. It also uses the *Picture* module, which contains the code for the *Picture*, *Picture::List* and *Picture::Index* classes. It is not available from CPAN, but it will be discussed later in this section. It takes care of all the handling of the images and HTML. The main program only parses the XML, and passes the information to the code in *Picture*.

❶ The program expects as its first argument on the command line the name of an XML file of the format discussed on page 155. It instantiates an *XML::Parser* object, and tells it which subroutines to call when it encounters the start or end of a tag or some text data. Following that, a *Picture::Index* object is created, which is defined in the *Picture* module. This is the data structure used to store all the information contained in the XML file.

❷ Next, the XML file is parsed, and the `$picture_index` object's `generate_output()` method is called, which actually generates all pictures, thumbnails and HTML files.

That is all the work that occurs in the main program. Of course, there is a lot more code to write—in particular, the subroutines that the XML parser object is to call. The first of these is the subroutine that will be called when a start tag has been encountered in the input file:

```perl
my $in_picture = 0;                    ❸ Declare state
my $in_text    = 0;                       variables

sub xml_start
{
    shift;
    my $element = shift;               ❹ The name of the element
    my %attrs = @_;                       and any attributes

    for ($element)
    {
        /^index$/    and
            $picture_index->set_option(%attrs);

        /^option$/   and
            $picture_index->set_option($attrs{name},
                                       $attrs{value});

        /^list$/     and
            $picture_index->add_list(%attrs);

        /^picture$/ and do
        {
            $picture_index->add_picture(%attrs);
            $in_picture = 1;
        };

        /^text$/     and
            $in_text = 1;
    }
}
```

❸ Two state variables are declared that will be used to track whether we are currently inside a picture tag or a text tag. We need to keep track of this so that in the text handler, `xml_char()`, we know whether we need to store the text fragments that are detected.

❹ The `xml_start()` subroutine is invoked each time an opening XML tag is detected, and the attributes of that tag are passed in as arguments. When the top node element is read, the attributes are merely passed on to the `$picture_index` object, which was defined in the main body of the program. When an `<option>` tag is encountered, its name and value attributes are also passed on as options to the `$picture_index` object. When a `<list>` or `<picture>` is seen, the corresponding method is called. The two state variables are set to certify that we can keep track of whether we're actually processing a picture or text at the moment. This allows us to ignore any textual data that isn't part of a text block in a picture tag.

The subroutines that are called when an XML end tag or character data are encountered are called `xml_end()` and `xml_char()`, and are defined as follows:

```
sub xml_end
{
    shift;
    my $element = shift;

    for ($element)
    {
        /^picture$/ and $in_picture = 0;
        /^text$/    and $in_text = 0;
    }
}

sub xml_char
{
    my $parser = shift;
    my $string = shift;
                                        Only if we're processing a
    if ($in_picture && $in_text)    ● picture's text tag
    {
        $picture_index->add_text($string);
    }
}
```

All that needs to be done in `xml_end()` is to reset the two state variables, and all that the `xml_char()` subroutine needs to do is to call the `add_text()` method if both the state variables are true.

This concludes the program that parses the XML file. It is now time to have a look at the *Picture* module. It contains code for three classes, *Picture::Index*, *Picture::List*, and *Picture*. The names of these three packages makes it clear that they reflect the data structure in the XML document.

The Picture::Index class

The *Picture::Index* class is responsible for the creation of the index pages, and the management of photo lists. It also contains convenient methods that forward information to the lists that are managed. Let's have a look at how *Picture::Index* is implemented:

```
package Picture::Index;
use strict;
use CGI qw(-no_debug);          ❶ For HTML output

our %options = (                    ❷ Default options
    out_dir        => '.',
);

sub new
{
    my $proto = shift;
    my %attrs = @_;
    my $class = ref($proto) || $proto;
    my $self  = {%options, %attrs, _lists => []};
    bless $self => $class;
}
```

❶ The *Picture::Index* class includes the *CGI* module, for generating HTML. That way we don't have to worry as much about correctly opening and closing tags, and can let a thoroughly debugged module do all the hard work for us.

❷ A package-wide %options hash is declared, which is used to initialize objects that are instantiated from this class. This can be seen in the new() method, which is defined next. The objects of the class are all instantiated with the contents of the %options hash, overridden with the arguments (stored in %attrs) and have a reference to an empty array added to the store picture lists. This array will be used to store the contained photo lists, which are implemented as *Picture::List* objects, discussed later.

The set_option() method can be used to set individual attributes for the class as a whole, or for individual objects.

```
sub set_option
{
    my $proto = shift;
    my %attrs = @_;
                                        Pass arguments on to
    Picture->set_option(@_);        ● the Picture class

    if (ref($proto))                ● Is this an object?
    {
        $proto->{$_} = $attrs{$_} for keys %attrs;
    }
    else
    {
        %options = (%options, %attrs);
    }
}
```

In any case, the call is forwarded to the *Picture* class, so that all attributes set in this subroutine become class defaults. If the method is called on an object reference, the object's options are changed, otherwise the class options are changed.

The add_list() method is used to create a new list in the index. This is accomplished by instantiating a new *Picture::List* object (discussed later), and pushing that onto the end of the array that contains all lists. At this time a file name is also assigned to this particular list, which will be used for the output phase.

```
sub add_list
{
    my $self  = shift;
    my %attrs = @_;
    my $list  = Picture::List->new(%attrs);
    my $num   = push(@{$self->{_lists}}, $list);
    $self->last_list->{filename} = "index$num.html";
}

sub last_list
{
    my $self = shift;
    $self->{_lists}->[-1];
}
```

The last_list() method can be used to get a reference to the last list added.

The add_picture() and add_text() methods just add a picture to the current list, or text to the current picture.

```
sub add_picture
{
    my $self = shift;
    $self->last_list->add_picture(@_);
}

sub add_text
{
    my $self = shift;
    $self->last_list->last_picture->add_text(@_);
}
```

This is done by forwarding the call to the current *Picture::List* or *Picture* object, which can be obtained through the method last_list() in *Picture::List* and the last_picture() method in *Picture*, which will be discussed later. There should be no surprises in this way of delegating work for anyone who is familiar with OO programming.

The only code left to write for this package is the code that actually generates the output files from the information provided:

```
sub generate_output
{
    my $self = shift;
    local(*OUT);
```

```perl
mkdir($self->{out_dir}) or
    die "Cannot create dir $self->{out_dir}"
        unless -d $self->{out_dir};

foreach my $li (-1 .. $#{$self->{_lists}})
{
    my $fn = "$self->{out_dir}/";
    $fn    .= ($li == -1) ?
             'index.html' :
             $self->{_lists}->[$li]->{filename};

    my $h = CGI->new();
    open(OUT, ">$fn") or
        die "Cannot open $fn: $!";
    print OUT
      $h->start_html(
        -title => $self->{title} || '',
        -bgcolor => '#ffffe7'
      ),
      $h->start_table(
        {-cellpadding => 10, -bgcolor => '#ffffe7'});

    foreach my $lj (0 .. $#{$self->{_lists}})
    {
        my $list = $self->{_lists}->[$lj];
        print OUT $list->index_entry($li == $lj);
    }
    print OUT
        $h->end_table,
        $h->end_html;

}
}
```

③ Make sure the output directory exists

④ A special case for the master index

● **Create an HTML file for the index of this list**

● **Get the index entry for the contained list**

❸ After making sure the output directory exists, a loop is set up over all the lists that were added, and for each list, the name of the output file is determined.

❹ There is actually one extra run of the loop for element −1. Its purpose is to create the *main* index, i.e., the index that has only the headers of the sections, with all sections closed (see figure 6.2). This inclusion is also the reason that the code creating the file name looks complex. If the loop index is −1, then the file name becomes index.html, otherwise the file name becomes whatever it was set to in the add_list() method discussed earlier.

The outermost loop creates all of the index documents. Each index document needs to have information about all the lists in it. Inside this loop, we need to loop again over all the lists, and ask each list to generate the HTML for its own entry by calling the index_entry() method. We will discuss this method in full later. The only argument it expects is a boolean value that tells it whether to generate only a header, or a full set of thumbnails. It needs to generate thumbnail lists only when the document we are currently generating is the index for the list in question; in other words, when $li == $lj.

The Picture::List class

We will now look at the code that manages the *Picture::List* objects. These objects represent individual lists of photos that belong together, and manage the order of these photos, as well as how they should look in an index entry.

```
package Picture::List;
use strict;
use CGI qw(-no_debug);

sub new
{
    my $proto = shift;
    my %attrs = @_;
    my $class = ref($proto) || $proto;
    my $self  = {%attrs, _pictures => []};
    bless $self => $class;
}
```

There is nothing surprising in the package header or its constructor. We use the *CGI* module again for the creation of the HTML involved, to save work and debugging. A new object gets initialized by using the arguments passed into the constructor, and a reference to an empty array is added. This array will be used to store all the pictures in this list.

To add those pictures, the method `add_picture()` is provided. The `add_picture()` method instantiates a new *Picture* object and pushes that onto the end of the discussed array.

```
sub add_picture
{
    my $self    = shift;
    my $picture = Picture->new(@_);
    push @{$self->{_pictures}}, $picture;
}

sub last_picture
{
    my $self = shift;
    $self->{_pictures}->[-1];
}
```

The method `last_picture()` is provided to get a reference to the current picture, so that outside code can easily obtain this information.

In the `generate_output()` method of the *Picture::Index* class, we discussed asking the *Picture::List* objects to generate the HTML for themselves. This is accomplished in the following code:

```
sub index_entry
{
    my $self = shift;
    my $selected = shift;
    my $h = CGI->new();
```

```perl
if ($selected)
{
    my $return =
      $h->Tr({-valign => 'top'},
        $h->td({-align => 'center', -width => 70},
          $h->a({-href => 'index.html'},
            $h->img({
              -src => 'deselect.gif',
              -width => 70,
              -height => 20,
              -border => 0,
              -alt => '-',
            }),
          ),
        ),
        $h->td({-bgcolor => '#ffd7d7', -width => '100%'},
          $h->tt($h->big($h->b($self->{description})))),
        ),
      );
    for my $picture (@{$self->{_pictures}})
    {
        $picture->generate_output;
        $return .= $picture->index_entry;
    }
    return $return;
}
else
{
    return
      $h->Tr({-valign => 'top'},
        $h->td({-align => 'center', -width => 70},
          $h->a({-href => $self->{filename}},
            $h->img({
              -src => 'select.gif',
              -width => 70,
              -height => 20,
              -border => 0,
              -alt => '+',
            }),
          ),
        ),
        $h->td({-bgcolor => '#ffd7d7', -width => '100%'},
          $h->tt($h->big($h->b(
            $h->a({-href => $self->{filename}},
              $self->{description}
            ),
          ))),
        ),
      );
}
}
```

● **Need to generate HTML for a selected list**

● **Need to generate HTML for an unselected list**

There are two main branches in this subroutine: ❶ one to generate HTML for a *selected* index entry, and ❷ one branch to generate HTML for an unselected index entry (see figure 6.2). The code in each of these branches is almost identical, and generates HTML for a table row representing the index entry for this picture list, with a little arrow picture in the left table cell, and the description of the list in the right.

If the list is currently selected, thumbnails of the photos in the list need to be printed, together with a short description. This is done by setting up a loop which calls the generate_output() method for each picture, and adds the result of that call to the current output. In this way, the *Picture::List* class delegates part of the work to the *Picture* class.

The Picture class

We will now have a look at the last package, which is responsible for all the image handling in this program.

```perl
package Picture;
use strict;
use CGI qw(-no_debug);          The Image::Magick module is
use Image::Magick;           ❺ needed for image sizing

our %options = (                    ❻ Default options
    pic_size        => 400,            for the photos
    thumb_size      => 70,
    source_dir      => '.',
    out_dir         => '.',
    thumb_dir       => 'thumbs',
    pic_dir         => 'pics',
    overwrite       => 0,
);

sub new
{
    my $proto = shift;
    my %attrs = @_;
    my $class = ref($proto) || $proto;
    my $self  = {%options, %attrs, text => ''};
    $self->{html_name}  = "$self->{name}.html";
    $self->{thumb_name} = "$self->{thumb_dir}/$self->{name}.jpg";
    $self->{pic_name}   = "$self->{pic_dir}/$self->{name}.jpg";
    bless $self => $class;
}
```

❺ The *Picture* class uses the *CGI* module for the HTML output, but it also needs *Image::Magick* to be able to read the source images, and write the resized and reformatted images for the web photo album and the thumbnails.

❻ As in the *Picture::Index* package, there is a %option hash that is used to provide defaults for the various attributes of the pictures. The attributes specify what the size of the images will be for the single pages (they will fit inside a 400 by 400 pixel square), and for the thumbnails (70 by 70 square maximum). The source images will be sought in the directory specified by source_dir, and there are three attributes that control the output directories: out_dir, thumb_dir and pic_dir. All of the HTML files will be written in out_dir, all full-size pictures in out_dir/pic_dir and all thumbnail pictures that are displayed in the indexes will be put in out_dir/thumb_dir. The overwrite attribute controls whether already existing images will be overwritten or left alone. Each of these attributes can be overridden by specifying an appropriate <option> tag in the XML file. The constructor for this class initializes an object with defaults copied from the %option hash, and sets up the file names of the various output files for this particular photo.

All these options can be changed per object, or for the whole class with the set_option() method:

```
sub set_option
{
    my $proto = shift;
    my %attrs = @_;

    if (ref $proto)
    {
        $proto->{$_} = $attrs{$_} for keys %attrs;     ● Set options for
                                                          the object...
    }
    else
    {
        %options = (%options, %attrs);      ● ...or the whole class
    }
}
```

All pictures, except for full-sized images and thumbnail images, can also have text associated with them. This text is added with the add_text() method:

```
sub add_text
{
    my $self = shift;
    $self->{text} .= shift;
}
```

Each photo can appear as an entry on an index page. The *Picture::List* class calls the index_entry() method to get the HTML when that is necessary, and that method is implemented as follows:

```
sub index_entry
{
    my $self = shift;
    my $h = CGI->new();

    return
      $h->Tr({-valign => 'top'},
        $h->td({-align => 'center', -bgcolor => '#ffd7d7'},
```

```
        $h->a({-href => $self->{html_name}},
          $h->img({
            -src => $self->{thumb_name},
            -width => $self->{thumb_width},
            -height => $self->{thumb_height},
            -alt => '',
            -border => 0,
          }),
        ),
      ),
      $h->td({-width => '100%'},
        $h->tt($self->{label}),
      ),
    )
}
```

This method generates HTML for a single table row with two cells. The left cell contains the image tag for the thumbnail, and the right side contains the picture label. Remember that this method was called from the index_entry() method in the *Picture::List* object, just after a call to generate_output() (see the code on page 114). The order of those two calls is important, because generate_output() is actually responsible for calling the method that sets the size of the thumbnail image:

```
sub generate_output
{
    my $self = shift;
    local(*OUT);

    my $pic_dir   = "$self->{out_dir}/$self->{pic_dir}";
    my $thumb_dir = "$self->{out_dir}/$self->{thumb_dir}";

    mkdir($pic_dir) or die "Cannot mkdir $pic_dir: $!"
        unless -d "$pic_dir";
    mkdir($thumb_dir) or die "Cannot mkdir $thumb_dir: $!"
        unless -d "$thumb_dir";

    $self->generate_images;                ● Generate all images

    $self->{text} =~ s#\n\s*\n#</p><p>#g;   ● Empty lines are
                                              paragraph separators
    my $h = CGI->new();
    my $html_name =                         ● Create the HTML
        "$self->{out_dir}/$self->{html_name}";    file for this photo
    open(OUT, ">$html_name") or
        die "Cannot open $html_name: $!";
    print OUT
      $h->start_html(
        -title => $self->{title} || $self->{name},
        -bgcolor => '#ffffe7'
      ),
      $h->table({-cellpadding => 20,
          -bgcolor => '#ffffe7'},
        $h->Tr({-valign => 'top'},
```

```
            $h->td({-bgcolor => '#ffd7d7',
                -valign => 'center'},
              $h->img({src => $self->{pic_name},
                width => $self->{width},
                height => $self->{height}}),     ● Put in the
              ),                                    image tag
            $h->td({-width => '100%'},
              $h->tt($h->p($self->{text})),      ● And write the text
            ),
          ),
        ),
      $h->end_html();
}
```

This method creates the single picture pages (see figure 6.3) for the photo album. Before doing this, the code first checks that the necessary output directories exist, creating them where necessary. Then the generate_images() method is called, which is responsible for making certain that the full-size picture and the thumbnail exist, and for reading in their dimensions. Since the rest of the code in this method is almost self-explanatory, we'll jump right ahead and have a look at generate_images():

```
sub generate_images
{
    my $self = shift;
    my $rc;
    my $im = Image::Magick->new();

    my $pic_name = "$self->{out_dir}/$self->{pic_name}";

    if (-f $pic_name && !$self->{overwrite})
    {
        warn "Won't overwrite $pic_name\n";        ● The image
        $rc = $im->Read($pic_name);                   already exists
        warn $rc if $rc;
    }
    else
    {
        foreach my $ext qw(tif tiff png jpg jpeg gif)   ┐ Find a
        {                                               ⑦ source
            $rc = $im->Read(                            ┘ image
                "$self->{source_dir}/$self->{name}.$ext");
            last unless $rc;
        }
        warn($rc), return if $rc;

        $im->Scale(geometry =>                          ● Create a web-
            "$self->{pic_size}x$self->{pic_size}");       ready resized
        $im->Set(filename    => $pic_name);               version of image
        $rc = $im->Write();
        warn $rc if $rc;
    }
```

```
$self->{width}  = $im->Get('width');                    ● Memorize
$self->{height} = $im->Get('height');                       dimensions of
                                                             image
my $thumb;
my $thumb_name = "$self->{out_dir}/$self->{thumb_name}";

if (-f $thumb_name && !$self->{overwrite})
{
    warn "Won't overwrite $thumb_name\n";               ❽ The thumbnail
    $thumb = Image::Magick->new();                          image already
    $rc = $thumb->Read($thumb_name);                        exists
    warn $rc if $rc;
}
else
{
    $thumb = $im->Clone();
    $thumb->Scale(geometry =>
        "$self->{thumb_size}x$self->{thumb_size}");     ● Create a
    $thumb->Set(filename   => $thumb_name);                 thumbnail
    $rc = $thumb->Write();                                  from current
    warn $rc if $rc;                                        image
}
$self->{thumb_width}  = $thumb->Get('width');           ● Memorize
$self->{thumb_height} = $thumb->Get('height');              dimensions of
}                                                            thumbnail
```

This is where all the image manipulation takes place. This subroutine checks whether
the output image already exists, and if so, it is read into the $im *Image::Magick*
object. Reading in the image has to be done in order to create a thumbnail version of
it, and we need to know its dimensions to generate decent HTML.

❼ If the image doesn't yet exist, the source_dir directory is checked for images with
the same base name and one of the extensions from a predefined list. If no matching
source images can be found, a warning is emitted and the subroutine is terminated. If
a source image can be found, it is read into the *Image::Magick* object, resized to fit
inside a square of pic_size pixels, and written to the output image location. Once
we are certain that we have an image loaded in $im, we store the image dimensions so
that they can be used to generate correct HTML image tags for it.

❽ If a thumbnail image already exists on disk, it is loaded into the $thumb *Image::Mag-
ick* object. If no thumbnail image exists, one is created by making a copy of the $im
object which contains the full-size image, resizing that copy, and writing it to disk.
Once we are certain a thumbnail exists, its dimensions are stored for future reference
while building the HTML.

To finish off the module, we need to return a true value.

```
"This is the end of Picture.pm";
```

Limitations of the program

In the current incarnation of this program, all the pictures need a unique name. This can be easily solved by prefixing the names of the resulting images with some mangled string that is based on the source directory from which the image was read.

The HTML for output is hard-coded in the *Picture* module. It would probably be more flexible to use template files, or to allow callbacks that actually create the HTML. However, to be fully flexible there, complicated code needs to be created. I judged it easier to just create new modules if I needed a different look and feel. Instead of creating fully new modules, it is often enough to use the classes presented here as parent classes, and to override only the parts of the code that need to be changed, i.e., the `generate_output()` and `index_entry()` methods. The general layout idea remains the same for all child classes, however. If a totally different layout is wanted, a totally new piece of code needs to be written.

The design of the three classes isn't as neatly organized and cleanly separated as it could be.

6.6   SUMMARY

In this chapter we've had a look at dynamically creating graphical content for the web. We have also discussed the (currently) most appropriate graphical formats for the web. And finally, we've had a look at some ways to automatically create static content—in this particular case, image directories, for display on a web site.

CHAPTER 7

Animations for the Web

Animations come in many sizes and shapes. Nowadays, most people immediately think of multi-frame GIF when the subject of animation is mentioned in the context of image manipulation or computer graphics, and only a few people think also of video formats, such as AVI, MPEG and QuickTime. There is a good reason for this: the video formats normally require quite a bit of knowledge of video compression, color spaces, frame rates, bit rates and other more obscure parameters. In other words: it isn't easy to work with video formats, and it has therefore become the domain of a small group of specialists with video editing tools. Video formats also have a limited application: they're meant for video, and not for general purpose animations. There exists no ideal tool to work with these formats aside from Perl, thus, this section will limit itself to animation for the web, which at the moment is the only other most widespread use of moving computer graphics.[1]

Animations on web pages are seldom useful. They're eye-candy, and are often an eye-sore. Many animations are created and published on the Web simply because it

---

[1] Of course, there are computer generated animations which are created for film or TV, but they generally don't get stored in a GIF format, or anything resembling that.

can be done. Some animations are created because the designers of the site treat the Web as an extension of television. In certain quarters it is believed that a Web site isn't up to par until it has something on it that moves gratuitously.

However, one thing that animations excel at is catching the attention of visitors to your web site. The human eye naturally gravitates toward anything that moves; thus, if you do put an animation to your web site, it should highlight the parts on which you want viewers to focus, over and above the rest of the page. Your company logo probably doesn't fall into this category. It also means that you should limit the number of animations on a page to the barest minimum to avoid sensory overload. If you've ever tried to read text on a page that has more than three animations in view, you'll know what I mean. Even subtle animations make it hard for people to concentrate on the content displayed in the midst of all the movement.

Then of course there is the area of advertising on the Web. We are all, by now, familiar with the banners, buttons, boxes, and other advertising material that we have to download to reach the content we are actually seeking. I'm probably not too far off the mark in believing that some 90 percent of animations on the Web are related to advertising. Because the goal of this advertising is to attract your attention and convince you to follow the link they represent, they are almost always intrusive and distracting. For this same reason, animation is perfectly suited to advertisements on web pages.

What exactly is an animation? In its simplest form, an animation is a sequence of images, displayed in succession to provide an illusion of movement or change. Video formats accomplish this by replacing the image with an entirely new one (although some compression formats actually avoid duplicating pixels or lines that are identical in the two images). Other animation formats allow you to position smaller images on top of a previous larger one, or even combine them. Yet other formats allow you to specify drawing primitives which are drawn and rendered on the fly, and can be moved around and transformed.

Let's have a look at the various file formats that can be used to present animations on web pages.

7.1 ANIMATION FILE FORMATS

Most of the animated illustrations served on Web pages are GIF format animations. The use of Macromedia Shockwave and Flash is increasing, because people are looking for ways to get around the limitations of the GIF format. There are, however, some other contenders that hopefully soon will gain a significant share in the animated web content. In this section we'll take a look at the most widely used animation file formats.

7.1.1 GIF

The GIF image format allows the creation of animations in a fairly simple and straightforward manner. The acceptance of GIF by the leading web browsers also attributed significantly to the widespread use of GIF animations. Ever since the introduction of animated GIF support in one of the earlier Netscape browsers, the use of this format has virtually exploded. Since the GIF format is the most widely used format, we'll be spending the bulk of this chapter on the creation of GIF animations.

There is, however, only so much that can be accomplished within the limits of the GIF specification. It was never meant to cover the sort of elaborate animations for which it is currrently used, thus resulting in large, inefficient blobs of data shuffled over the Internet so someone can present you with a banner slightly more eye-catching than their competitor's banners. Add to that the fact that everyone in the world now has to pay royalties whenever they create a GIF image and compress it (see section 2.1.1, on page 17), and it's no wonder that people have started looking for other solutions.

Unfortunately, the GIF format will be around for some time yet, mainly due to the fact that mainstream browsers are very slow in accepting the alternative formats discussed in this chapter and elsewhere. For several years to come there will be a legacy of obsolete browsers that cannot deal correctly with PNG and MNG formats but that perfectly parse and render images stored as GIF.

7.1.2   MNG

The Multi-image Network Graphics format (see section 2.1.4, "MNG," on page 19) addresses these issues. It is an open, nonproprietary format that has been specifically designed to support efficient, well compressed animations, using techniques and formats from both the PNG and JPEG standards. At this time the MNG standard is still in development, although some applications (notably ImageMagick) already support it. It avoids the application domain of formats that currently cover video compression, and is therefore unlikely to ever include sound. MNG support in web browsers is still very limited and relies on users finding and installing a plug-in.

SEE ALSO   Plug-ins to support MNG for Netscape Navigator (Linux, Win32) and Internet Explorer (Win32) are listed on http//www.libmng.com/plugins/.

7.1.3   Macromedia Flash

Macromedia Flash animations are slightly different from GIF animations. They are internally formatted differently, and support all kinds of interesting operations geared toward creating animated and interactive content. A Flash application is actually much more than mere animation, although it is often used only for that. The format is proprietary, and, although the players are free, a license fee is required for software that creates the animations. There is no decent way to work with the Macromedia formats from within Perl,[2] so we won't spend any more time on it.

---

[2]   Since this was written, several projects have been started to make this possible, and these projects are in various stages of development. If you do a search on http://www.google.com/ for the keywords *flash* and *perl*, you will find several of them.

SVG

For animations that should not be implemented as bitmapped frames, the Scalable Vector Graphics format (see section 2.1.5, "SVG," on page 19) will prove to be an important player. Many GIF animations can be better implemented as Macromedia Flash animations, and in many places where Flash animations are now used, the SVG format will be an appropriate, nonproprietary replacement. Support for the SVG format can be expected in the next release of the major browsers since it has been adopted by the World Wide Web Consortium as a candidate recommendation for a standard.

Apart from these four formats there really isn't much available that is widely supported, or looks like it might be widely supported in the near future. Many graphics packages use their own format to store animations (such as ImageMagick's MIFF format), but it is unlikely that support for these will ever be available in mainstream web browsers.

7.2   *GIF ANIMATIONS*

Because at this moment GIF is the only widely supported animated image format that can be created from within Perl, we'll discuss it in more depth. There are several parameters that are important for animated GIFs, which you will encounter in examples in this chapter.

GIF animations are built up from a sequence of images that can be of a different size, as long as they're smaller than the first image. The GIF format supports a few options which can be set per image or frame, and one global-only option. The following provides gives a short description of each:

loop

First there is the loop parameter, which is really a Netscape extension. This global parameter controls how often an animated sequence is played. If this is set to 0, the animation will loop forever.

delay

This parameter can be set for the whole sequence at once, and for each individual frame. It expresses how long to wait (in hundredths of a second) before displaying the next image in the sequence. It can have a value between 0 and 65,535, which is just under 11 minutes. If this is set to 0, the animation will be displayed as fast as possible, and will be at different speeds depending on the client and its environment.

dispose

The GIF format defines a disposal method, which is one of the following:

0	No method specified.
1	Do not dispose; the graphic is left as is.
2	Restore to background color. The area used by the graphic is restored to the background color.
3	Restore to previous. The area used by the graphic is restored to what it was before displaying this graphic.

Method 3 is not implemented in all clients out there; notably, some older versions of Netscape will not be able to deal with this correctly.

transparency

While this last one is a general GIF attribute and not limited to animations, it is still important, because it can exert an influence over how the frames in a GIF animation are combined. Unfortunately, this is dependent on the program used to display the animation.

Each frame in a GIF animation can have its own size, offset and color palette. The first frame has to be the largest one in the sequence, and none of the other frames is allowed to extend past the borders of this initial frame. That means that if the canvas size for your animation is 200 by 300 pixels, the initial image should have that size, and all of the other images should be less than or equal to that size. If any of the following images has an offset, it should be smaller than the first image by at least the magnitude of the offset. Many applications will actually allow violations of these rules but, strictly speaking, they should be obeyed in any case.

7.3   PERL AND ANIMATIONS

Creating animations is a highly specific task, and most animations need to be created manually, because you have to shift pixels, adjust timing, and generally fiddle around until everything is as it should be. There are very few animation tasks that can be automated, but nonetheless, you will occasionally find yourself in a situation in which you want to automatically generate animated graphics. The various sections in this chapter offer a short indication of how you can achieve that task, using Perl and its modules.

Even if you don't directly create the animations from within Perl, you can still use it to prepare the images from which you are going to build the animation. Instead of translating, blurring, or resizing 20 times manually, let Perl take care of that: you import the result into an image editor that can work with the animation file format, and you fine-tune it.

To create animations in Perl, the options are fairly limited. The only two packages I know of that can be used to create animations are the *Image::Magick* and *Gimp* modules, both of which are capable of creating GIF and MNG output. There is no Perl module to create SVG, let alone SVG animations. *Image::Magick* can read SVG, but it cannot output it. Since SVG is an XML-based text format, however, it isn't difficult to create an SVG file from within a Perl program. All that's needed is a detailed knowledge of the file format, but that is not really a Perl issue. An example of how to create SVG output, albeit not animated in this case, can be found in appendix C.

There are some tasks that you will find yourself facing regularly when creating animations. The next few sections will discuss some of these tasks, and provide suggestions on how to automate them. Few of the upcoming examples are likely to be full animations that one would use on their own, but they could conceivably be players in a larger project. For example, you could make a company logo pop up on top of a chart that shows how successful it has been over the last quarter. Or you could make it disappear if the results weren't that great.

7.4 REPEATEDLY APPLYING A FILTER

Interesting effects in animations can be achieved by repeatedly applying the same filter, such as a blur, shear, resize or translation. Repeating these effects can make objects appear out of thin air, rotate into view, or zoom into existence. All of these involve using the same base image and transforming or moving it according to some rules. Each application of these rules results in a frame or part of a frame being incorporated into a larger animation. When the image size changes, for example with a shear, resize, or crop, the resulting frames will have boundaries that are different from the preceding images. In this case, you might need to adjust some of the frame-positioning parameters to make certain the resulting images overlap in the way you intended. We will see more on that in section 7.4.2.

First, we will look at how to repeatedly apply a filter to slowly increase the visual effect that a single pass of that filter would have. Stringing together the resulting images into an animation can provide some interesting effects.

7.4.1 Example: making objects appear

Sometimes you will want to make it look like an object in your animation appears out of nothing. This can be achieved by starting with an image that you want to be the end result, and repeatedly applying a blurring type of filter to it. If, at the same time you also adjust the brightness, you'll find that it looks like your image slowly disappears, or dissolves into nothing. All you need to do now to create the illusion that the object is appearing is reverse all the frames of the sequence you just created. The following program uses *Image::Magick* to do exactly that:

```
use Image::Magick;                     Set the number of
my $frames = 10;              ❶ output frames

my $im = Image::Magick->new();
my $rc = $im->Read('logo.png');
die $rc if $rc;
                                        ❷ Copy the input image, and
my $frame = $im->Clone();                  create the frames
for (1 .. $frames)
{
    $frame->Spread(amount => 5);
    $frame->Blur(order => 3);           ❸ Modify the
    $frame->Modulate(                      next frame
        brightness => 100 + 75/$frames);
    unshift @$im, $frame->Clone();    ❷
}
```

```
$rc = $im->Quantize(colors => 256,
                    dither => 1,
                    global_colormap => 1);
warn $rc if $rc;
$im->Set(delay => 10, loop => 1);
$rc = $im->Write('logo-spread.gif');
die $rc if $rc;
```

❹ **Reduce the palette size**

❺ **Set GIF parameters, and save the animation**

❶ The program starts by setting `$frames` to the total number of animation frames. We will work backward through the animation, and put the frames that are generated at the start of the image sequence. The last frame is the image itself, which is read from disk.

❷ A copy of the image object is made, and this copy is subjected to three filtering operations for each frame that is needed. At the end of each loop, a copy of the frame is pushed to the front of the current animation with `unshift`, thus creating a reverse sequence of frames that are progressively changed by the three filters.

❸ The filters chosen to do this job are `Spread()`, `Blur()` and `Modulate()` to adjust the brightness. The first two will spread and smear out the pixels of the original image, making it look more and more blurred after each pass. At the same time, the brightness of the image is increased by a certain factor to make it more vague and lighter. I've found that for most images a total amount, over all frames, of about 75 percent is a good value, but for darker images you might need to adjust that.

❹ Since this animation is destined for the Web we'll optimize it slightly and make sure that all frames in the animation use the same color map by calling `Quantize()`.

❺ We set the delay time of each frame to 1/10th of a second, make sure that we only go through the animation once (since it makes no sense to repeat it), and save it to a file. The result of all of this can be seen in figure 7.1.

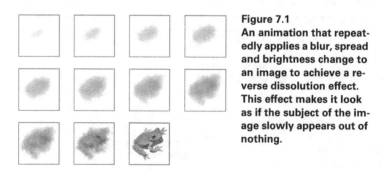

Figure 7.1
An animation that repeatedly applies a blur, spread and brightness change to an image to achieve a reverse dissolution effect. This effect makes it look as if the subject of the image slowly appears out of nothing.

Instead of the three filters used in this example, you can use any of the special effects mentioned in appendix A, as long as they don't change the size of the image they operate on. If you do need to change the size of the image, some extra steps will be required to align everything properly. We will see an example of this in the next section.

To make this a more usable program, you could consider parsing the command line arguments, and allowing the user to specify the number of frames, the total amount of brightness change and the amount of spread and blur applied. It could also show you a preview with the `Animate()` function, if requested.

7.4.2 Example: zooming in on an object

The GIF format specifies that the first image in a multi-frame animation determines the bounding box of the animation, and that none of the following frames are allowed to go beyond that border. If your software doesn't automatically clip these frames, you will have to remember to do it yourself. In the case of *Image::Magick,* the clipping happens automatically, but you are still responsible for making certain that the first image indicates the desired size of the total animation. Of course, when images are smaller than the background, you also need to position them correctly, unless you want them all to appear in the top left corner.

Suppose you want to create an animation in which you zoom in on the same image used in the previous example. If you merely apply the same program as above, and replace the three filters with a call to `Resize()` or `Scale()`, you'll find that the result will be an animation that does not work. This would be because the first frame in the animation is also the smallest, resulting in a bounding box that can't accommodate the later images. Depending on the software used to create and display this animation, the result can be surprising, and it might even cause a crash.

The following program is very similar to the one presented before, but adds all the necessary code to control the size and layout of different sized frames in an animation.

```
use Image::Magick;

my $frames = 10;

my $im = Image::Magick->new();
my $rc = $im->Read('logo.png');        ❶ Read the image, and get
die $rc if $rc;                           its width and height
my ($im_width, $im_height) =
    $im->Get('width', 'height');

my $background = $im->Clone();         ❷ Create a background
$background->Colorize(fill => '#ffffff',   image for the
                      opacity => 100);     animation
warn $rc if $rc;
```

❶ First, the image that will become the last frame is read in, and its width and height are determined.

❷ This image is cloned and the clone is filled with a white color. This copy will become the background, i.e., the first frame, of the animation.

```
my $frame = $im->Clone();    ❸ Copy the image
for (1 .. $frames)
{
```

```
$frame->Resize(geometry => '75%');
my ($frame_width, $frame_height) =
    $frame->Get('width', 'height');
my $offset_x = ($im_width  - $frame_width )/2;
my $offset_y = ($im_height - $frame_height)/2;
$rc = $frame->Set(page => "+$offset_x+$offset_y");
warn $rc if $rc;
unshift @$im, $frame->Clone();
}
unshift @$im, $background;
```

4 **Modify the copied image**

5 **Add the background as the first image**

3 The image is cloned again, as in the last example, to create the individual frames of the animation.

4 For each iteration, the image is resized to 75 percent of its current size, and the width and height of the result are determined. These dimensions are used to calculate the offsets needed to center this frame with respect to the background, and the page image attribute is set accordingly. Then the frame is added to the start of the $im object.

5 The last frame to be added (to the start) is the image background that was created earlier.

```
$rc = $im->Quantize(dispose => 1,
                    colors  => 256,
                    dither  => 1,
                    global_colormap => 1);
warn $rc if $rc;
$im->Set(delay => 10, loop => 1);
$im->[0]->Set(delay => 0);
$im->[$#$im]->Set(page => '+0+0');
```

6 **Reduce the color palette size**

7 **Set the offset for the last frame**

6 As in the previous example, we quantize the color palette of the animation, so that all frames use a global palette, and we set the delay of all frames to 1/10th of a second. The first frame does not need to be displayed for any amount of time, so its delay is reset to 0.

7 The last frame, which is the original image, does not yet have a page offset, so we set that now, before saving the image. If we didn't explicitly set it, it would end up with the same offset as the frame before it, which is of course not what we want.[3]

The result of this program can be seen in figure 7.2.

---

[3] This might be a bug in ImageMagick, and is possibly going to be fixed in a future release.

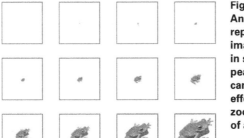

Figure 7.2
An animation created by repeatedly resizing an image, and positioning it in such a way that it appears centered on the canvas. This creates an effect similar to a camera zooming in on the subject of an image.

If you want to save this zooming animation in a format that doesn't support frame offsets, such as MPEG, you will find that you end up with a corrupt video. This is because *Image::Magick* will not automatically attempt to correct for features that are not present in the output format because it assumes that you know what you are doing, and you intend to do exactly that. Since we do know what we are doing, we can solve the problem by using the Coalesce() method on the image sequence before we save it.[4]

```
my $im2 = $im->Coalesce();
warn $im2 unless ref $im2;
$rc = $im2->Write('logo-zoom.mpg');
warn $rc if $rc;
```

7.5   ANIMATED TEXT

Often you'll find yourself playing with text on animated graphics. There are many, many ways that text can be displayed in an animation or part of an animation. The techniques in the previous sections can be used, of course, but text has the unique quality that it is made up of individual words and letters. Animations can make use of that.

The following program will take a string, and display the letters one by one in the same spot, spelling out the full contents of the string.

```
use Image::Magick;

my $string = "Hello World";
my $img = Image::Magick->new();

my $letter_img = Image::Magick->new(size => '40x40');
$letter_img->Read('xc:white');
```

❶ Create a template for a single letter

---

[4]   At least, this is how it is *supposed* to work. However, in *Image::Magick* 5.2.3 and 5.2.4 this is broken. Hopefully it will be fixed for the next release.

```
foreach my $letter (split //, $string)
{
    push @{$img}, $letter_img->Clone();
    $img->[$#$img]->Annotate(
        text    => $letter,
        font    => '-*-arial-bold-r-*-*-36-*-*-*-*-*-*-*',
        gravity => 'Center',
        fill    => 'red',
    );
}

$img->Set(loop => 0, delay => 20, dispose => 2);
$img->[$#$img]->Set(delay => 200);
$img->Transparent('white');

$img->Write('spell.gif');
```

❷ Process the individual letters

❸ Set the animation options and save it

The program is initialized by including *Image::Magick*, setting a string, and creating an object that will hold the animation frames. Next, a template image for a letter is created and given a white background.

❷ The string is split into its individual letters, and for each letter, the template image is cloned. This clone is added to the overall image array, and `Annotate()` is used to put some text on the image.[5]

❸ After all letters have been written to a frame, the loop parameter is set to 0 (for an ever-repeating animation), and the general image delay is set to 20/100 of a second. For the final frame, the delay is set to 2 seconds.

This is not a very useful animation on its own, but it could be used as part of a larger project. It can also be made more interesting with some special fonts, such as Gallaudet, for which the characters consist of little people. You could make them walk, sit or jump, simply by passing in the correct string.

7.6   ANIMATED CHARTS

You might occasionally wish to show the evolution of a certain set of data over time, or you may want to add some life to a lackluster pie chart. One way to do that is by animating them. We'll show a simple example that builds a set of pie charts with *GD::Graph::pie*, each of them slightly rotated. It uses *Image::Magick* to string all those pie charts together in an animated GIF.

---

[5] Note that the font string in the example is an X font string. ImageMagick supports the use of X fonts, TrueType fonts (with the help of the freetype library) and PostScript fonts (with the help of Ghostscript). Also see the description on page 278 in appendix A. Note that on plastforms where you don't have an X server available, you might need to use a font name such as "Arial-Bold" and an explicit point size of 36.

```
#!/usr/bin/perl -w
use strict;
use GD::Graph::pie;
use GD::Graph::Data;
use Image::Magick;

my $ani = Image::Magick->new();

my $data = GD::Graph::Data->new();
$data->read(file => 'pie.dat', delimiter => ',')
    or die $data->error;

for (my $angle = 0; $angle < 360; $angle += 20)
{
    my $chart = GD::Graph::pie->new(200, 200);
    $chart->set(start_angle => $angle);
    my $gd = $chart->plot($data) or die $chart->error;
    $ani->BlobToImage($gd->png);
}

$ani->Set(loop => 20);
$ani->Set(delay => 50);
$ani->Write('pie-im.gif');
```

❶ Get the data for this chart

❷ Create the frames, using a different start angle for the pie

❸ Set the animation options and save it

First of all we create an *Image::Magick* object, $ani, that will be used to store the individual frames of the animation.

❶ Then we read in the data for our *GD::Graph* chart into a *GD::Graph::Data* object. It is read from a file of the following form:

```
Sydney,165
Adelaide,98
Perth,114
Melbourne,148
Brisbane,119
```

❷ We set up a loop that increments an angle from 0 to 340 degrees in 20 degree steps. Inside this loop we create a *GD::Graph::pie* object,[6] and set its start_angle attribute. We plot the pie, and add the PNG output to the $ani image object with the BlobToImage() method.

❸ When all the pies have been created, we set some attributes for the animation, and save it as a GIF. The result is a pie chart that slowly rotates clockwise. A few of the frames are shown in figure 7.3.

---

[6] In the current implementation of *GD::Graph*, an object cannot be reused, so we need to create a new object for each pie chart.

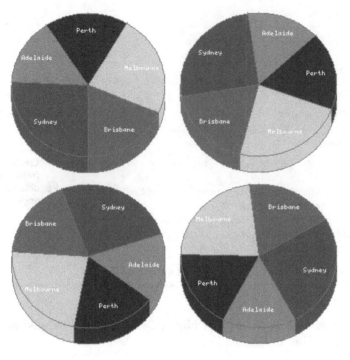

Figure 7.3
Four frames out of an animation created by a succession of calls to the *GD::Graph::pie* module. For each call the rotation of the pie is specified slightly higher, which creates an animation of a rotating pie.

Of course, this is just an example, and not a particularly impressive one, but if you have a series of data that evolves over time, animating that in a sequence of charts can be quite illustrative.

7.7 ANIMATIONS WITH THE GIMP

It is also possible to create animations with the *Gimp* modules, the Perl interface to the Gimp image manipulation program. If you have ever worked with the Gimp, or with PhotoShop, you'll have no trouble following the flow of the program. If you don't know how the Gimp works, it would be worthwhile to obtain a copy and start familiarizing yourself with it.

SEE ALSO To fully explain the complete Gimp interface is outside of the scope of this book, and I suggest reading *Grokking the Gimp* [23] to learn more about how the Gimp works, and checking out the Gimp Developers FAQ at http://www.rru.com/meo/gimp/faq-dev.html for more on general programming for the Gimp. You can find lots of documentation on the Gimp at http://www.gimp.org/docs.html. There is also a tutorial available for Perl Gimp users at http://imagic.weizmann.ac.il/ dov/gimp/perl-tut.html.

The following program creates an animation which is very much like the one presented in the previous section. It also interfaces with *GD::Graph* to create an animation of a rotating pie chart:

```perl
#!/usr/bin/perl -w
use strict;
use GD::Graph::pie;
use GD::Graph::Data;
use Gimp qw(:auto);
use Gimp::Fu;

my $data = GD::Graph::Data->new();
$data->read(file => 'pie.dat', delimiter => ',')
    or die $data->error;

register
    "rotating_pie",
    "Rotating Pie",
    "This creates a rotating pie",
    "Martien Verbruggen",
    "Martien Verbruggen (c) 2000",
    "2000-02-21",
    "<Toolbox>/Xtns/Perl-Fu/rotating pie",
    "*",
    [
        [PF_INT32, "width", "Width", 200],
        [PF_INT32, "height", "Height", 200],
        [PF_INT32, "start", "Start Angle", 0],
        [PF_INT32, "end", "End Angle", 360],
        [PF_INT32, "step", "step angle", 20]
    ],
    \&chart_animation;

exit main();
```

❶ Register the program

❷ Define some controls for the program

❸ Define the subroutine to be called

❹ Call the Gimp

The program starts off, as usual, by including the modules it needs. This time we need to use both the *Gimp* and *Gimp::Fu* modules to be able to interact with the Gimp.

❶ Before being able to interact with the Gimp, or to be called from the Gimp, a program needs to register itself. The first eight arguments to the register() function define how the function will appear in the Gimp's plug-in registry and in the menus of the program.

❷ The ninth argument is an array reference, whose contents define a few controls that will pop up on a dialog box when a user selects the plug-in from within the user interface, and some default values for the variables set therein.

❸ These variables will be passed in as arguments to the subroutine given as the last argument.

❹ After the registration is finished, the main() function is called. This function is defined by the Gimp plug-ins, and will call the subroutine chart_animation() when this program is run from the command line, as opposed to from within the Gimp. The program exits with the same status as that returned by the main() subroutine.

A Gimp drawing is built up of layers. When exporting a Gimp image as a GIF, each layer becomes a frame in the resulting animation. The parameters for each frame in the animation are read from the name of the layer, as will be explained shortly. The following subroutines create these layers, and combine them in a single image:

```perl
sub chart_animation
{
    my ($width, $height, $start, $end, $step) = @_;      ❺ Read the
    my $img = Image->new($width, $height, RGB);              arguments
                                                             and create a
                                                             new image
    for (my $angle = $start; $angle < $end; $angle += $step)
    {
        my $chart = chart_img(
          $width, $height, $angle);                       ❻ Create a new chart
        $chart->selection_all();                             and put it in the
        $chart->get_active_layer->edit_copy();               selection buffer

        my $lyr = Layer->new($img, $img->width, $img->height,
            RGB, "Pie (100ms) (combine)", 100, NORMAL_MODE);
        $lyr->add_layer(-1);
        my $sel = $img->active_drawable->edit_paste(0);
        $sel->floating_sel_anchor();
        $img->selection_none();              Add a new layer and  ❼
    }                                        paste the selection
                                             buffer into it
    return $img;
}
```

❺ The chart_animation() subroutine accepts the five parameters set up in the registry as arguments, and creates a new Gimp image of the specified height and width. As in the previous program that used *Image::Magick*, a loop is set up for the angles of the rotating pie chart.

❻ For each angle to be plotted, a new chart is created with the chart_img() subroutine, which we will define momentarily. This subroutine returns a Gimp image object, of which we make a copy into the selection buffer.

❼ We create a new layer. The GIF animation parameters are stored in the name of the layer, as that is where the GIF export plug-in expects to find them. The layer is added to the top of the layer stack, and the current selection (which contains a copy of the chart) is pasted onto the layer. Since a paste in the Gimp always results in a *floating* selection, we make sure to anchor it to the layer. To prevent accidental problems, we also make certain that nothing else in the overall image is selected, before continuing with the next iteration of the loop.

The chart_img() function is responsible for creating a single chart in the animation sequence.

```perl
sub chart_img
{
    my ($w, $h, $angle) = @_;
```

```
my $chart = GD::Graph::pie->new($w, $h);
$chart->set(start_angle => $angle);
my $gd = $chart->plot($data) or die $chart->error;

my $file = "/tmp/pie.$$";
open(TMP, ">$file") or die $!;
print TMP $gd->png;
close TMP;

my $img = file_png_load(RUN_NONINTERACTIVE, $file, $file);

unlink $file;
return $img;
}
```

It does this by changing the start angle for the start between successive calls. Since there is no way to pass image data to the Gimp via a scalar, a temporary file is used to store the result of the *GD::Graph::plot* call, which is loaded with one of the Gimp's built-in functions: `file_png_load()`. The resulting image object is returned to the caller, who is responsible for adding it to another image, or performing any other work with it as needed.

This program can be used to create charts from within the Gimp. To make it more usable, one would need to allow for many more options to be passed into it—where to find the data would be an important one.

7.8   SUMMARY

In this chapter we've had a look at some ways in which GIF animations can be created from within Perl, and what issues are involved. It shouldn't be too difficult to combine pieces of information from this chapter into larger programs that create animations. Generally speaking, you will create most animations in an interactive program, but you might find it useful to be able to programmatically create the frames for a larger animated project. The files created by the short programs presented can be imported into a larger animation, and positioned correctly from within an interactive program. It will at least save you the trouble of having to manually create 20 or more frames by repeatedly applying the same set of filters and rules. That's the sort of work computers do best.

C H A P T E R   8

Resizing and combining images

Images are not always available exactly the way you want them. Often you have to sharpen, blur, enlarge or shrink them, or apply special effects to make them fit in with another set of images. Perhaps you want to assert your copyright on a picture by adding a watermark. There is likely a set of business rules to apply to images to prepare them for publication on your web site or any other medium you use, or you might decide to combine multiple images to form a composite image.

There are several ways in which you can manipulate the contents of an image, or multiple images, with Perl modules. Some modules provide standard functionality, such as scaling, cropping and filtering, all at a high level. Examples of modules that do this include *Image::Magick* and, to a lesser degree, *GD*. When you need functions that fall outside of the scope of these modules' standard operations, you can write your own code that deals with the individual pixels of the image.

This chapter provides a description of the modules and their methods usable in manipulating the contents of a single image, or in combining multiple existing images. If you need to implement a certain functionality that the modules don't directly provide, look at the methods for working with individual pixels, described in chapter 12.

8.1 SCALING AND CROPPING AN IMAGE

Image::Magick is really the only module that provides direct scaling and resizing functionality, and it does this in a most flexible and accessible way. It provides several methods for resizing images, each with a slightly different application domain:

- *Scale().* scales an image by calculating the average color of the source pixels that contribute to a destination pixel. (See also page 272.)

- *Zoom().* does the same as `Scale()`, but additionally applies a filter, and optionally blurs the resulting image. (See also page 276.)

- *Sample().* resizes an image using *pixel sampling*, giving the resulting pixel the color of the most applicable source pixel. Essentially, no new colors will be introduced in the resized image. If you are working with images that have a fixed palette you want to preserve, this is the method to use. (See also page 271.)

- *Magnify().* doubles the size of an image. This is equivalent to `Scale()` with a geometry of 200 percent. (See also page 264.)

- *Minify().* halves the size of an image. This is equivalent to `Scale()` with a geometry of 50 percent. (See also page 265.)

- *Transform().* does the same as `Scale()`, but instead of acting on the current image, it returns the result as a new image. In addition to scaling, this method can crop and apply a filter to the returned image, which often results in significantly more attractive results. (See also page 275.)

8.1.1 Image::Magick geometry specification

Most of these methods, except `Minify()` and `Magnify()`, accept a geometry parameter which expresses the desired size to which the image should be scaled. This geometry string is quite flexible, and can be used to achieve various scaling effects. A full explanation can be found in "Geometry" section of appendix A, on page 277, but we'll have a look at some typical applications here:

```
# Resize an image to fit within 300 by 300 pixels
$im->Scale(geometry => '300x300');

# Resize an image to 300 by 300 pixels exactly
$im->Scale(geometry => '300x300!');

# Resize an image to twice its size
$im->Scale(geometry => '200%');
# or
$im->Magnify();

# Resize an image to twice its horizontal size, and half
# its vertical size
$im->Scale(geometry => '200%x50%');

# Create a new image which is half the size of the old one
$im2 = $im->Transform(geometry => '50%');
```

```
# Resize the image to half size, but keep the current
# set of colors
$im->Sample(geometry => '50%');
```

8.1.2 Cropping an image

To crop an image, the Crop() and Transform() methods can be used. Crop() acts upon the object on which it was invoked, while Transform() returns a new image object based on the current one:

```
# Crop the current image to 100 by 100 pixels, starting
# at an offset of 20 pixels horizontally, and 30 vertically
$im->Crop(geometry => '100x100+20+30');

# Do the same, but create a new image
$im2 = $im->Transform(crop => '100x100+20+30');
```

Other image deformation methods

There are several other methods that displace an image's pixels (e.g., Rotate(), Shear() and Roll()). Section A.5 on page 250 contains a reference to all *Image::Magick* methods, and it is a advisable to at least become familiar with them.

SEE ALSO   Section 6.5 on page 100 contains some code for creating thumbnail versions of images using both *GD* and *Image::Magick*.

8.2 COMBINING IMAGES

Some of the reasons for combining images include: Watermarking your artistic property, applying borders, or shaping an image by cutting out a part based on another image. There are many ways that a creative mind can devise to combine images. This section deals with a few methods for doing this using Perl modules.

8.2.1 Combining GD images

GD offers only a few methods to combine images, and they all simply overlay one image on top of another. To combine two *GD::Image* objects, the following methods are available:

```
$image->copy($src_image, $x_dst, $y_dst, $x_src, $y_src, $width, $height)
```

Copy a rectangle from $src_image onto $image. The rectangle is defined by the coordinate of the upper-left corner ($x_src, $y_src), and the dimensions $width and $height. The upper-left corner of the copy will be located at the destination image coordinates ($x_dst, $y_dst).

```
$image->copyMerge($src_image, $x_dst, $y_dst,
  $x_src, $y_src, $width, $height, $opacity)
```

This method does the same things as copy(), but allows the specification of the amount of transparency in the overlay image. The parameter $opacity can be a value between 0 and 100, where 0 means fully transparent (which has the same effect as not doing anything), and 100 means fully opaque (which has the same effect as copy()).

```
$image->copyMergeGray($src_image, $x_dst, $y_dst,
    $x_src, $y_src, $width, $height, $opacity)
```

This is identical to copyMerge(), except that it converts the pixels in the destination rectangle to grayscale before performing the merge.

```
$image->copyResized($src_image, $x_dst, $y_dst,
    $x_src, $y_src, $dst_width, $dst_height, $src_width, $src_height)
```

If you need to resize the rectangle to be copied, you can use this method. It takes the same parameters as copy(), but allows you to specify the width and height of the destination rectangle. The source rectangle will be resized to fit these new dimensions.

Figure 8.1 shows an example of what can be done with each of these operations.

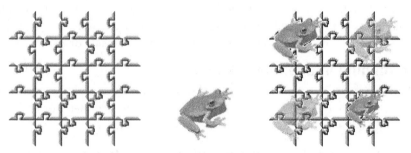

Figure 8.1   Overlaying images with *GD* methods copy() **(top left),** copyResized() **(bottom right),** copyMerge() **(top right) and** copyMergeGray() **(bottom left).**

The code used to produce this image is:

```
use GD;

# 150x150 grayscale image of a jigsaw pattern
open(IN, 'jigsaw.png') or die "jigsaw.png: $!";
my $dst = GD::Image->newFromPng(*IN) or
    die "jigsaw.png is not a PNG file";
close(IN);

# 64x64 RGB image of a frog
open(IN, 'logo.png') or die "logo.png: $!";
my $src = GD::Image->newFromPng(*IN) or
    die "logo.png is not a PNG file";
close(IN);

my ($dst_width, $dst_height) = $dst->getBounds();
my ($src_width, $src_height) = $src->getBounds();

my $x_offset = $dst_width  - $src_width;
my $y_offset = $dst_height - $src_height;
my $scale = 0.75;
my $opacity = 50; # percent
```

```
$dst->copy($src, 0, 0, 0, 0,
    $src_width, $src_height);
$dst->copyMerge($src, $x_offset, 0, 0, 0,
    $src_width, $src_height, $opacity);
$dst->copyMergeGray($src, 0, $y_offset, 0, 0,
    $src_width, $src_height, $opacity);
$dst->copyResized($src, $x_offset, $y_offset, 0, 0,
    $scale * $src_width, $scale * $src_height, $src_width, $src_height);

open(OUT, '>jigsaw-logo.png') or
    die "Cannot open jigsaw-logo.png for write: $!";
binmode OUT;
print OUT $dst->png;
close(OUT);
```

In each instance the whole source image is copied onto the destination image. In the case of the merge methods, an opacity of 50 percent is specified, and for copyRe-sized() the image is scaled by a factor of 0.75 ($scale) in both directions. The variables $x_offset and $y_offset are used to determine coordinates that will leave enough room for the destination rectangle to fall inside of the image.

8.2.2 Combining Image::Magick images

With *Image::Magick* there are additional possibilities for combining images, using the Composite() method (see page 255). The compose parameter can take the values shown in table 8.1.[1]

Table 8.1 *Image::Magick*'s composition operators in action. The left column is the result of the application of the given composition operator to the left original, with the right original as the composite. The right column displays the result of the reverse. Note that the two images have a different size.

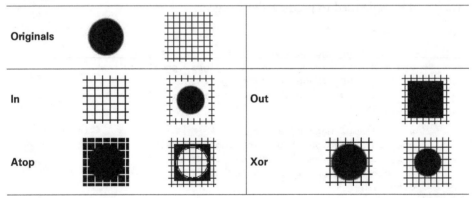

Continued on next page

---

[1] The value of the image argument is called the composite, and the image that the Composite() method works on is, logically, called the image.

CHAPTER 8   *RESIZING AND COMBINING IMAGES*

Table 8.1 *Image::Magick's* composition operators in action. The left column is the result of the application of the given composition operator to the left original, with the right original as the composite. The right column displays the result of the reverse. Note that the two images have a different size. *(continued)*

Plus			**Minus**		
Add			**Subtract**		
Difference			**Over**		

- *Over.* The composite obscures the portions of the image that are overlapped. If the composite has an alpha channel, the pixels of the image will be proportionally obscured.

- *In.* The composite replaces the pixels of the image, which will be removed. The alpha channel of the composite is preserved only if the image also has an alpha channel.

- *Out.* The shape of the composite is cut out from the image, leaving nothing.

- *Atop.* The composite obscures portions of the image that are overlapped. Alpha channels are not used.

- *Xor.* The result is the exclusive or of the two images. Alpha channels can produce quite interesting results.

- *Plus.* The result is the sum of the individual channels of the two images, with overflows cropped to the maximum allowable value for a pixel (255 for each component). The alpha channel is ignored.

- *Minus.* The result is the subtraction of the individual channels of the composite from those of the image, with underflows cropped to 0. The alpha channel is ignored.

- *Add.* The result is the sum of the individual channels of the two images, modulo 256.

- *Subtract.* The result is the subtraction of the individual channels of the composite from those of the image, modulo 256.

- *Difference.* The absolute value of image subtracted from composite.

- *Bumpmap.* Apply a shading filter to image, using the composite as a bump map.

- *Replace.* Replace the pixels of the image with the pixels of the composite where the two overlap. Ignore and discard alpha channel information.

- *ReplaceRed, ReplaceGreen, ReplaceBlue.* Replace a specific color channel in the image with the same channel in the composite image. The other channels are left untouched.

- *ReplaceMatte.* Replace the matte channel of the image with that of the composite. If the composite is a grayscale image or bitmap without a matte channel, the image will be used as the matte channel. For examples of the use of this operator, see sections 8.2.3 and 12.4.2, "Transparency and Image::Magick," on page 230.

  The Replace operators have been removed from *Image::Magick* 5.2.9, and a set of new operators has taken their place: Copy, CopyRed, CopyGreen, Copy-Blue and CopyMatte.

- *Blend.* Blend the two images with the specified opacity. The opacity defaults to 0 (fully transparent).

```
$image->Composite(
    compose => 'Blend',
    image   => $composite,
    opacity => 75,
);
```

  This operator does not work correctly from *Image::Magick* 5.2.3 onward, and has been removed from 5.2.9.

- *Displace.* Use the composite as a displacement map for image. The values of the pixels in the composite image determine how far the pixels in the image will be displaced to the left or right. A fully black pixel in the displacement map will cause a maximum displacement in the positive direction, and a white pixel a maximum displacement in the negative direction. A neutral gray will not displace the pixel.

  The geometry parameter can be used to specify a horizontal and vertical displacement scale, as HORxVER. If unspecified, these default to 20x20.

- *Modulate.* Modulate the brightness and saturation of the original image with the values of the composite image. A base saturation and brightness can be specified with a geometry parameter, as BRIGHTNESSxSATURATION in percent.[2]

```
$image->Composite(
    image    => $composite,
    compose  => 'Modulate',
    geometry => '32.5x48.3',
);
```

---

[2] The saturation component is ignored in all versions of *Image::Magick* before 5.2.4.

There is, of course, nothing stopping you from using both *Image::Magick* and *GD* to combine images. You can easily read an image in with one module, do some work on it, and then transport it to the other module for further manipulation or drawing. See section 4.3, "Combining GD and Image::Magick," on page 53 for methods to do this.

8.2.3   Adding a watermark to an image

Adding a watermark to an image can be accomplished in two ways: visibly and invisibly. Adding a visible watermark is normally done to assert ownership of the copyright on an image in a clear way, and when compromising the visual integrity of the image does not present a problem.

Watermarks with GD

To add a visual watermark to an image, you can overlay your company logo or some text onto the image. The *GD* copyMerge() method (see page 140) provides a good way to overlay an image which is mostly transparent onto another image. We will discuss how a small program takes a logo file and an image file, and produces an image with the logo overlaid. The program starts as follows:

```
#!/usr/local/bin/perl -w
use strict;
use GD;
use Getopt::Long;

sub usage
{
<<EOF;
Usage  : $0 [options] logo image output_file
Options:
    --opacity N     specify opacity of logo in percent.
    --gravity SPEC  specify where the logo should end up.
                    One of North, NorthEast, NorthWest,
                    South, SouthEast, SouthWest, East,
                    West, or Center.
EOF
}

my $gravity = 'SouthEast';        ● Set some
my $opacity = 50;                   defaults

GetOptions(
    'gravity=s'     => \$gravity,
    'opacity=i'     => \$opacity,
) or die usage();

die usage() unless @ARGV >= 3;
```

As the usage() subroutine specifies, this program takes the name of an input logo file, the name of the image on which to overlay the logo, and the name of an output file. It pastes the logo on top of the image, using the opacity and gravity specified.

```perl
my $watermark_file  = shift;
my $image_file      = shift;
my $out_file        = shift;

my $image = GD::Image->new($image_file) or
    die "GD cannot read $image_file: ",
        $! ? "$!\n" : "unknown error\n";
my $watermark = GD::Image->new($watermark_file) or
    die "GD cannot read $watermark_file: ",
        $! ? "$!\n" : "unknown error\n";

my ($x, $y) = calculate_coords($gravity,
    $image, $watermark);

$image->copyMerge($watermark, $x, $y,
    0, 0, $watermark->getBounds(), $opacity);

open(IM, ">$out_file") or die "$out_file: $!";
binmode(IM);
print IM $image->png;
close(IM);
```

❶ Read the input images

❷ Calculate destination coordinates of watermark

❸ Merge the two images

● Save the resulting image

❶ This program uses the internals of *GD* to autodetect the image format[3] instead of opening the files itself, which makes it necessary to distinguish between two cases of errors that might cause `GD::Image->new()` to fail: the errors that set the `$!` variable, and those that don't. If `$!` is not set when an error occurs, the string *unknown error* is appended to the error message. While this is hardly enlightening, it is slightly more elegant than having no error message at all.

❷ The coordinates where the watermark image should be placed are determined with a call to `calculate_coords()`, which is covered later.

❸ For this simple program, the logo is always copied as a whole onto the image. This is accomplished by using the call to `$watermark->getBounds()` to specify the width and height of the rectangle to copy. For a program such as this it is hardly useful to allow these parameters to specify anything other than the whole logo, so we don't provide any command-line switches for them.

```perl
sub calculate_coords
{
    my ($grav, $dst, $src) = @_;
    my ($dst_width, $dst_height) = $dst->getBounds();
    my ($src_width, $src_height) = $src->getBounds();

    my $x = ($dst_width  - $src_width )/2;
    my $y = ($dst_height - $src_height)/2;

    for ($grav)
    {
        /^North/i and $y = 0;
        /^South/i and $y = $dst_height - $src_height;
```

● Default to Center

---

[3] Using the `GD::Image::new()` method to autodetect the image format requires *GD* version 1.30 or newer.

```
        /West$/i  and $x = 0;
        /East$/i  and $x = $dst_width - $src_width;
    }
    return ($x, $y);
}
```

The destination coordinates $x and $y are calculated from the gravity specification by the `calculate_coords()` subroutine. The gravity specification has been deliberately chosen to match that of *Image::Magick*, which makes it easier to replace *GD* with *Image::Magick*, should the need arise, and it provides us with a fairly consistent interface. There are no explicit checks in place to verify that the gravity specification is a valid one, since all invalid specifications will cause the logo to be centered on the output image.

The result of this program can be seen in figure 8.2.

Figure 8.2
Watermarks added to an image by overlaying a logo using *GD* and *Image::Magick*. Both images were generated with the opacity set to 60 percent, and all other command line parameters left at the default value.

Watermarks with Image::Magick

We will now look at an equivalent program, but with a few more options, e.g., using *Image::Magick*. This program has more options because there are more possibilities for watermarking images with *Image::Magick*.

```
#!/usr/local/bin/perl -w
use strict;
use Image::Magick;
use Getopt::Long;

sub usage
{
<<EOF;
Usage  : $0 [options] logo image output_file
Options:
    --opacity N     specify opacity of logo in percent.
    --gravity SPEC  specify where the logo should end up.
                    One of North, NorthEast, NorthWest,
                    South, SouthEast, SouthWest, East,
```

```
                        West, or Center.
     --emboss           Create an 'embossed' watermark.
     --tile             Tile the watermark all over the image.
EOF
}

my $gravity      = 'SouthEast';
my $compose      = 'Over';
my $opacity      = 50;
my %opts         = ();
my $rc;

GetOptions(
    'emboss'     => sub{ $compose = 'Modulate' },
    'opacity=f'  => \$opacity,
    'gravity=s'  => \$gravity,
    'tile'       => sub{ $opts{'tile'} = 1 },
) or die usage();

die usage() unless (@ARGV >= 3);
my ($wm_file, $in_file, $out_file) = @ARGV;
my $watermark = Image::Magick->new();
$rc = $watermark->Read($wm_file);
die $rc if $rc;
my $image = Image::Magick->new();
$rc = $image->Read($in_file);
die $rc if $rc;
```

❶ Set some defaults

❷ Read the input images

❶ The main variable in this code fragment is `$compose`, which will be used to identify what sort of watermark we want to create. If the `emboss` option is specified, the program will create watermarks that look as if they are stamped into the image; otherwise it will create the watermark by simply overlaying the second image. The value this variable has is the value of the compose attribute that we'll be passing to the `Composite()` method later on in the program.

❷ After the options have been read, and the necessary variables have been declared, the source and watermark images are read from disk. Then, depending on whether the emboss option was specified, the real work can begin:

```
if ($compose eq 'Over')          ❸ Create a normal watermark
{
    my ($w, $h) = $watermark->Get("width", "height");
    my $mask    = Image::Magick->new(size => "${w}x${h}");
    my $g       = 255 - $opacity/100 * 255;
    my $color = sprintf "#%02x%02x%02x", $g, $g, $g;
    $mask->Read("xc:$color");
    my $cur_mask = $watermark->Clone();
    $cur_mask->Channel('Matte');
    $rc = $mask->Composite(
        image    => $cur_mask,
        compose => 'Plus');
    warn $rc if $rc;
    $rc = $watermark->Composite(
```

```
            image   => $mask,
            compose => 'ReplaceMatte');
        warn $rc if $rc;
    }
    elsif ($compose eq 'Modulate')
    {
        $rc = $watermark->Shade(azimuth => 30, elevation => 30);
        warn $rc if $rc;
        $opts{'geometry'} = $opacity,
    }
```

④ Create an embossed watermark

❸ Surprisingly, in *Image::Magick* we need to do quite a bit of work to achieve the same effect as with the presented methods for *GD*.[4] First of all, we need to create a new image, which will be used as a transparency mask to add the desired opacity to the watermark (see also section 12.4.2, "Transparency and Image::Magick," on page 230). This image is created the same size as the watermark, and filled with a uniform gray calculated from the specified opacity. The matte channel from the original watermark is then extracted, and combined with the mask. This ensures that wherever the original watermark had a higher transparency (lower opacity) the original values are preserved. Finally, the new alpha mask is added back into the original watermark.

❹ If, instead, the emboss option was specified, and therefore the composition method is Modulate,[5] the job becomes a lot easier. The original watermark is embossed with the Shade() filter, which ensures that areas with a uniform color become a medium gray. This embossed watermark is then used to modulate the pixels in the original image. Wherever the watermark has a neutral gray, the original pixels remain the same. The more the colors of the pixels in the watermark deviate from middle gray, the more the colors of the original image will be influenced. Figure 8.3 shows what can be done with this option, and what the intermediate embossed watermark looks like.

Now that we have created the watermark image, and prepared all the options that are needed to call Composite(), we combine the images, and save the result to disk:

```
$rc = $image->Composite(
    image      => $watermark,
    compose    => $compose,
    gravity    => $gravity,
    %opts);
warn $rc if $rc;

$rc = $image->Write($out_file);
die $rc if $rc;
```

❺ Combine the image with the watermark

❻ Output the result to disk

---

[4] In versions of ImageMagick before 5.2.4, the Blend operation for the Compose() method could be used to merge images. However, this has been broken since 5.2.4 and removed from 5.2.9. The method here is more elaborate, but probably works in more versions.

[5] See the description on 144. This composition operator, as well as the tile option, requires *Image::Magick* 5.2.3 or later.

5 The `Composite()` method is called on the original image, with the modified watermark image as a composite. All the other options have been set earlier in the program.

6 Because we use the `Write()` method from *Image::Magick,* it is possible to specify any image format and file name that the module can understand. You can use the special file name `'-'` to output the result to STDOUT, or just specify a file name with a known extension to save the output in that format.

The result of this program without the emboss option can be seen in figure 8.2, next to an image produced with the earlier presented *GD* program. As you can see, the output is fairly similar. The output of this program with the emboss option can be seen in figure 8.3.

Figure 8.3
Watermarks added to an image by modulating it with an embossed logo (far left), using *Image::Magick*. The image in the middle was produced with the opacity set to 60 percent and the gravity to NorthWest, and the one on the right was produced with an opacity of 25 percent and the tile option.

Occasionally, putting a logo in the corner of an image is not enough to assert ownership, and you want to ensure that the image is useless when copied, but that the general idea of the picture is still visible. For this purpose, you can tile a logo all over the image, with a very low opacity.

Hiding information in an image

If altering the visual appearance of an image is not an option, an invisible watermark can be added with a technique called steganography. Steganography is the general technique (some people would say art) of hiding information in other data in such a way that a third party cannot, or is very unlikely to, detect this information. Apart from all the illicit applications that come to mind, it can also be used to hide digital watermarks in graphics. *PerlMagick* conveniently provides a very simple means to do this:

```
$image = Image::Magick->new();
$image->Read('leopard.tif');

$watermark = Image::Magick->new();
$watermark->Read('logo.png');
$image->SteganoImage(image => $watermark, offset => 14);
$image->Write('png:leopard-st.png');
```

Read in the image in an *Image::Magick* object (in real code you would check for errors), read in the watermark image, and call the `Stegano()` method. Then write the image to disk in a suitable nonlossy format.

Later, if you want to check whether an image that is yours contains the watermark, you need to know the original size of the watermark, and the offset you used.[6]

```
$hidden = Image::Magick->new(size => "64x64+14");
$hidden->Read('stegano:leopard-st.png');
$hidden->Write('png:logo-st.png');
```

An example of an image treated this way can be seen in figure 8.4.

Figure 8.4
This picture contains a steganography watermark, which is invisible. The little frog on the top right is the original image hidden in the photo, and the little frog on the bottom right is the extracted image.

The image itself looks untouched, but it does contain the watermark. Note that this method of steganography does not actually store all the information of the original watermark in the image, but a simplified grayscale version of it.

Unfortunately, *Image::Magick*'s steganographic method is not especially robust. It will withstand some blurring and such of the image, but cropping or conversion to a lossy image format such as jpeg or gif might make the watermark irretrievable, which may not be a problem with the way this is implemented in *Image::Magick*, but more a deficiency in the steganography method itself. To protect your images from thievery, you would be better off using other means, such as good copyright statements and legal advice. Steganography is too easy to beat.

8.3   SUMMARY

In this chapter we have seen the most commonly used ways in which images are transformed, from adding a watermark to resizing images. With these methods as a base you should be able to achieve most effects you want. In chapter 12 we'll be looking at more customized ways to manipulate images.

---

[6] Reading of stegano images was broken in versions 5.2.7 and 5.2.9 of ImageMagick. If you want to run this example, either use 5.2.6 or before, or 5.3.0 and later.

One area of image manipulation that was not described, but that might be of interest, is the application of special effects. Of course, many special effects can be achieved through convolution filters, and this is often the way they are implemented in image manipulation software (see also chapter 12). Appendix A contains a list of all the methods available through *Image::Magick*, including the special effect filters that it provides. It also includes example figures illustrating each effect. If you need to apply a blurring or solarizing filter, I suggest you take a look at that appendix.

Three-dimensional graphics

The title of this chapter is a bit of a misnomer, since it is actually about the creation of two-dimensional images of three-dimensional scenes. People in the 3D business tend to use the term *computer graphics*[1] as if only 3D rendering matters, but that is too narrow. There are, after all, many computer graphics applications that have nothing to do with three-dimensional objects and projections, as can be seen in the other chapters in this book.

Even in the field of 3D computer graphics, there are vastly different areas with different requirements. On the one end of the scale there are the photo-realistic rendering engines attempting to create images of 3D scenes that look as realistic as possible. Many inventive and sophisticated algorithms are used to add a touch more realism to the texture of an object, the focus of a virtual camera lens, or the way light diffracts and diffuses in air. These rendering engines generally take a great number of CPU cycles (and sometimes memory) to render a single frame, and many frames are necessary to create animated films such as Jurassic Park, Toy Story, or Shrek.

---

[1]   Something else to note is that the computer graphics business often uses the acronym CGI for Computer Graphics and Imaging. This has, of course, nothing to do with the Common Gateway Interface as discussed in chapter 6.

On the other end of the scale, one can find high-speed three-dimensional game engines. These engines tend to emphasize speed over realism, and employ many algorithms that produce a reasonable looking effect in the least amount of computing time. Often you'll find the implementations of these algorithms in hardware, for example on the graphics card in your computer, to speed up the process to its limits. Most applications that use engines similar to these are interactive applications, such as games, 3D model viewers, or architectural programs that allow you to walk through the design of your new house.

In this chapter we'll discuss how to use some Perl interfaces to the 3D rendering libraries, OpenGL and RenderMan. These two libraries represent the two ends of the scale of realism versus speed, and between the two of them they cover almost any need you might have in the area of three-dimensional computer graphics. Unfortunately, there are no modules for Perl that allow working with 3D vector graphics, so we won't discuss that subject.

In discussing the modules, we will mainly touch on how to use them, what the differences between these modules and their C counterparts are, and what the Perl-specific gotchas are. This will allow you to pick up any documentation that has been written for the C APIs (and there is quite a bit of that), and translate that to the equivalent Perl code, with this chapter as a guide.

We won't see any implementations of 3D algorithms here, because, frankly, I don't believe this should be done in Perl, yet. This is one area of computing where Perl is just too bulky and slow to be really useful. It is much wiser to delegate the hard work of three-dimensional rendering to lower-level code, as provided by the *RenderMan* and *OpenGL* modules.

To be able to comfortably work with these packages, you will need to have some trigonometry, and especially vector and matrix algebra knowledge. While it may be possible to create a three-dimensional scene by trial and error, it is definitely a big help to understand what the various translations, rotations and shears mean and what they do to your carefully constructed objects.

9.1 OPENGL

OpenGL is an API created and developed by Silicon Graphics Inc. (SGI), initially only for their hardware. It offers programmers a transparent interface to the rendering capabilities of the graphics hardware in a computer, and allows them to use the faster routines there instead of ones implemented in software. Many graphics cards support OpenGL nowadays, and libraries are available for many platforms. Apart from the commercial SGI OpenGL version, the Mesa 3D library is an excellent and free Open Source implementation. If you are running an operating system that doesn't have an OpenGL implementation installed, you can obtain the Mesa 3D libraries from http://www.mesa3d.org/.

The main goal of the OpenGL libraries is to provide quick access to hardware-driven graphics rendering. This makes it particularly useful for people who have to create complex real-time animations, such as those used in computer games and viewers for three-dimensional objects such as architectural plans. OpenGL can be used to create reasonably realistic scenes, but the emphasis is on speed.

In addition to the core OpenGL library, the *OpenGL* module also provides access to the libraries which have become, more or less, standard companions of OpenGL: GLUT, GLU and GLX. GLUT is a platform-independent interface to window management, menus, and other windowing tools. It is limited, but allows one to write portable code for the various windowing environments in use. GLU is a library built on top of OpenGL that provides some higher order functionality using the primitives of OpenGL, so that you don't have to write too much code to create a ball every single time. GLX is the OpenGL extension to the X window interface, and is therefore useful only if you're working with an X11 server.

SEE ALSO   Another alternative, if you're looking for a windowing environment for your application that is portable and works well with OpenGL, is the Simple DirectMedia Layer (SDL) library, available as a set of Perl modules. Look for the *SDL::sdlpl* or *SDL::OpenGL* modules, or for the distribution SDL-sdlpl on your nearest CPAN mirror.

The OpenGL library was originally written in C, and C APIs don't always translate nicely and directly into Perl. Let's have a look at how the C API is made available to Perl callers. Before reading on, it might be a good idea to get a copy of the OpenGL specification and API from http://www.opengl.org/ (see references [24,25]).

9.1.1   OpenGL library functions in Perl

Almost all OpenGL library functions can be translated directly into Perl subroutines that are callable from your program. The name of the C OpenGL function is available as a Perl function, and works the same way. However, there are some exceptions to this, and this section deals with those exceptions.

Functions that use array arguments in the C API to return values, such as `glGet-Integerv()` and `glGetFloatv()`, have a counterpart in the Perl API with a _p suffix, and they return the values in the more usual Perl way. For example, to attain the dimensions of the current viewport in OpenGL, the C code would look like:

```
#include <GL/gl.h>
GLint viewport[4];
glGetIntegerv(GL_VIEWPORT, viewport);
```

after which the *x* and *y* coordinates and the width and height are available in that order in the viewport array. In Perl, this code becomes

```
use OpenGL;
my ($x, $y, $width, $height) = glGetIntegerv_p(GL_VIEWPORT);
```

As you can see, this looks much closer to the way functions normally operate in Perl.

Functions that take pointers to strings to be filled as the result of the API call are available under several names: first of all, there is the function name with a _c suffix, for which an *OpenGL::Array* object must be supplied in place of the pointer argument. The second way to call these functions is with an _s suffix, in which case it takes a Perl string argument in place of the pointer. The function name with no arguments is, in most cases, an alias to the function name with the _s suffix, but it's safer to just call the one you mean. For example, to read the pixels from the current viewport, using the variables from the preceding code:

```
my $rgba;
glReadPixels_s($x, $y, $width, $height, GL_RGBA, GL_UNSIGNED_BYTE, $rgba);
```

NOTE   In versions before 0.52 of the *OpenGL* modules, it was necessary to pre-allocate the string that you passed off to these functions, because the module failed to allocate memory for them on its own. This has been fixed in newer versions, and I strongly suggest that you get one if at all possible (see section 3.2.10, "OpenGL," on page 32, for more information on where to get newer versions). If, for some reason, you can't install a newer version of the module, you will need to do something like:

```
my $rgba = "X" x ($width * $height * 4 * 1);
glReadPixels_s($x, $y, $width, $height, GL_RGBA,
   GL_UNSIGNED_BYTE, $rgba);
```

Needless to say, this tends to be error-prone, because you have to take into account what GL_RGBA and GL_UNSIGNED_BYTE mean for the number of bytes to allocate, and you have to maintain this code. Perl programmers are just not used to having to allocate their memory, and they shouldn't have to.

The OpenGL library and the associated utility libraries (GLX, GLU and GLUT) have undergone periodic changes. The *OpenGL* module supports most of the old versions, and several support libraries for OpenGL. Exactly what gets exported to your name space is, as usual, controlled by the arguments to the import function for *OpenGL*. Here are some alternatives:

- use OpenGL;
- use OpenGL qw(:constants :functions);
- use OpenGL qw(:constants glReadPixels);
- use OpenGL qw(:all);

The module allows export of all the functions and constants defined in the OpenGL API, as well as their special Perl adaptations, and it defines a set of tags that can be used to export groups of them. The tags are listed in table 9.1.

Table 9.1 The *OpenGL* import tags. The default tag (if nothing is specified) is :old. Note that some of these tags are combinations of some of the others.

:all	All the current API functions and constants.
:old	All the old, original API functions and constants.
:glconstants	All the constants from the OpenGL library.
:gluconstants	All the constants from the GLU library.
:glutconstants	All the constants from the GLUT library.
:glxconstants	All the constants from the GLX library.
:oldconstants	All the old, original API constants.
:constants	All the current API constants.
:glfunctions	All the current functions from the OpenGL library.
:glufunctions	All the functions from the GLU library.
:glutfunctions	All the functions from the GLUT library.
:glxfunctions	All the functions from the GLX library.
:oldfunctions	All the old, original API functions.
:functions	All the current API functions.

If no labels are specified, the default exported functions are the same as if the :old label were specified. Note that if you specify another label and still want the old functions and constants available, you have to also specify :old explicitly. If you don't use :old, then none of the functions that start with `glp` are available. To import absolutely everything into your name space, use the following:

```
use OpenGL qw(:all :old);
```

9.1.2 Capturing your OpenGL output

Due to the way OpenGL was designed—as an interface to hardware for high speed graphical rendering—every OpenGL application requires a window or screen for its output. The drawing doesn't occur in some memory buffer in the OpenGL libraries, but the commands are sent, where possible, directly to the hardware responsible for its display.

This is all well and good if you're writing a game or a three-dimensional walk-through viewer for an architectural program, but less handy when you are trying to produce a copy of your rendering to keep on file, perhaps for printing in a book such as this one. Because this is an area often overlooked in discussions on the OpenGL library, and because it places this section more closely within the range of the rest of the book, I'll discuss how to read your screen buffer and create an image on disk.

To capture an image you have to read the pixels of the window displayed by the OpenGL client. Luckily, they needn't be read one by one; instead you can make a single call to a function provided by the OpenGL library: glReadPixels().[2] Before doing so, however, you need to make a decision on which channels interest you and tell the OpenGL library how you want it to convert the pixels into values. Before discussing the particulars, let's look at a subroutine that can be used to capture any part of the currently displayed window to an image file. We use the *Image::Magick* module to translate the raw information that comes from the call to glReadPixels(), and to save the file to disk.

```
use OpenGL qw(:all);
use Image::Magick;

sub gltIMCapture
{
    my $file = shift;
    my $rgba;
    my ($x, $y, $width, $height) =
        @_ == 4 ? @_ : glGetIntegerv_p(GL_VIEWPORT);      ❶ Get size of window
                                                             to save

    glFinish();
    glPushClientAttrib(GL_CLIENT_PIXEL_STORE_BIT);        ❷ Save the
    glPixelStorei(GL_PACK_ROW_LENGTH, $width);               current state
    glPixelStorei(GL_PACK_ALIGNMENT, 1);

    glReadPixels_s($x, $y, $width, $height,               ❸ Get the
                GL_RGBA, GL_UNSIGNED_BYTE, $rgba);            pixels

    glPopClientAttrib();

    my $im = Image::Magick->new(
                size    => "${width}x$height",            ❹ Create an
                magick => 'RGBA');                           Image::Magick object
    my $rc = $im->BlobToImage($rgba);                        from the pixels
    warn($rc), return if $rc;
    $im->Write($file) if $file;
    return $im;
}
```

❶ If the user has passed in four arguments that define the rectangle to be captured, these arguments are used. Otherwise, the dimensions of the current window are requested and used.

❷ The first thing we do is call glFinish(), to make sure that the OpenGL drawing functions are all completed. If we don't do that, we run the risk of reading out pixels from a frame buffer that is only half complete. This is followed by a call to glPushClientAttrib() to save all the current pixel settings, after which we can change them to our liking with glPixelStorei(). Once we have read the pixels into $rgba we reset the settings by calling glPopClientAttrib().

---

[2] Also see the note on page 156 for some information on glReadPixels().

❸ ❹ The pixels are read into a long string of bytes with values for the red, green, blue and alpha channel, which can be read directly into an *Image::Magick* object with the `BlobToImage()` method. All we need to do then is save the image. To allow the user to postprocess the image, we return a reference to the *Image::Magick* object.

This routine can be very handy to have around when you are writing OpenGL applications that need to be able to take snapshots of the rendered scenes. The example program in section 9.1.3 uses this routine to allow the user to save a snapshot of the current window on screen. We will put it in a library of OpenGL tools, which we can expand in the future, and write a little application that uses it to create two images:[3]

```
#!/usr/local/bin/perl -w
use strict;
use OpenGL qw(:all :old);
require "OpenGLTools.pl";

sub triangle
{
    glBegin    (GL_TRIANGLES);
    glColor3f (0.0, 0.0, 0.0);
    glVertex2f(0.0, 0.0);
    glColor3f (0.5, 0.5, 0.5);
    glVertex2f(30.0, 0.0);
    glColor3f (1.0, 1.0, 1.0);
    glVertex2f(0.0, 30.0);
    glEnd      ();
}

glpOpenWindow (width => 250, height => 250);
glLoadIdentity();
gluOrtho2D     (0.0, 30.0, 0.0, 30.0);
glClearColor  (1.0, 1.0, 1.0, 0.0);
glClear       (GL_COLOR_BUFFER_BIT);

triangle();

gltIMCapture("OpenGLcap1.png", 50, 50, 100, 100);
gltIMCapture("OpenGLcap2.png");
```

This is a basic OpenGL application that draws a triangle, filled with a smooth gray-scale gradient. Once the drawing is finished, it captures part of the window, and the whole window with the previously discussed `gltIMCapture()` function, and saves these captures to files which can be seen in figure 9.1.

You might have noticed that the program presented contains floating point values everywhere, while Perl doesn't really care about these sorts of things. The truth is that integer values would have worked just as well, but I like to be explicit. It also comes

---

[3] In case you noticed the odd spacing in this code: I often vertically align the brackets around the arguments to OpenGL function calls, because I find it slightly more legible. Some people think it's awful.

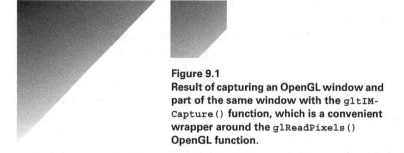

Figure 9.1
Result of capturing an OpenGL window and part of the same window with the `gltIM-Capture()` **function, which is a convenient wrapper around the** `glReadPixels()` **OpenGL function.**

in handy when I decide that parts of these programs need to be ported to C, in which case there is less work to do if all the constants are already in the correct format.

9.1.3 Example: a planetary system

OpenGL is normally used for more complex tasks than what we've seen up until now. We'll discuss an interactive application that is a very simplistic simulation of a small ball orbiting another ball, while being orbited by an even smaller ball. The result of this application can be seen in figure 9.2.

Figure 9.2 **Output of an OpenGL program emulating the movement of three balls around each other in a vaguely planet-like configuration. The first picture shows the initial display, and the second picture shows the display after 255 virtual days.**

No effort has been made to accurately implement the laws of physics, so don't assume that we are really discussing the movement of three planets. The following application may not appear useful as is, but it can serve as a skeleton for virtually any OpenGL application, because it includes nearly everything such an application needs. The only thing that you need to add are real functionality and possibly menus and such. All those additions fit in the main structure of this program.

We start by including the *OpenGL* module and the tool library we talked about in the previous sections. Since we measure time in our fictitious solar system in days, we create a variable for that, and set it to the beginning of time. We also store the default name of a file to which we send viewport captures. We then write our main program, using the GLUT library functions to do most of the work for us:

```perl
#!/usr/local/bin/perl -w
use strict;
use OpenGL qw(:all);
require "OpenGLTools.pl";

my $day = 0;
my $filename = "capture.png";

glutInitDisplayMode    (GLUT_SINGLE|GLUT_RGBA|GLUT_DEPTH);
glutInitWindowPosition(0, 0);
glutInitWindowSize    (500, 250);
glutCreateWindow      ($0);
init                  ();
glutReshapeFunc       (\&reshape);
glutKeyboardFunc      (\&key_pressed);
glutSpecialFunc       (\&key_pressed);
glutDisplayFunc       (\&display);
glutMainLoop          ();
```

❶ The display is initialized to a single buffer window that can hold RGBA pixels, and the depth buffer is enabled, since we want to make sure that objects that should be in front of each other actually appear that way. We then initialize and create a window, and set up all of the default variables in the init() subroutine.

❷ GLUT works by running through an event loop and calling user-defined callback functions whenever something interesting happens. We tell the library which callback functions we want to use when a window is resized, a key is pressed, or we need to draw our planets.

> **NOTE** We need to register two functions to be called when a key gets pressed: one for normal keys, and one for special keys. This is because in C these two events can't easily be handled by the same function, since normal keys are passed as unsigned characters and special keys as integers. In Perl that distinction doesn't exist, so we can register the same function twice. There is nothing stopping you from writing two separate functions to deal with these separate sets of keys, which might make rewriting your application as a C program slightly easier.

❸ Once the application is properly set up and initialized, we enter the GLUT main event loop, and start running.

The init() function sets up all the default values for this application, such as the lighting, texture of the materials, and shading.

```perl
sub init
{
    glMaterialfv_p(GL_FRONT, GL_SPECULAR, 1, 1, 1, 1);
    glMaterialfv_p(GL_FRONT, GL_SHININESS, 50);
    glLightfv_p   (GL_LIGHT0, GL_POSITION, 1, 1, 1, 0);
    glShadeModel  (GL_SMOOTH);
    glEnable      (GL_DEPTH_TEST);
```

```
glEnable     (GL_LIGHTING);
glEnable     (GL_LIGHT0);
glClearColor (1.0, 1.0, 1.0, 0.0);
}
```

A default material is created with `glMaterialfv()`, and a light is set up. The depth testing routines are enabled, without which we would not know which planet was in front and which in the back. The lights are switched on, and the default background color is set with `glClearColor()`.

The `reshape()` subroutine is called by the GLUT main loop immediately after the window is created, and every time it is resized. It is responsible for setting up any variables and OpenGL parameters that depend on the window size:

```
sub reshape
{
    my ($w, $h) = @_;

    glViewport   (0, 0, $w, $h);
    glMatrixMode (GL_PROJECTION);
    glLoadIdentity();
    gluPerspective(35.0, $w/$h, 1.0, 20.0);
    glMatrixMode (GL_MODELVIEW);
    glLoadIdentity();
    glTranslatef (0.0, 0.0, -5.0);
}
```

This subroutine is passed the new width and height of the window as its arguments. These arguments are used to set up a viewport and perspective, in such a way that the objects in the window will be scaled in the same way the window was scaled, without distorting the aspect ratio.

Immediately after `reshape()` is called, the subroutine that does the actual drawing, `display()`, is invoked.

```
sub display
{
    my $rot_planet_axis = (360 * $day)     % 360;
    my $rot_moon        = (360 * $day/28)  % 360;
    my $rot_planet      = (360 * $day/365) % 360;

    glClear(GL_COLOR_BUFFER_BIT | GL_DEPTH_BUFFER_BIT);

    glPushMatrix();
      glColor3f        (1.0, 1.0, 0.8);                  Draw the sun
      glutSolidSphere(1.0, 20, 20);
      glRotatef        ($rot_planet, 0.0, 1.0, 0.0);
      glTranslatef     (2.0, 0.0, 0.0);
      glPushMatrix     ();
        glRotatef        ($rot_moon, 0.0, 1.0, 0.0);
        glTranslatef     (0.5, 0.0, 0.0);
        glColor3f        (0.5, 0.5, 0.5);                Draw the little
        glutSolidSphere(0.05, 10, 10);                  moon
      glPopMatrix      ();
```

```
        glRotatef        ($rot_planet_axis, 0.0, 1.0, 0.0);
        glColor3f        (0.0, 0.0, 0.8);
        glutSolidSphere(0.2, 15, 15);                ● Draw the planet
    glPopMatrix();
}
```

This subroutine doesn't get any arguments, so it relies on global variables that have been set. In this particular case, there is only one variable we depend on, and that is the time, which is stored in $day. This time is used to calculate rotations for the planet itself ($rot_planet_axis), the planet around the sun ($rot_planet), and the moon around the planet ($rot_moon). In OpenGL, all rotations and translations are relative to the current coordinate system.

In this subroutine, glPushMatrix() is used to save the state of the coordinate system each time, before it is changed for one of the planets. It is then restored with glPopMatrix() once a planet has been drawn. The first call to glRotatef() applies to both the little moon and the planet, but the second call to glRotatef() only applies to the little moon, since it falls between a glPushMatrix() and glPop-Matrix() call. This is the normal way in which relative transformations are handled in OpenGL, so it's a good idea to be familiar with this technique.

This application would not be very interesting if we had no way to change what is displayed, so we'll write the subroutine that gets called when a key is pressed:

```
sub key_pressed
{
    my ($key, $x, $y) = @_;

    $key == GLUT_KEY_LEFT    and $day -= 7;
    $key == GLUT_KEY_RIGHT   and $day += 7;
    $key == GLUT_KEY_UP      and $day++;
    $key == GLUT_KEY_DOWN    and $day--;
    $key == 27               and exit(0);      #ESCAPE

    $key == ord('s')         and save_snapshot();
    $key == ord('n')         and set_filename();

    glutPostRedisplay();
}
```

The numerical value of the key that was pressed is passed in as the first argument, and the coordinates of where the pointer was at the moment that the key was pressed get passed as the second and third arguments. The last two in this application are of less concern, so we'll disregard them. Whenever the left or right arrow keys are pressed, we increment or decrement $day by 7, and whenever the up or down arrows are pressed, we increment or decrement by 1. This allows the user to move our solar system forward and backward in time, in steps of a day or a week. When the escape key is pressed, we exit from the program.

When the s key is pressed, we save a snapshot of the current screen to disk, and when the n key is pressed, we prompt the user for a new filename for saving the next snapshot. The definition of the two subroutines that get called when the s or n key are pressed are as follows:

```
sub set_filename
{
    print "Enter a new file name for output: ";
    chomp($filename = <STDIN>);
    $filename .= ".png" unless $filename =~ /\./;
}

sub save_snapshot
{
    print "Saving to $filename\n";
    gltIMCapture($filename);
}
```

The subroutine `set_filename()` is called when the n key is pressed, and it prompts for a new filename on standard input. In a real application this would probably be replaced by code that would pop up a dialog box, and accept input that way, but for the sake of simplicity we will forgo that here. The subroutine `save_snapshot()` is invoked when the s key is pressed, and it calls the previously discussed `gltIMCapture()` to save the whole window to a file.

9.1.4   OpenGL summary

In this section we've had a look at how the *OpenGL* module works, how to create a three-dimensional interactive application with it, and how to save the contents of OpenGL windows to files with the help of *Image::Magick*. Of course, OpenGL can also be used to create two-dimensional graphics, but its strength is the rendering of three-dimensional scenes.

> **SEE ALSO**   You should now be able to take a good book on OpenGL (like the Red Book [26] or the Blue Book [27]) and use this section to translate all the C code into Perl. Also, you can find a great deal of information on the OpenGL site at http://www.opengl.org/. These books can tell you about all the other possibilities OpenGL offers, and how to implement them.

9.2   RENDERMAN

The *RenderMan* module is intended as an interface to the Blue Moon Rendering Tools (BMRT), which is a combination of a RenderMan compliant library and a rendering engine. The RenderMan Interface Standard was developed by Pixar Animation Studios for their own internal use, and has become something of a standard in the 3D computer graphics world. Pixar published the interface, and several programs now implement a RenderMan-compliant interface. Some call Render-Man the PostScript of the 3D computer graphics world. PostScript is a device-independent description language for two-dimensional graphics, and RenderMan is the same for three-dimensional graphics primitives. In my opinion that is where most of the analogy ends.

The device-independence of the RenderMan standard means that it does not prescribe how to render the scene it describes. It only delineates what is to be rendered, and leaves it up to the engine to pick a method and algorithm to do this. It is free to use ray tracing or scan lines or any other rendering method it chooses, as long as it renders the whole scene. It mainly prescribes a set of instructions that can be used to define where objects are in a scene, what material they're made of, what sort of lighting there is, how to move and transform objects, what sort of camera should be emulated, and so forth.

Perhaps the largest part of creating satisfactory and realistic renderings is the definition of the shaders, which define the textures of almost everything in the RenderMan world. In other words, the shaders define how something will look: they make objects look metallic or plastic, for example. If you want your objects to look bumpy, rusty, shiny or transparent, or you want your company logo to appear on one of your objects, you create a shader for it.

Knowing the RenderMan API isn't going to net you any spectacular results by itself. There is a lot of knowledge to attain before you'll be able to create great animations or renderings. This chapter will not teach you how to use the RenderMan API or the shader language that performs all those neat little tricks you've seen in films. That would require a whole book on its own, and in fact such books have been written. Two good books about RenderMan are *The RenderMan Companion* [28] and *Advanced RenderMan* [29]. While the former has been around for awhile, it's still a good introduction to the whole concept behind RenderMan. The latter goes somewhat farther and shows some advanced usage of the API. I strongly recommend at least one of these books if you seriously want to use the *RenderMan* module.

In the example in this chapter we will avoid using any of the advanced features of RenderMan, simply because they would distract too much from the purpose of this section, which is to show you that the module is there, and how to use it. If you read one of the above-mentioned books, you'll realize just how easy it is to translate what is in there into Perl code using the *RenderMan* module.

It is probably a good idea to keep a copy of the RenderMan interface specification handy while reading through this section. The official version can be found on Pixar's website [30], and the RenderMan FAQ [31] has some more useful pointers.

9.2.1 How to use the module and the BMRT

The Blue Moon Rendering Tools are a collection of programs and a library that renders three-dimensional scenes described by the RenderMan Interface specification. Some of the tools are meant to render or preview scenes, and some are meant to compile shaders or preprocess images to be used as texture maps. The documentation that comes with the BMRT adequately explains these tools, but I'll offer a short summary here, mainly because the *RenderMan* module refers to them as output methods.

The *RenderMan* module can be used to directly invoke the BMRT previewer or the rendering engine to produce graphics output, but it can also be used to create a RIB (RenderMan Interface Bytestream) file. This file can then be fed to another rendering engine, such as Pixar's Photorealistic RenderMan. The content of this file will resemble your program code quite closely, and is almost a direct translation of all the calls that can be made to the *RenderMan* API. To select which of the output methods you want, you specify either `rgl`, `rendrib`, or a file name to the `Begin()` method. If nothing is specified to the `Begin()` method, the RIB output will be printed to STD-OUT, and you can pipe it directly into a tool that will read it. Some of these tools come with the BMRT and we'll have a short look at them.

To preview a RIB file, you can use the *rgl* program, which displays your drawing primitives as simple shapes and uses Gouraud shading instead of full rendering. This can provide a quick and handy check as to whether your animation is running as it should, and whether the movements are correct before you spend vast amounts of computing power on rendering the full scenes.

To actually render the scenes in all their glory, use the *rendrib* program. This produces high-quality images that are either displayed on your screen or written to a file, depending on the settings contained in the bytestream it is rendering. It uses ray tracing and radiosity to render the scenes, and produces surprisingly good looking images.

9.2.2   The RenderMan language binding for Perl

The Perl implementation for the RenderMan API follows the C implementation very closely, but there are, of course, a few differences. First, all function names in the C library start with the string `Ri`, such as `RiBegin()` and `RiEnd()`. The Perl equivalents do not use this prefix, but use instead the same names as in the RIB files. All types in the C version start with `Ri`, but since we don't need to worry about types in Perl, that will not concern us. The constants in the C library all begin with `RI_`, and this is the same for the Perl module.

The arguments to the Perl functions can be passed much more conveniently than the arguments to their C equivalents. All parameter lists are passed as hash references in the Perl functions, while in the C API they need to be passed in as separate arguments, which all have to be pointers, terminated by the constant `RI_NULL`. For example, the function to set up a light source is defined as

```
RtLightHandle
    RiLightSource( shadername, parameterlist )
    RtToken     shadername;
```

or, for the RIB binding

```
LightSource name sequencenumber parameterlist
```

The C version returns a handle to a light source, which can be used for further operations later on. In the RIB version the equivalent of that handle is the sequence number. The Perl version of this function will follow the C API most closely, meaning that it returns a handle to a light source, and it takes two arguments: a shader name and an optional hash reference containing the parameters to this shader.

In C you would have to call `RiLightSource()` in the following manner:

```
RtLightHandle alight;
RtFloat intensity = 0.5;
alight = RiLightSource("ambientlight",
                       "intensity", &intensity, RI_NULL);
```

In Perl, you call it in this way:

```
$alight = LightSource("ambientlight", {intensity => 0.5});
```

which, at least to me, seems much more readable and convenient. For completeness, this is the equivalent RIB call:

```
LightSource "ambientlight" 1 "intensity" [0.5]
```

One further point to note is that all arrays, matrices, and other types are implemented as one-dimensional arrays of doubles in the Perl module. The elements of a two-dimensional matrix in this one-dimensional array are organized row by row. In other words, all the elements of the first row come first, then all the elements of the second row, and so on. This is important to know if you plan to create vectors and matrices for use by the *RenderMan* module.

9.2.3   Example: A rotating cube of cubes

As always, an example program is the best way to show how the *RenderMan* module can be used, so in this section we'll be writing a program that creates an animation of a rotating group of objects. You will probably want to keep a copy of the RenderMan API specification (see [30]) around, so you can look up what some of the functions do, and what their arguments mean.

This program is loosely based on one of the example programs that comes with the BMRT distribution. It creates a cube of (by default) 3 by 3 by 3 smaller cubes, and rotates this whole structure around. Optionally, the individual objects can rotate in the opposite direction. As an extra, to demonstrate how seamlessly BMRT joins solid bodies together, these small cubes will intersect with a slightly larger sphere to form a single solid body. And while the whole structure is rotating, the individual small objects will shrink until they have disappeared in the last frame.

We'll start with the modules used by this program, and its help message:

```
#!/usr/local/bin/perl -w
use strict;
use RenderMan;
use Getopt::Long;

sub usage
{
<<EOF;
Usage  : $0 [options] [rendrib | rgl | RIB filename]
```

```
Options:
      --number N     the number of objects per side
      --frames N     the number of frames
      --rotation F   the amount to rotate per frame
      --nocubes      don't draw the cubes
      --nospheres    don't draw the spheres
      --reverse      reverse the rotation on the small objects
      --basename     the base of the filename to save the
                     individual frames
EOF
}
```

All of this speaks sufficiently for itself. The options in the usage() subroutine are all given defaults, which are then potentially overwritten by processing the command line arguments to the program with the GetOptions() function from the standard *Getopt::Long* module:

```
my $nframes   = 50;
my $number    = 3;
my $rotation  = 10.0;
my $cubes     = 1;
my $spheres   = 1;
my $basename  = "frame";
my $reverse   = 0;

GetOptions (
      "frames:i"      => \$nframes,
      "number:i"      => \$number,
      "rotation:f"    => \$rotation,
      "cubes!"        => \$cubes,
      "spheres!"      => \$spheres,
      "reverse!"      => \$reverse,
      "basename:s"    => \$basename,
) or die usage();
```

By default, the program will generate 50 frames, wherein the cube is rotated 10 degrees between frames. Thus, the cube will rotate slightly less than one and a half times over the whole animation. The program defaults to drawing both the little cubes and the spheres (controlled by the variables $cubes and $spheres), which will rotate in the direction of the large cube. If the --reverse argument is specified, they will rotate in the opposite direction, which means that from the camera's point of view, they will not rotate at all. Run the program if you want to see how that looks, or see figure 9.3.

Now that we have gathered all the information we need from the user, it is time to start the actual output.

```
Begin(shift or ());        ❶ Begin RenderMan output

for my $frame (1 .. $nframes)
{
    my $filename = sprintf "$basename%03d.tif", $frame;
```

```
FrameBegin($frame);
  Display($filename, RI_FILE, RI_RGBA);
  Format(512, 384, 1);
  Imager("background", {"background" => [1, 1, 1]});
  ShadingRate(1.0);

  Projection("perspective");
  Translate(0.0, 0.0, 1.5);
  Rotate(40.0, -1.0, 1.0, 0.0);

  WorldBegin();
    LightSource("ambientlight", {intensity => 0.5});
    LightSource("distantlight", {intensity => 0.5});
    Surface("plastic");

    my $rot   = $rotation * $frame;
    my $scale = ($nframes - ($frame - 1))/$nframes;
    Rotate($rot, 0.0, 0.0, 1);
    render_objects($number, $scale, $reverse * -$rot);
  WorldEnd();
FrameEnd();
}

End();
```

❷ Specify output parameters

❸ Set up our viewpoint

Set up lights and default material

❹ Render the cubes

❶ We pass the first remaining argument from the command line to the Begin() method, or, if there was no argument, the empty list.[4] We need to perform this check to avoid warnings from Perl about uninitialized variables being used. Then we set up a loop to create the number of frames that are to be rendered.

❷ The output of the rendering program should go to the file names specified by the Display() method. Instead of RI_FILE we could have used RI_FRAMEBUFFER to indicate that the output should be sent to a screen. The size of the output file is set to 512 by 384 pixels, with a pixel aspect ratio of 1; and the background color of the image is set to white with the Imager() call. We then set up Phong shading by specifying a shading rate of at least once per pixel.

❸ We proceed by setting up our viewpoint and perspective by rotating and translating the global coordinates around, after which we can start with the definition of the *world* in which we will be working. The first items to be defined in our world are the lights and the default material.

❹ After that is completed, we set up some variables and call render_objects(), which is a subroutine that is responsible for drawing the spheres and cubes on the grid that was specified by the arguments.

```
sub render_objects
{
    my ($n, $s, $r) = @_;
```

❺ Initialize the arguments

---

[4] On some platforms the presented code does not work correctly, even though it should. You may have to replace this line with something like Begin(shift or "output.rib").

```
    return unless $n > 0;

    AttributeBegin();                          ⑥ Transform the
    Translate(-0.5, -0.5, -0.5);                 coordinate system
    Scale(1/$n, 1/$n, 1/$n);
    for my $x (1 .. $n)
    {
      for my $y (1 .. $n)
      {
        for my $z (1 .. $n)
        {
          my @color = map { $_/$n } ($x, $y, $z);   ⑦ Set the color of the
          Color(@color);                               object
          TransformBegin();
          Translate($x - 0.5, $y - 0.5, $z - 0.5);  ⑧ Transform the
          Rotate($r, 0, 0, 1);                         coordinate system
          Scale($s, $s, $s);
          cube(0.8)                      if $cubes;  ⑨ Draw the
          Sphere(0.5, -0.5, 0.5, 360) if $spheres;     object
          TransformEnd();
        }
      }
    }
    AttributeEnd();
}
```

❺ The subroutine takes as its arguments the number of objects to render, and the scale and angle at which to render them. We return immediately if the number of requested objects is smaller than or equal to zero.

❻ We push the current state of the attributes onto the attribute stack with `Attribute-Begin()`. All the changes we make to attributes, such as the coordinate system, are local until the corresponding call to `AttributeEnd()`. After we have saved the current state, we change it by modifying the translation and scaling. We then set up three nested loops; one for each side of the large cube we're drawing.

❼ Inside the innermost loop we set the color of the object we're going to draw, based on the coordinates of the object we're drawing. This means that the color over the cube as a whole will gradually change between objects.

❽ We save the state of the current transformation matrix with `TransformBegin()`, and change the coordinate system to draw a single small object, which can be made up of a cube, a sphere, or a combination of both, depending on the variables `$cubes` and `$spheres`.

❾ We draw the cube and the sphere with `Sphere()`, which is a function provided by the RenderMan library, and `cube()`, a function we provide ourselves. Once that is accomplished, we restore the transformation matrix to the value it had before we drew this small object. All that is left for us to do now is to provide the code that actually draws a solid cube, or rectangle.

```
my @cube_sides;        ⑩ Array to hold cube vertices
BEGIN
{
  @cube_sides = (
    [-1,-1, 1, -1,-1,-1,  1,-1,-1,  1,-1, 1],  # bottom
    [-1,-1, 1, -1, 1, 1, -1, 1,-1, -1,-1,-1],  # left
    [ 1, 1,-1, -1, 1,-1, -1, 1, 1,  1, 1, 1],  # top
    [ 1, 1,-1,  1, 1, 1,  1,-1, 1,  1,-1,-1],  # right
    [ 1,-1, 1,  1, 1, 1, -1, 1, 1, -1,-1, 1],  # back
    [-1, 1,-1,  1, 1,-1,  1,-1,-1, -1,-1,-1]); # front
}

sub cube
{
    my $sx = shift || 1;         ⑪ The scaling parameters in all
    my $sy = shift || $sx;          three directions
    my $sz = shift || $sy;

    TransformBegin();
    Scale($sx/2, $sy/2, $sz/2);           ⑫ Scale and draw
    Polygon(4, { "P" => $_ }) for (@cube_sides);   the cube
    TransformEnd();
}
```

⑩ The array @cube_sides holds the coordinates that define the six sides of a cube
with sides of length 2 centered around the origin. These coordinates have to be
defined in a certain order to make sure that the normal of each of the sides points in
the correct direction. We simply define a cube with sides of length 2 here, and scale it
appropriately in each direction to create a smaller or larger cube, or stretch it when we
want rectangular sides.

⑪ The subroutine cube() takes three optional arguments, which are the scaling factors
in the x, y and z directions. If the scaling in the z direction isn't specified, it defaults to
the scaling factor in the y direction. If that isn't specified, it defaults to the scaling factor in the x direction, and if that isn't specified, it defaults to 1. So, if only one argument is given, the cube is scaled uniformly in all three directions, according to that
argument. If no argument is given, a cube with side 1 will be drawn.

⑫ The coordinate system is scaled according to the arguments. Notice that we divide
the arguments by 2, to account for the fact that the cube defined by @cube_sides
has sides of length two. By dividing each scaling factor by 2, we ensure that we are
working on a cube with sides 1. Once the coordinate system is set up, we draw our six
polygons that define the six sides of the cube. The Polygon method takes as its first
argument the number of vertices, and as its second argument a parameter list. In this
case the only parameter is P, which defines a list of points, and its value is a reference
to an array holding the coordinates of these points.

Figure 9.3 shows a few frames out of the animations created with this program, using
the default settings and with the --reverse flag specified.

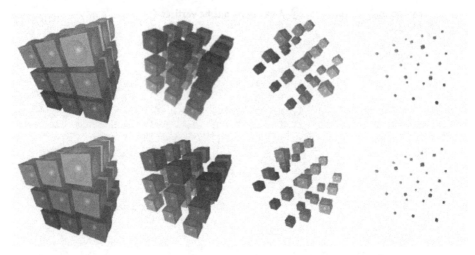

Figure 9.3 Output of the RenderMan example program discussed in the text, run once with no arguments, and once with the `--reverse` argument specified. When the `--reverse` argument is specified, the smaller cubes will rotate in the opposite direction of the whole block of cubes, which means that they don't rotate at all, relative to the camera point of view.

As you can see, for the default program the cube as a whole rotates and the smaller objects rotate identically, as if they're fixed inside of the larger cube; and as time progresses, the objects get smaller. When the `--reverse` argument is specified to the program, the small objects no longer rotate relative to the camera viewpoint, but they now seem to rotate inside of the larger cube.

In this section it has been demonstrated that it is perfectly feasible to write a RenderMan program in Perl. All the hard work is done during the rendering phase, so there is really no reason, performancewise, not to use Perl for this. However, this doesn't mean that you can get by with less than serious computing power to render scenes more complex than this. Photorealistic rendering is very CPU intensive, and if you are serious about it, you want to get your hands on some fast hardware.

9.3   SUMMARY

In this chapter we have seen how to use the Perl interfaces to OpenGL and Render-Man. We have noted that OpenGL may be used for renderings that require high speed or real-time response, and that RenderMan is the one to use when the output must be as realistic as possible.

Special topics

In the following chapters you will find topics that require more thought about graphics programming, and programming in general. We get closer to the basics of graphics manipulation and creation, and will discuss some techniques that can be used to build your own set of tools for graphics programming in Perl.

Chapter 10 features thoughts about how to design and write your own graphics modules, and what to be aware of while doing this.

Chapter 11 provides a discussion of text placement and the calculations that go with the tasks of text alignment and wrapping.

Finally, the manipulation of individual pixels and channels in an image is discussed in chapter 12. Also in this chapter you will find techniques to use C from within Perl to make these operations go faster than can be achieved in pure Perl.

Writing your own graphics modules

When you find yourself writing or copying the same code over and over again, it's a good time to think about creating your own libraries. This can be done simply by taking some of the subroutines out of the scripts and putting them in a generally accessible library file. To make sure that the subroutines in those library files don't interfere with the names in your script, put them in their own name space or package. And if you name and install your library file appropriately, you have a module, because as the *perlmod* documentation tells us: A module is just a package that is defined in a library file of the same name, and is designed to be reusable.[1]

For example, the code for the *Image::Size* package lives in the file Size.pm in the directory Image, somewhere in the path that Perl searches for library files. The code was designed to be reusable, and thus, it is a module.

---

[1] Actually, this is not the whole story; you can have multiple packages in a module, and you can have a single package spread out over several source files. You can even add to packages in your main program. But when you start doing that, you are moving away from what a module is for.

Another reason to group code in a package and put it in a module, is that you plan on writing an object-oriented interface to that code. Perl's OO functionality is tightly linked with packages, and cannot exist without them. A class in Perl is just a package that contains subroutines that expect an object reference or class name as their first argument, and an object reference is just a reference blessed into the current class.

You might even write a group of modules that all work together, like the GDText-Utils package, wherein each class performs a distinct function, and all classes work together. Or you could write a set of related classes that are all originally designed as utilities for another class. For example, the DBI database interface uses as its drivers for each different database type a class in the DBD:: name space.

All of this is, of course, true in general for sensible Perl software design. The most important reasons for a discussion of these topics are, first, that many graphics applications are particularly well suited to an object-oriented model, and therefore benefit substantially from being written that way, as they become easier to understand, maintain and use. Second, there is also the more practical observation that there are many different Perl modules available for working with graphics. Each of these modules has its own interface, which is often terribly different from any other interface. Writing your own modules that provide a unifying front end to each interface can be very beneficial, especially if you have to write code that works with several modules or interfaces. We will see in the following section how to deal with that.

10.1 INTERFACE DESIGN

Suppose you need to write a program that draws a clock to display a time in an attractive manner. You look around the CPAN, and decide that the *Image::Magick* module is exactly what you need to do this. You write the prototype program shown in listing 10.1 on page 178, and it works to your satisfaction. Since you are writing this for *Image::Magick* version 5.2, which has a different interface from the previous versions, you include the version number on the use line to prevent runtime errors when people try to use it with an older version.

You make a CGI program out of this code (see chapter 6, "Graphics and the Web," to find out how to do this), and install it on the company web server. After a few weeks your webmaster informs you that your application takes up too much CPU time. You decide to rewrite it using *GD*, because that is lighter on the CPU [2] than *Image::Magick*. After a bit of coding, you come up with the prototype in listing 10.2 on page 179.

As can be seen in figure 10.1, the result is very similar to the *Image::Magick* version of the clock.

---

[2] A benchmark shows a difference of a factor 10 for the clock examples in listings 10.1 and 10.2 for versions of *Image::Magick* before 5.2.5. Newer versions will be much less CPU hungry.

Figure 10.1
Two clocks, the left one is drawn with *Image::Magick*, and the right one with *GD*.

You can now create your clock almost 20 times faster, but it cost you a good deal of coding effort because of the interface differences between the two modules.

One week later, your employer wants you to draw the clock in a perspective and apply some filters to it to make it look more attractive, which is something that cannot be directly done in *GD*. Thus you have to rewrite it, using *Image::Magick* again, and of course you need to incorporate the changes that you made in the meantime. By this time, you start to wish that both packages had the same interface.

Then, to top it off, your marketing department wants a printable version, one that scales nicely. And this is the point at which you fully understand why having one drawing interface with a set of pluggable drivers for the various output formats would be a big help.

The presented listings are for the two versions of the clock drawing program are similar in many places, but different enough to make rewriting them for another graphics module quite a bit of work and susceptible to the introduction of bugs. This chapter will look at how to separate the similarities and differences, and to place those two parts of the code in independent reusable libraries.

Listing 10.1   Drawing a clock, using *Image::Magick*

```perl
use Image::Magick '5.2';
use constant PI => 4 * atan2(1,1);
my $R = 60;
my $xc = my $yc = $R;

my $clock = Image::Magick->new(size => (2*$R+1).'x'.(2*$R+1));
my $rc = $clock->Read('xc:white');
die $rc if $rc;
$clock->Draw(primitive => 'Circle', fill => '#dfdfdf',
    stroke => '#dfdfdf',points => "$xc,$yc $xc,0");

# Draw the hour markers
for (my $angle = 0; $angle < 2 * PI; $angle += 2 * PI/12)
{
    my $x1 = $xc +       $R * cos($angle);
    my $y1 = $yc +       $R * sin($angle);
    my $x2 = $xc + 0.8 * $R * cos($angle);
    my $y2 = $yc + 0.8 * $R * sin($angle);
    $clock->Draw(primitive => 'Line', stroke => '#00007f',
        points => "$x1,$y1 $x2,$y2");
}

# Get the hour and minute
my ($min, $hour) = (localtime())[1,2];
$hour %= 12;    # go from 24 hour time to 12 hour time
my $min_angle  = 2 * PI * $min/60 - PI/2;
my $hour_angle = 2 * PI * ($hour/12 + $min/(12*60)) - PI/2;

my $xmin  = $xc +        $R * cos($min_angle);
my $ymin  = $yc +        $R * sin($min_angle);
my $xhour = $xc + 0.75 * $R * cos($hour_angle);
my $yhour = $yc + 0.75 * $R * sin($hour_angle);

# Draw the hands
$clock->Draw(primitive => 'Line', stroke => '#000000',
    linewidth => 2, points => "$xc,$yc $xmin,$ymin");
$clock->Draw(primitive => 'Line', stroke => '#000000',
    linewidth => 2, points => "$xc,$yc $xhour,$yhour");

# And put some decoration on the clock
$clock->Draw(primitive => 'Circle', fill => '#ff0000',
    points => "$xc,$yc $xc,".($xc - $R * 0.1));

$rc = $clock->Write($ARGV[0]);
die "Cannot write $ARGV[0]: $rc" if $rc;
```

Listing 10.2   Drawing a clock, using *GD*

```perl
use GD;
use constant PI => 4 * atan2(1,1);
my $R = 60;
my $xc = my $yc = $R;

my $clock = GD::Image->new(2 * $R + 1, 2 * $R + 1);
my $white = $clock->colorAllocate(255, 255, 255);
my $grey = $clock->colorAllocate(223, 223, 223);
my $red = $clock->colorAllocate(255, 0, 0);
my $blue = $clock->colorAllocate( 0, 0, 127);

$clock->arc($xc, $yc, 2 * $R, 2 * $R, 0, 360, $grey);
$clock->fillToBorder($R, $R, $grey, $grey);

# Draw the hour markers
for (my $angle = 0; $angle < 2 * PI; $angle += 2 * PI/12)
{
    my $x1 = $xc +       $R * cos($angle);
    my $y1 = $yc +       $R * sin($angle);
    my $x2 = $xc + 0.8 * $R * cos($angle);
    my $y2 = $yc + 0.8 * $R * sin($angle);
    $clock->line($x1, $y1, $x2, $y2, $blue);
}

# Get the hour and minute
my ($min, $hour) = (localtime())[1,2];
$hour %= 12;    # go from 24 hour time to 12 hour time
my $min_angle  = 2 * PI * $min/60 - PI/2;
my $hour_angle = 2 * PI * ($hour/12 + $min/(12*60)) - PI/2;

my $xmin  = $xc +        $R * cos($min_angle) ;
my $ymin  = $yc +        $R * sin($min_angle) ;
my $xhour = $xc + 0.75 * $R * cos($hour_angle);
my $yhour = $yc + 0.75 * $R * sin($hour_angle);

# Draw the hands
my $brush = GD::Image->new(2, 2);
$brush->colorAllocate(0, 0, 0);
$clock->setBrush($brush);

$clock->line($xc, $yc, $xmin , $ymin , gdBrushed);
$clock->line($xc, $yc, $xhour, $yhour, gdBrushed);

# And put some decoration on the clock
$clock->arc($xc, $yc, 0.2 * $R, 0.2 * $R, 0, 360, $red);
$clock->fillToBorder($R, $R, $red, $red);

open(OUT, ">$ARGV[0]") or die "open $ARGV[0]: $!";
print OUT $clock->png();
close(OUT);
```

10.1.1　Coordinate transformation

One point that is immediately obvious in the discussed programs is that the standard Cartesian coordinate system is not very convenient for drawing a clock. We are constantly calculating *x* and *y* coordinates from the more natural lengths and angles that we really want to work with, and we often need to translate things to the center of the image. What we really want to be able to do is have a coordinate system that fits the task: one that has its origin in the center of the image, or any other place we like, and that works with angles and radii. However, the drawing routines for the libraries we use, *GD* and *Image::Magick,* use Cartesian coordinates. Therefore. we will need to be capable of transforming Cartesian coordinates into polar ones and back (see figure 10.2).

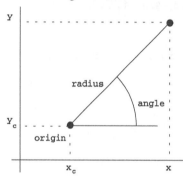

Figure 10.2
The relationship between the Cartesian and polar coordinates as used by the *Coordinate* module. This module transforms a given Cartesian coordinate pair into its polar equivalent, or the reverse. Optionally, the origin can automatically be translated.

For this purpose we will write the *Coordinate* module, which is just a small collection of handy subroutines and constants.

```
package Coordinate;
require Exporter;
@Coordinate::ISA = qw(Exporter);
@Coordinate::EXPORT =
    qw(PI set_origin get_origin polar2cart cart2polar);

use constant PI => 4 * atan2(1,1);

my $xc = 0;
my $yc = 0;

sub set_origin { ($xc, $yc) = @_ }          ● Set or get the Cartesian
sub get_origin { ($xc, $yc) }                 coordinates of the origin

sub polar2cart          ● Translate polar
{                         to Cartesian
    my ($r, $angle) = @_;
    return ($xc + $r * cos($angle),
            $yc + $r * sin($angle))

}

sub cart2polar          ● Translate Cartesian to polar
{
    my ($x, $y) = @_;
```

　　　　　　　　　CHAPTER 10　WRITING YOUR OWN GRAPHICS MODULES

```
        return (sqrt(($x - $xc)**2 + ($y - $yc)**2),
                atan2($y - $yc, $x - $xc))
}

1;
```

If a program uses this module it automatically imports all of the defined subroutines and constants into its namespace:

```
use Coordinate;

set_origin(100, 100);
my ($radius, $angle) = cart2polar(30, 20);
my ($x, $y) = polar2cart(25, 4 * PI / 3);
```

In addition to a conversion from polar to Cartesian coordinates and vice versa, these subroutines also perform translations of the origin. This means that the polar coordinates don't necessarily have the same origin as the Cartesian coordinates. Note that this particular version of this module only allows one coordinate base for your whole program. The origin coordinates are not set per call, but program-wide.

10.1.2   Choosing your drawing primitives

Now that we have a module that allows us to easily convert between Cartesian and polar coordinates, it is time to have a good look at the code to see what sort of objects we need to be able to draw, and what the parameters are that each object needs.

Breaking the clock down into its constituent parts, we derive the following list:

- *Face.* The face of the clock is a filled circle of a specific color around the image center. The size is specified by the radius of the circle.

- *Hands.* The hands of the clock are lines that start at the center, and have the attributes length, width, angle and color.

- *Hour markers.* The hour markers are lines that start at a distance from the center, and have a certain length, width, angle and color.

- *Decoration.* The decoration at the center is a filled circle, like the face of the clock.

This means we need one drawing primitive for a circle, and two different ones for lines. However, if we look again at the two line types, we can see that the lines that start at the center of the clock are really just a special case of the lines that start at a certain offset, namely for an offset of 0. So now we have two drawing primitives that can be defined as follows:

- *filled_circle(radius, color).* Draw a filled circle around the center with the specified *radius* and *color*.

- *line(start, stop, angle, color, width).* Draw a line along an *angle* between *start* and *stop* distances from the center, with attributes *color* and *width*. For the purpose of ease of use, the *width* attribute is optional, and will default to something useful, depending on the driver.

We decide that angles should be specified in radians, and colors are specified as strings starting with a '#', and containing 3 pairs of two characters with a hexadecimal value between 00 and FF. This color specification is like the one used for SVG and for HTML.

We will put the class of modules that implement this interface in the *Canvas::Polar* name space. This name space is generic enough that it isn't tied to the clock alone, but could be extended with methods for drawing pie charts or anything else that works nicely in polar coordinates. In the next sections we'll develop this interface for *GD* and *Image::Magick*. Appendix C contains code examples for other output.

10.1.3 Implementing the interface

Apart from providing the drawing primitives described in section 10.1.2, a good driver should be reusable, and as flexible as possible. There are several ways in which this can be done, and we'll discuss a few standard Object Oriented programming techniques.

Inheriting from Image::Magick

One way of writing a driver that reimplements a drawing interface for a particular drawing package is by inheritance, a so-called *is-a* relationship. The class that is the driver is basically just the same as the original class, but with a few extra methods, possibly overriding some of the parent methods. Let's have a look at how this could be done for the *Image::Magick* implementation of this driver:

```
package Canvas::Polar::ImageMagick;
use Image::Magick '5.2';
use Coordinate;
use strict;
@Canvas::Polar::ImageMagick::ISA = qw(Image::Magick);

sub new
{
    my $proto = shift;
    my $class = ref($proto) || $proto;
    my ($width, $height, $bgcolor) = @_;
    my $self = $class->SUPER::new(size => "${width}x$height");
    $self->Read("xc:$bgcolor");
    return bless $self, $class;
}
```

We give the package a name, include the *Coordinate* and *Image::Magick* modules, and set up inheritance with the @ISA array. The new() method shows that we simply instantiate an *Image::Magick* object through the built-in SUPER pseudo class. We use the standard Read() method that comes with *Image::Magick* to initialize an image that is filled with the specified background color. The reference contained in $self is, of course, an *Image::Magick* object, so we rebless it into our current class before returning it to the caller.

The methods that actually do the drawing are, as determined by the design in the previous section, `line()` and `fill_circle()`:

```
sub line
{
    my $self = shift;
    my ($r1, $r2, $angle, $color, $width) = @_;
    my ($x1, $y1) = polar2cart($r1, $angle);
    my ($x2, $y2) = polar2cart($r2, $angle);

    $self->Draw(primitive => 'Line',
                stroke    => $color,
                linewidth => $width || 1,
                points    => "$x1,$y1 $x2,$y2");
}

sub fill_circle
{
    my $self = shift;
    my ($radius, $color) = @_;
    my ($xc, $yc) = get_origin();
    my $yr = $yc - $radius;

    $self->Draw(primitive => 'Circle',
                fill      => $color,
                stroke    => $color,
                points    => "$xc,$yc $xc,$yr");
}

1;
```

These two methods translate the polar coordinates to Cartesian ones, using the functions provided by the *Coordinate* module discussed in section 10.1.1, and call the appropriate *Image::Magick* methods with these calculated coordinates.

The implementation of the previous class basically means that the returned canvas object *is* an *Image::Magick* object, with all the attributes and methods of that class. That might not be desirable. It is conceivable that we want none of the functionality of the underlying driver to be exposed to the user of the canvas object, maybe to prevent the user from directly drawing on it, or applying filters to it. Another reason to avoid this sort of inheritance is to prevent naming conflicts between the driver and interface class you're writing.

Incorporating a GD::Image object

To avoid these problems, you can use a *has-a* relationship, by making the driver object a contained attribute of the canvas interface. *GD* is a good example for this, because it already defines a method with the name `line()`. If we don't want to overload that name,[3] we can do something akin to the following:

---

[3] It is not impossible to overload `line()`, or any other method for that matter, it just isn't always the most appropriate action to take.

```perl
package Canvas::Polar::GD;
use GD;
use Coordinate;
use strict;

sub new
{
    my $proto = shift;
    my $class = ref($proto) || $proto;
    my ($width, $height, $bgcolor) = @_;
    my $self = {canvas => GD::Image->new($width, $height)};
    bless $self, $class;
    $self->_set_color($bgcolor);
    return $self;
}

sub gd
{
    my $self = shift;
    $self->{canvas};
}
```

This object is implemented, traditionally, as a hash reference. One of the attributes that we store is the *canvas* attribute, which contains a reference to a *GD::Image* object. If an object is contained this way, it can be a good idea to provide methods that offer the user access to this object's functionality, unless of course, you definitely do not want this. For this module we've chosen the easy way out, by providing a method that simply returns that contained object. For an example on how this could be used, see the next section.

Next, we need to define a few helper methods that will be used internally to translate the color notation into something palatable by *GD*, and to be able to draw lines with various widths using a *GD::Image* brush.

```perl
sub _rgb { map hex, unpack "x A2 A2 A2", shift }

sub _set_color
{
    my $self = shift;
    my $color = shift;
    # Check to see if the color already exists
    my $index = $self->{canvas}->colorExact(_rgb($color));
    return $index unless $index == -1;
    # If not, allocate it
    return $self->{canvas}->colorAllocate(_rgb($color));
}

sub _set_pen
{
    my $self = shift;
    my ($color, $width) = @_;

    return $self->_set_color($color) unless $width;
```

```
    my $brush = GD::Image->new($width, $width);
    $brush->colorAllocate(_rgb($color));
    $self->{brush} = $brush;
    $self->{canvas}->setBrush($brush);
    return gdBrushed;
}
```

These methods are only meant to be called internally in this module, and by certain modules that inherit from it. Therefore, by convention, their names start with an underscore. The _rgb() subroutine returns a list of the three color components contained in the string that we are using as a color specification. This list is needed for the various color allocation methods in *GD*. The _set_color() method is used to select a color from the current *GD* palette, or to allocate a new one if it doesn't already exist. The _set_pen() method is used to emulate line thickness in *GD*, since it natively only draws in one thickness. This is performed by setting the drawing brush to a square image of the specified color, and designating that brush as the active drawing pen, instead of a plain color.

All that is left now is the implementation of the methods that form our drawing interface, i.e., the line() and fill_circle() methods.

```
sub line
{
    my $self = shift;
    my ($r1, $r2, $angle, $color, $width) = @_;
    my ($x1, $y1) = polar2cart($r1, $angle);
    my ($x2, $y2) = polar2cart($r2, $angle);

    my $gd_color = $self->_set_pen($color, $width);
    $self->{canvas}->line($x1, $y1, $x2, $y2, $gd_color);
}

sub fill_circle
{
    my $self = shift;
    my ($radius, $color) = @_;
    my $gd_color = $self->_set_color($color);
    my ($xc, $yc) = get_origin();

    $self->{canvas}->arc($xc, $yc,
        2 * $radius, 2 * $radius, 0, 360, $gd_color);
    $self->{canvas}->fillToBorder(
        $xc, $yc, $gd_color, $gd_color);
}

1;
```

It now has become fairly easy to write a clock-drawing program, using virtually any driver that implements the interface discussed.[4] Some drivers (for example, text-based

---

[4] Implementations of this driver for the SVG format and for PostScript are presented in appendix C.

displays or drivers that work with inches and centimeters instead of pixels) would require some extra functionality that translates the clock sizes into more appropriate sizes for their particular type of display. This could be done by introducing a resolution attribute in your interface. Some drivers might not have an OO interface, but that needn't present a problem either. As long as the Canvas class provides the two described methods, the clock will happily draw itself. The details of how that happens are now neatly hidden behind our interface specification.

10.2 AN OO IMPLEMENTATION OF A CLOCK

Now that we have an abstract drawing interface with all the primitives needed to draw a clock, we can rewrite the programs from section 10.1 using the driver implementations for *GD* and *Image::Magick*. But we still will have quite a bit of code in each program. What this abstraction step has given us is the possibility to switch from driver to driver without altering our main program.

Suppose that we need to maintain two programs: one that creates a PNG image of a clock for a web page, and one that needs to import a variety of images to draw a clock on that. The interface to *GD* is the logical choice for the first one. Because of its speed and its flexibility in the number of image formats it can handle, *Image::Magick* is the logical choice for the second one. But we don't want to have to write all the code for the actual drawing of the clock twice. Instead, we want to be able to use a code fragment such as:

```
use Clock;
use Canvas::Polar::GD;

my $canvas = Canvas::Polar::GD->new(121, 121, '#ffffff');

my $clock = Clock->new(
    radius       => 60,
    hand_color   => '#000000',
    face_color   => '#dfdfdf',
    marker_color => '#00007f',
    center_color => '#ff0000',
);
$clock->draw($canvas, 60, 60);

open(OUT, ">GDclock2.png") or die $!;
binmode(OUT);
print OUT $canvas->gd->png;
close(OUT);
```

In this example, the code that deals with the drawing of the clock is independent of the actual object we draw on.[5] The only information we need to pass in is which canvas to use. What we have actually done with that canvas, and what we will do with it

---

[5] ...apart from the units, which are in pixels for both. Even this can be dealt with by allowing for a resolution attribute in the driver modules if other units are wanted

CHAPTER 10 *WRITING YOUR OWN GRAPHICS MODULES*

outside of the drawing code for the clock, is of no concern to the clock. Nor should it be. All the clock needs to know is that the canvas driver passed to it has all the methods needed to draw a clock.

Let's have a look at a possible implementation of this magical *Clock* class:

```perl
package Clock;
use Coordinate;

my %defaults = (
    face_color   => '#FFFFFF',
    hand_color   => '#000000',
    marker_color => '#00007F',
    center_color => '#7F0000',
    radius       => 50,
    when         => time(),
);

sub new
{
    my $proto  = shift;
    my $class  = ref($proto) || $proto;
    my $self   = { %defaults, @_ };
    bless $self => $class;
    return $self;
}
```

The constructor creates a hash reference and initializes it with the values from the hash %defaults, followed by whatever it gets passed as arguments. This ensures that any arguments passed in will *override* the defaults. By default, our clock will take the current time as the time to display, but the user can override this in the arguments.

The module contains only one further method that does all the hard work.[6]

```perl
sub draw
{
    my $self = shift;
    my ($canvas, $x, $y) = @_;
    set_origin($x, $y);

    my $R = $self->{radius};

    $canvas->fill_circle($R, $self->{face_color});

    for (my $angle = 0; $angle < 2*PI; $angle += 2*PI/12)
    {
        $canvas->line($R, 0.8 * $R, $angle,
            $self->{marker_color});
    }
```

● **Draw the face of the clock**

● **Draw the hour markers**

---

[6] A real-life production implementation of this class could have many other methods; a method to set the time being the most obvious one.

```
my ($min, $hour) = (localtime($self->{when}))[1,2];
$hour %= 12;                                    ● Convert from 24 hour
my $min_angle  = 2*PI * $min/60 - PI/2;            time to 12 hour time
my $hour_angle =
    2*PI * ($hour/12 + $min/(12 * 60)) - PI/2;

$canvas->line(0, $R, $min_angle, $self->{hand_color}, 2);
$canvas->line(0, 0.75 * $R, $hour_angle,
    $self->{hand_color}, 2);

$canvas->fill_circle(0.1 * $R, $self->{center_color});   ● Put some
}                                                            decoration on
                                                             the clock
1;
```

This method does much the same work as the code in the two programs in section 10.1, but in fewer lines and with less complexity. The main reason for the decrease in complexity is that we have provided it with a driver that can draw the graphical elements in terms that are natural to the problem. The good news is that we don't need to clutter the code with conversions between angles and coordinates.

The result of all this can be seen in figure 10.3.

Figure 10.3
Two clocks, drawn with the two different drivers for the *Clock* module. The left image was produced with a driver based on the *Image::Magick* module, and the right image with one based on the *GD* module.

10.3   SUMMARY

Hopefully, it has been made clear that good software design and abstraction are not only matters of elegance, or limited to pedantic discussions on Usenet and at universities. The object-oriented code presented is much more maintainable and reusable than the two previous examples. More importantly, especially for graphics programming, it is much harder to create bugs and definitely easier to track them down, because each code fragment is aimed only at solving a very small part of the overall problem and is stated in the terms best suited to the problem at hand.

Another point that I hope has been sufficiently conveyed is how naturally OO fits in with programming graphics interfaces. Not only does the world of graphics programming translate well into an OO model, but, more practically, these techniques provide us with a means of hiding the specific ways in which the low-level graphics primitives are implemented for the various drivers like *GD* and *Image::Magick* or the various output formats like SVG or PostScript.

SEE ALSO   The `perlsub`, `perlmod`, `perlmodlib`, `perltoot`, `perlobj` and `perlbot` manual pages explain in more detail how Perl's OO model works. Damian Conway [32] has written an excellent book on object oriented programming in Perl.

C H A P T E R   1 1

Controlling text placement

Most drawing primitives in graphics manipulation are fairly straightforward: you determine the size of the object you want to draw, decide where you want it to appear, and draw it. The number of parameters and the difficulty in positioning these objects is limited, because of the simplicity of their shape and the predictability of their size. You draw a circle with a certain radius around a center, and you automatically know what the bounding box of this circle is going to be. When you draw a polygon, it is easy enough, with some basic geometric mathematics, to determine what its bounding box is going to be.

Text objects have slightly more demanding requirements, at least when you start working with proportional typefaces. You cannot easily predict the size of the text object you will be drawing, because the way proportional typefaces are rendered and spaced is quite complex. If you fix the point size of the text, the height is known, but the width depends on the text, the individual characters, the spacing of these characters, and the potential kerning that occurs. If your drawing package allows you to fix the width of the box in which the text appears, then you cannot easily predict the resulting height.

If you knew the internal parameters of all characters in the font you are working with, and all the parameters that go with the font and the particular rendering engine, then you could, in theory, predict the outcome. However, the result is so sensitive to such an array of parameters, that this is hardly ever successful. The *Font::TTF* modules could theoretically be used to make these sorts of predictions, but not without a lot of work, and not with great accuracy.

Most of the time, or almost always, you are not interested in the precise details of the text rendering that goes on behind the scenes, and you certainly don't want to have to do all the calculations that go with the positioning of proportional characters. What concerns you is the size of the box you are going to draw, which you'd like to know before actually drawing. The reasons for needing to know these things include wanting to be able to center the box accurately on some point in your graphic, or to organize multiple text boxes in a rather precise way.

The rest of this chapter talks about how to determine these sizes and parameters, and how to use this information to make text go precisely where you want it to. Alignment, spacing and sizing of text strings in the two most popular drawing packages for Perl, *GD* and *Image::Magick*, will be discussed and demonstrated.

SEE ALSO   For basic instructions on how to produce text with *GD*, see section 4.1.3, "Drawing text with GD." and for *Image::Magick* see section 4.2.5, "Drawing text with Image::Magick."

11.1   *DETERMINING TEXT SIZE*

In order to correctly position a string on an image it is important that you understand how the specific graphics package in use renders the font on the page. The parameters you need to know are the horizontal and vertical size of the string in pixels, and the handle on the bounding box.

11.1.1   Text sizes in *GD*

The *GD* module can draw text in two ways: with a limited set of built-in fonts, and with TrueType fonts from a user-specified file. These two types of fonts have different API calls, and wildly different metrics; dealing with alignments of strings drawn with the different fonts is not even similar.

The metrics for a string drawn with the built-in fonts and one with a TrueType font are shown in figure 11.1.

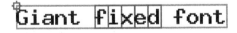 

Figure 11.1   The size parameters and handles for strings with *GD*. For fixed-width fonts, the only parameters of importance are the width and height of the single characters and the handle is located at the upper- left corner of the string. For TrueType fonts, the parameters of importance consist of the coordinates of the bounding box around the whole string to be drawn, and the handle is located at the baseline of the font.

The handle for a string drawn with a built-in font is the top left corner of the bounding box for the text, the size of the bounding box is the height of a single character, and the width is the width of a single character multiplied by the number of characters:

```
$text_width   = gdGiantFont->width * length($string);
$text_height  = gdGiantFont->height;
# or
$text_width   = GD::Font->Giant->width * length($string);
$text_height  = GD::Font->Giant->height;
```

For TrueType fonts, the situation is slightly more complex. The handle on the bounding box is the baseline of the font. The letters will be drawn on a (normally horizontal) line through this point, the resulting string will have a part above and a part below the handle. If invoked as an object method, the stringTTF() method will draw a string on a *GD* canvas, and return the coordinates of the bounding box of the complete string. If this method is invoked as a class method, i.e., as GD::Image->stringTTF, it will return the bounding box of the text, but without actually drawing it. In this way, you can obtain the size of the text before you draw it.

So, to calculate the size of a TrueType font string, you can do something such as:

```
$string = 'Some Text';
@bounds = GD::Image->stringTTF(0, '/usr/share/fonts/ttfonts/arialbd.ttf',
                14, 0, 0, $string);
die $@ unless @bounds;
$text_width   = $bounds[2] - $bounds[0];
$text_height  = $bounds[1] - $bounds[7];
```

See section 11.2, "Aligning text in graphics." for an example on how to use this information to correctly align strings with *GD*.

11.1.2   Text sizes in Image::Magick

There is no documented method for *Image::Magick* to predict the size of a text string,[1] but it can be obtained by making use of *Image::Magick's* built-in LABEL file type. Since the *Image::Magick* object is implemented as a reference to an array containing separate images, we can do something like the following:

```
$im = Image::Magick->new();
# ...
$im->Set(
    font => '@/usr/share/fonts/ttfonts/arialbd.ttf',
    pointsize => 12
);
# Create a new image in the object
$rc = $im->Read("label:$string");
if (!$rc)
{
```

---

[1] For versions of *Image::Magick* 5.2.6 and before, there was no such method. Version 5.3.9 of *Image::Magick* provides the user with the QueryFontMetrics() and QueryFont() methods, Unfortunately, this addition arrived too late to allow changes to this chapter before publication.

```
    $text_width  = $im->[$#$im]->Get('width');
    $text_height = $im->[$#$im]->Get('height');
}
else
{
    warn $rc;
}
# Get rid of the temporary image
pop @$im;
```

It would be helpful if *Image::Magick* provided a rapid access method for this sort of information, because the method outlined above is a spectacular 100 times slower than the `stringTTF()` method in *GD*, and is not exactly elegant either.

Even though *Image::Magick* does not provide a direct method to obtain the size of a text fragment, we can write our own, and insert it into the *Image::Magick* namespace:

```
sub Image::Magick::TextSize
{
    my $im  = shift or return;
    my $str = shift or return ();

    my $rc = $im->Read("label:$str");
    return () if $rc;
    my $l = pop @$im;
    return $l->Get('width', 'height');
}
$im = Image::Magick->new();
$im->Set(
    font => '@arialbd.ttf',
    pointsize => 12
);
($text_width, $text_height) = $im->TextSize($string);
```

This extends the *Image::Magick* class with the capability of providing you with width and height information about a string to be drawn, much as the `stringTTF()` method does for *GD*. We still do not have as much information as `stringTTF()` provides, nor is the information as accurate. We are also lacking a reliable position with regard to the baseline of the font, which is needed to draw lines of text word by word. We'll be seeing more about this in section 11.2.

NOTE One can argue over whether adding a method to a class at runtime is wise or not. There is the risk of trampling on symbols in a namespace which isn't really yours; you could accidentally redeclare a method that already exists; or you could change the value of a package variable. Of course, if you run Perl with the -w option it will warn you about re-declaration of subroutines; and if you make sure to scope your variables with my, you don't change anything but that which is lexically local to your subroutine.

However, it is probably preferable, in most cases, to create a subclass of *Image::Magick*, and add the methods you need to that class. Of course, you have to rewrite all your code to create objects of your subclass instead of *Image::Magick*, but normally that shouldn't be too much work.

```perl
package myImage::Magick;
use Image::Magick;
@myImage::Magick::ISA = qw(Image::Magick);

sub TextSize
{
    my $im  = shift or return;
    my $str = shift or return ();

    my $rc = $im->Read("label:$str");
    return () if $rc;
    my $l = pop @$im;
    return $l->Get('width', 'height');
}

package main;

$string = 'Some Text';
$im = myImage::Magick->new();
$im->Read('gradation:white-black');
$im->Set(
    font => '@/usr/share/fonts/ttfonts/arialbd.ttf',
    pointsize => 12
);
($text_width, $text_height) = $im->TextSize($string);
```

If the amount of extra functionality you need is reasonably large and complex (say more than a few subroutines), then writing a subclass for use in your code is probably the preferred way to go. If all you want to do is to add a little bit of functionality for reuse in one program, then it is easier to just insert a method in the namespace of the class you are working with.

11.2 ALIGNING TEXT IN GRAPHICS

Aligning text to a center point or left or right margin is one of the most frequent operations you will find yourself performing with text objects. Apart from the horizontal alignment, there is also vertical alignment. You might like to put some text in the upper right corner of a box you drew, or a copyright notice on the bottom right corner of a photograph. This section discusses how to achieve alignment of text with the help of the modules under discussion, and a little bit of work on your own part.

11.2.1 Aligning text with *GD*

The *GD* module doesn't provide built-in functionality to position text centered on or with its right side aligned to a point. It is, however, possible to write something ourselves, with the help of the techniques described in section 11.1.

In order to have full control over text positioning, at least a minimal set of positional parameters is required: a horizontal left, center or right alignment and a vertical top, center or bottom alignment. The following code presents a subroutine that can draw text aligned in all sorts of ways, using the *GD* module:

```
sub alignStringTTF
{
    my $gd = shift;
    my ($valign, $halign) = splice @_, 7, 2;
    my @bb = GD::Image->stringTTF(@_) or return;
    my ($x, $y) = @_[4,5];

    SWITCH: for ($halign || 'left')
    {
        /^right/i  and $x -= ($bb[2] - $bb[0]),
            last SWITCH;
        /^center/i and $x -= ($bb[2] - $bb[0])/2,
            last SWITCH;
    }
    SWITCH: for ($valign || 'baseline')
    {
        /^top/i    and $y -= ($bb[7] - $y),
            last SWITCH;
        /^center/i and $y -= ($bb[1] + $bb[7])/2 - $y,
            last SWITCH;
        /^bottom/i and $y -= ($bb[1] - $y),
            last SWITCH;
    }

    return $gd->stringTTF(@_[0..3], $x, $y, $_[6]);
}
```

This subroutine takes a *GD::Image* object as its first argument. It then takes arguments 7 and 8, as the vertical and horizontal alignment parameters. There should now be 7 arguments left, which should be exactly the same as the arguments to the stringTTF() method in the *GD* module, meaning that this method has the same calling signature as the stringTTF() method, except that it optionally accepts the two alignment parameters at the end of the list.

When the arguments have been processed, the bounding box of the text is determined and, based on the given alignment parameters and the bounding box, new *x* and *y* coordinates for the call to stringTTF() are calculated. Once that is done, the standard stringTTF() method gets called with the same parameters that were given to this method, except that the *x* and *y* coordinates have been replaced with ones that align the bounding box differently. The logical ORs in the SWITCH lines are there because both alignment parameters might be undefined; for example, because they were not specified. We don't want warnings when that happens, so we provide a default value. This default value can be anything, but in this case we use it to document what stringTTF() does by default.

The following code demonstrates how this subroutine can be used to align and position text to produce figure:

```
use GD;
my $gd = GD::Image->new(300, 60);
my $white = $gd->colorAllocate(255,255,255);
my $black = $gd->colorAllocate(  0,  0,  0);
my $green = $gd->colorAllocate(  0,255,  0);
my $gray  = $gd->colorAllocate(127,127,127);
$gd->line(0,  30, 300, 30, $gray);
$gd->line(150, 0, 150, 60, $gray);

my @args = ('/usr/share/fonts/ttfonts/arialbd.ttf', 24,
    0, 150, 30, 'A string');
alignStringTTF($gd, $black, @args, 'bottom', 'right');
alignStringTTF($gd, $green, @args, 'top',     'right');
alignStringTTF($gd, $green, @args, 'bottom');
alignStringTTF($gd, $black, @args, 'top');
```

Figure 11.2   Text alignment with *GD*. The four True-Type font strings were aligned in four different ways to the center point of the image by determination of the bounding box of the string to be drawn, and an appropriate repositioning of the drawing handle.

Having a fairly simple subroutine like `alignStringTTF()` around saves you a lot of work in calculating where your text goes, and it makes your program more elegant and readable as well. Because we wrote the subroutine in such a way that it accepts a *GD::Image* object as the first argument, you could even consider putting it in the *GD::Image* name space, which would make it available as a normal method for a *GD::Image* object. As written, it should behave identically to the standard `stringTTF()` method, except that it accepts these extra alignment parameters. To make it more robust, you could consider subjecting the argument list to a more rigorous inspection.

Later in this chapter, in section 11.2.2, we will see more on abstracting this sort of work out into reusable subroutines.

11.2.2   Aligning text with Image::Magick

Image::Magick provides some rough alignment functionality for text, through the use of the gravity parameter (see also section A.6, "Common method arguments," on page 276) in the `Annotate()` method.[2] The best way to illustrate the use of these parameters is with some code:

---

[2] The gravity parameter for text with the Draw method is somewhat unreliable, at least in version 5.2.3.

```perl
use Image::Magick;
my $im = Image::Magick->new(size => '400x50');

# Set image defaults
$im->Set(stroke        => 'red',
         fill          => 'red',
         font          => 'Helvetica',
         pointsize     => 24);
$im->Read('xc:white');

# Draw some lines
$im->Draw(primitive    => 'line',
          stroke       => 'blue',
          points       => '0,25 400,25');
$im->Draw(primitive    => 'line',
          stroke       => 'blue',
          points       => '200,0 200,50');

$im->Annotate(text     => 'Align NorthEast',
              geometry => '+200+25',
              gravity  => 'NorthEast');
$im->Annotate(text     => 'Align NorthWest',
              geometry => '+200+25',
              gravity  => 'NorthWest');
$im->Annotate(text     => 'Align South',
              geometry => '+200+25',
              gravity  => 'South');
```

which produces the image in figure 11.3.

Align NorthEast|Align NorthWest
Align |South

Figure 11.3   Text alignment with *Image::Magick*. The strings were aligned with the gravity parameter set to NorthEast, NorthWest and South respectively.

Image::Magick always approximately aligns the baseline of the string to the coordinates given, if the gravity is of a *North* type. Because it isn't possible to obtain the coordinates of the bounding box of a string with (older versions of) *Image::Magick*, more customized positioning of text, as in the *GD* examples in the previous section, cannot be achieved. There is no way to calculate how far the text sticks out above or below the baseline. The only retrievable information is the approximate size of the string to be drawn, and that is simply not sufficient for precise text positioning. In newer versions of *Image::Magick* the QueryFontMetrics() method could be used to obtain the necessary information.

11.3   WRAPPING TEXT

You will sometimes find yourself in a situation in which you need to place a large string on an image which is longer than your image is wide. You can, of course, manually break up the string and draw individual strings, but every time the text changes it has to be done again. It would be terribly handy if you had some code that did line wrapping for you.

While correct typesetting of text is a nontrivial matter and requires a full knowledge of the typeface with which you are working, an adequate approximation can be achieved even by a relative novice. You break the string up into words,[3] and put the individual words on the canvas, all the time keeping track of the number of pixels left in this line. The number of parameters needed to do all this is quite large: the font name, font size, spacing between the lines, left and right border, top, color, alignment parameters, and others if you need more flexibility. That means that if you implement this as a single subroutine, the call to it would look something like:

```
wrap_text($gd_image, $fontname, $fontsize, $line_space,
    $color, $left, $right, $top, $text);
```

This looks fairly nasty, and each time you add a new capability to your subroutine, the interface to that subroutine changes slightly. It can be made a bit less rigid by allowing the arguments to come in as a hash:

```
wrap_text($gd_image,
    font        => $fontname,
    font_size   => $fontsize,
    color       => $color,
    line_space  => $line_space,
    left        => $left,
    right       => $right,
    top         => $top,
    text        => $text
);
```

This is already a major improvement, since it doesn't require the user of the interface to remember exactly what the order of arguments is, and it allows easier provision of defaults. It is still limited by the single subroutine call, and the only interaction possible is to call it. There is no feedback regarding the size the box will be, for example. Of course, you can provide yet another function to create that information.

A better way to provide an interface to your text wrapping code is to put all this functionality in a class of its own (see also chapter 10). It is possible for us to subclass *GD::Image*, but that isn't very convenient. One reason is that *GD::Image* is implemented as a reference to a scalar, which doesn't allow us to easily store object-specific information that we want to use. Another reason is that, even though this example will only use GD, the idea is not really entirely specific to GD. With some effort it could be rewritten for any graphics package that provides the basic information we will need for this module.

To produce a picture like the one shown in figure 11.4, we would rather not write code that does all the calculations for each box and word separately, and repeat that

---

[3] ...or tokens, split up by spacing

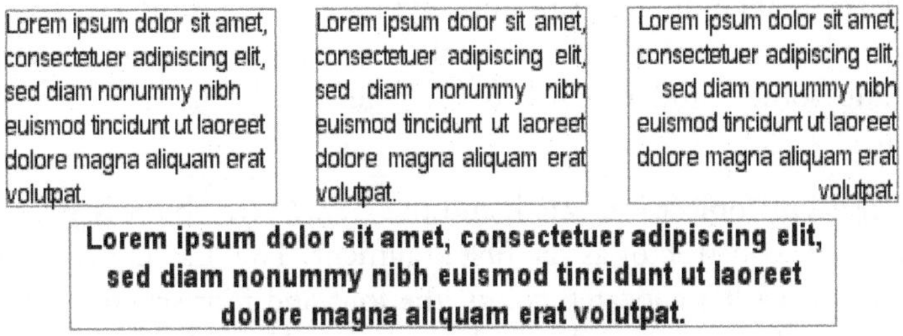

Figure 11.4 Examples of text wrapping and justification with the *GD* module. All the necessary calculations were done with the *GDTextWrap* module presented in the text.

each time we need to create a text box. Instead we would like to be able to write something approximating the following:

```
use GD;
use GDTextWrap;

my $gd = GD::Image->new(450,170);
my $white = $gd->colorAllocate(255,255,255);
my $black = $gd->colorAllocate(  0,  0,  0);
my $blue  = $gd->colorAllocate(127,127,255);
```

❶ Create a GD::Image object

```
my $text = <<EOSTR;
Lorem ipsum dolor sit amet, consectetuer adipiscing elit,
sed diam nonummy nibh euismod tincidunt ut laoreet dolore
magna aliquam erat volutpat.
EOSTR

my $wp = GDTextWrap->new($gd,
    font       => '/usr/share/fonts/ttfonts/Arialn.ttf',
    font_size  => 10,
    top        => 10,
    line_space => 4,
    color      => $black,
    text       => $text,
);
```

Create a GDTextWrap object ❷

```
$wp->set(align => 'left', left => 10, right => 140);
$gd->rectangle($wp->get_bounds, $blue);
$wp->draw();
$wp->set(align => 'justified', left => 160, right => 290);
$gd->rectangle($wp->get_bounds, $blue);
$wp->draw();
$wp->set(align => 'right', left => 310, right => 440);
$gd->rectangle($wp->get_bounds, $blue);
$wp->draw();
$wp->set(align => 'center', left => 40, right => 410,
    font => '/usr/share/fonts/ttfonts/Arialnb.ttf',
    font_size => 12, top => 110);
$gd->rectangle($wp->get_bounds, $blue);
$wp->draw();
```

❸ Draw a box with text

❶ This code starts by including *GD* and our hypothetical module *GD TextWrap*. Next, a *GD::Image* object is created and some colors are allocated for it. A variable $text is declared and some standard pseudo Latin text to be used in the text boxes is assigned to it.

❷ Then, a *GD TextWrap* object is created, and the *GD::Image* object is associated with it by passing it to the constructor as the first argument. The drawing color of the object is set to one of the earlier allocated colors, the font and font size to something agreeable, the text to the Latin phrase, the top boundary to 10, and a line spacing is chosen.

❸ Now it is time to start drawing some boxes. First, the alignment and left and right bounding parameters are set. Then, a blue rectangle the size of the bounding box is drawn by using a postulated method called `get_bounds()` that gives us coordinates exactly in the manner that the `rectangle()` method wants. Finally, the `draw()` method is called. This is repeated for three more boxes to produce figure 11.4.

All of the above looks like approximately the amount of code we would like to write to produce text boxes. Unfortunately, the hypothetical module *GD TextWrap* does not exist,[4] so we will have to write it ourselves. We start by creating the main module file GDTextWrap.pm. In this file we put the code for the class *GD TextWrap*. In Perl, a class is not much more than a package, so:

```
package GDTextWrap;
$GDTextWrap::VERSION = 0.10;
use strict;
use GD;
use Carp;
```

As good module developers, we put a version number in the module file, and because we don't want to spend too much time debugging, we include the *strict* pragma. We also include the standard *Carp* module so that errors from within our class are dealt with in a slightly more elegant manner.

We have a good idea of the parameters we'll need, so we define some default values which we can use in the constructor.

```
my %attribs = (
    left        => 0,
    right       => undef,
    top         => 0,
    line_space  => 2,
    font        => '/usr/share/fonts/ttfonts/arialbd.ttf',
    font_size   => 12,
    color       => undef,
    align       => 'justified',
    text        => undef,
);
```

---

[4] or at least, it didn't when this was written. See section 11.3.1 for more information.

The reason that some of these are present but undefined is that this hash will not only be used for the default values of the attributes, but also, as we will see later, in the set method to check for the validity of the attribute names.

Next we define a constructor, an initialization method and a set method:

```
sub new        ❶ The constructor
{
    my $proto = shift;
    my $class = ref($proto) || $proto;
    my $gd    = shift;
    ref($gd) and $gd->isa('GD::Image')
        or croak "Not a GD::Image object";
    my $self  = { gd => $gd };
    bless $self => $class;
    $self->_init();
    $self->set(@_);
    return $self
}

sub _init       ❷ The initializer
{
    my $self        = shift;
    $self->{$_}     = $attribs{$_} foreach keys %attribs;
    $self->{color}  = $self->{gd}->colorsTotal - 1;
    $self->{right}  = ($self->{gd}->getBounds())[0] - 1;
}

sub set       ❸ The set() method
{
    my $self = shift;
    my %args = @_;
    foreach (keys %args)
    {
        exists $attribs{$_} or
            do { carp "No attribute $_"; next };
        $self->{$_} = $args{$_};
    }
}
```

❶ The constructor won't be much of a surprise to anyone familiar with Perl's OO model. It uses an anonymous hash as the base for an object. We shift off the first argument (which is really the bit before the arrow in the call), and make sure that we know which class we belong in. We then take the second argument and make sure that it is a *GD::Image* object. We create an anonymous hash reference containing a reference to that object, bless it into the current class and continue by calling the _init()[5] method and the set() method with the remaining arguments.

---

[5] Following the normal conventions, we start the names of methods that are not part of the public interface with an underscore.

❷ The _init() method sets the attributes of the object to the default values which were stored in the hash %attributes, and computes some valid values for the color and right attributes from the *GD::Image* object passed to the constructor: It sets the color to be used to the last color in the object's palette, and the right boundary equal to the image width, less one pixel.

❸ All that the set method does is treat its arguments as a hash of attribute names and values and, checking that each one is valid, assigns them to the object's attributes. The other two public methods are defined as follows:

```
my $dry_run = 0;          ❹ Variable to allow
                             simulation of drawing
sub get_bounds
{
    my $self = shift;
    $dry_run = 1;
    return $self->draw(@_);
}

sub draw        ❺ Draw the text
{
    my $self = shift;
    $self->_set_font_params();

    my $y = $self->{top} + $self->{font_up};
    my @line = ();
    foreach my $word (split(' ', $self->{text}))
    {
        my $len =
            $self->_get_width(join(' ', @line, $word));
        if ($len > $self->{right} - $self->{left} && @line)
        {
            $self->_draw_line($y, 0, @line) unless $dry_run;
            @line = ();
            $y += $self->{font_height} + $self->{line_space};
        }
        push @line, $word;
    }

    $self->_draw_line($y, 1, @line) unless $dry_run;    ❻ Draw a line

    $dry_run = 0;

    $self->{bottom} = $y + $self->{font_down};
    return (                                        ❼ Return the
        $self->{left}, $self->{top},                   bounding box
        $self->{right}, $self->{bottom}                coordinates
    )
}
```

④ The lexically scoped variable `$dry_run` controls whether the draw routines actually draw, or only do the calculations necessary for the drawing. This is important if we want to be able to determine how large the box to be drawn will be before actually drawing it. The `get_bounds()` method does provide us with that possibility. It sets `$dry_run` to a true value, and then calls the `draw()` method to do the real work.

⑤ The `draw()` method calls `_set_font_params()` which, as the name suggests, sets up some parameters for the font we will use, such as how many pixels this font extends above and below the baseline (`font_up` and `font_down`), and the total height of the font (`font_height`). Once those are known, the y coordinate for the first baseline is set up, and we start looping over each word in the text to draw. In the loop, we calculate the length that a line would be if we added the current word with the call to `join()`. If that length is larger than the width of the box, *and* there is already a word in the line,[6] we draw the current line (see later for a description of `_draw_line()`), but only if this is not a dry run. We empty the current line and increment the y coordinate with the height of the font and the line space. If the length is not larger than the width of the box, we simply add the current word to the current line.

⑥ When we run out of words, we still have the current line in the buffer `@line`, so we need to draw that.

⑦ To finish off, we reset the `$dry_run` variable to 0, and calculate the bottom of the box we've just drawn by adding the number of pixels that the font sticks out below the baseline to the *y* coordinate. We then return the coordinate pairs of the top left and bottom right corner of the box.

To figure out the required font parameters, we need to do quite a bit of work:

```
my ($test_string, $space_string, $n_spaces);

BEGIN
{
    $test_string .= chr($_) for (0x21 .. 0x7e);
    $space_string = $test_string;
    $n_spaces = $space_string =~ s/(.{5})(.{5})/$1 $2/g;
}
```

Set up the font ⑧ parameters

```
sub _set_font_params
{
    my $self = shift;
    my @bb1 = GD::Image->stringTTF(0,
        $self->{font}, $self->{font_size}, 0, 0, 0,
        $test_string);
    my @bb2 = GD::Image->stringTTF(0,
        $self->{font}, $self->{font_size}, 0, 0, 0,
```

---

[6] We need to check this in case the current word we're adding is longer than the box is wide.

```
                $space_string);
        # Height of font above  and below the baseline
        $self->{font_up} = -$bb1[7];
        $self->{font_down} = $bb1[1];
        # Height of font in total
        $self->{font_height} =
            $self->{font_up} + $self->{font_down};
        # width of a space
        $self->{space} =
            (($bb2[2]-$bb2[0]) - ($bb1[2]-$bb1[0]))/$n_spaces;
    }
```

8 The _set_font_params() method is responsible for establishing some font metrics, like the maximum height of the font above and below the baseline, and the average width of a space character. It does this by getting the bounding boxes for a string
($text_string) which contains the standard printable characters (the characters
with an ordinal value between 33 and 126), and the same string with a number of
spaces inserted ($space_string).[7] These strings are calculated at compile time in
the BEGIN block shown.

Since *GD* draws TrueType fonts on the baseline, the top and bottom of the bounding
box give us the first two wanted parameters, namely the values for the font_up and
font_down attributes. The difference in width between the first and second bounding boxes gives us the width of all spaces in the second string, which we divide by the
number of spaces to obtain the average width of a space.

The method used in draw() to calculate the width of a text line is defined as follows:

```
sub _get_width
{
    my $self = shift;
    my $string = shift;
    my @bb = GD::Image->stringTTF(0,
        $self->{font}, $self->{font_size}, 0, 0, 0, $string);
    return @bb ? ($bb[2] - $bb[0]) : 0;
}
```

This method returns the width in pixels of a string when drawn with the current font
and font size. It is also used in the following, rather drawn out, method:

```
sub _draw_line
{
    my $self = shift;
    my $y    = shift;
    my $last = shift;          ● Needed for justified lines
```

_____

[7] This will work for most regular fonts, and for many of the fancier fonts. It might work less reliably for
nonwestern font encodings and character sets. Note that simply getting the bounding box of a string
containing only a single space does not work.

```
SWITCH: for ($self->{align})
{
    /^just/i    and !$last and do
    {
        $self->_draw_justified_line($y, @_);
        last SWITCH;
    };

    my $line = join(' ', @_);
    my $len  = $self->_get_width($line);

    /^right/i   and do
    {
        my $x = $self->{right} - $len;
        $self->{gd}->stringTTF($self->{color},
            $self->{font}, $self->{font_size},
            0, $x, $y, $line);
        last SWITCH;
    };
    /^center/i  and do
    {
        my $x = ($self->{left} + $self->{right})/2 -
            $len/2;
        $self->{gd}->stringTTF($self->{color},
            $self->{font}, $self->{font_size},
            0, $x, $y, $line);
        last SWITCH;
    };

    my $x = $self->{left};
    $self->{gd}->stringTTF($self->{color},
        $self->{font}, $self->{font_size},
        0, $x, $y, $line);
}
}
```

● **The default action is left justification**

The _draw_line() method draws a single line of text. The first argument is the y coordinate of the baseline of the current line. The second argument is a flag that tells us whether this is the last line in a box. We need to know this for justified paragraphs, for which the last line is normally placed flush left. The other arguments are the words to be positioned on the line.

We determine what sort of alignment we need for the current line by checking the align attribute and the passed in $last argument. We can draw the line quite simply for left, right, and centered alignment: calculate the x coordinate, and draw the string. For right alignment the x coordinate is simply the length of the line to the left of the right side of the box. For centered text it's slightly more complex: The middle (average) of the left and right sides of the box, minus half the length of the line. Left aligned text starts at the left side of the box.

The case for justified text is a bit more difficult, which is why we use a separate method for it—which is the last method in this module:

```perl
sub _draw_justified_line
{
    my $self = shift;
    my $y    = shift;
    my $x    = $self->{left};

    my @lengths = ();
    my $length = 0;

    foreach my $word (@_)
    {
        my $len = $self->_get_width($word);       ❾ Calculate length
        push @lengths, $len;                         of individual
        $length += $len;                             words
    }
                          Calculate average
    my $space =       ❿ space between words
        ($self->{right} - $self->{left} - $length)/($#_ || 1);

    for (my $i = 0; $i < $#_; $i++)
    {
        $self->{gd}->stringTTF($self->{color},
            $self->{font}, $self->{font_size},     ⓫ Draw all
            0, $x, $y, $_[$i]);                       words except
        $x += $lengths[$i] + $space;                  the last one
    }

    $x = $self->{right} - $lengths[-1];
    $self->{gd}->stringTTF($self->{color},          ● Draw the last word
        $self->{font}, $self->{font_size},
        0, $x, $y, $_[-1]);
}

$GDTextWrap::VERSION;       ⓬ Every module should return a true value
```

❾ To draw a justified line, we need to calculate what the total amount of space on a line is. The only way to find that out is by adding up the lengths of the individual words, and subtracting the sum from the width of the box. The first loop does that and more: apart from determining the total width taken up by words, it also stores the individual length of each word in an array. This we do in order to avoid recalculating these while drawing the words in the second loop.

❿ Once we know the amount of space needed for the words, we determine the total amount of whitespace left on the line and divide that by one less than the number of words to get the length of a single space. The actual expression we divide by is ($#_ || 1) which is one less than the number of words, or 1 if there is only one word. This prevents division by zero.

⓫ Next, we draw the words starting at the left margin. After each word we move the width of that word plus the amount of calculated whitespace to the right to draw the next word. We do this for all the words except the last one. To ensure that the last word neatly aligns with the right of the box, that is exactly where we draw it: we set the *x* coordinate as many pixels left of the right margin as the word is long, and draw the word. This avoids any rounding errors that might have crept in during the previous calculations.

⑫ And of course, since a module needs to return a true value, we return one, in this case the contents of the $VERSION variable.

11.3.1 The GD::Text modules

The code presented in the previous sections, in a cleaned up and much more robust version, has been released to CPAN under the name GDTextUtils. So why did we spend so much time on this, you ask?

The previous sections are useful if you ever need to do the same sort of work for a different module. Sure, for *GD* all the hard work is done, but what if a new module is released two weeks after this book hits the shelves? Or what if *Image::Magick* suddenly starts providing enough information about its string placement to be able to do all this?[8] When that happens, you should be able to get the code from the previous sections to work with some minor changes. At least you will (hopefully) understand the principles that underlie the positioning of text.

The GDTextUtils package currently contains three modules: *GD::Text*, which provides information about all fonts that *GD* can deal with, without worrying about whether it is a TrueType or built-in font, and which *GD* method to call. It is also the base class for *GD::Text::Align*, which lets you draw text. The interface to the drawing routines are again independent of the underlying font, except that some of the functionality will be missing for built-in fonts, e.g., built-in fonts don't rotate. The *GD::Text::Wrap* module allows you to define a left and right margin between which you want a string to be wrapped, justified in the various ways.

The *GD::Text* modules can draw strings in any specified font that is valid in *GD*. They will pick up TrueType fonts from a directory you specify, either with an environment variable TTF_FONT_PATH, or though the use of the method font_path(). You can create a *GD::Text* object that tries out a few fonts in a specified order, and picks the first one that matches. This allows you to have best case and worst case behavior, without running the risk of failure, because you can always specify a built-in font as the last one. You needn't even specify the extension of the TrueType font files, as long as it is .ttf.

The usage of the modules and objects is quite straightforward and well documented, so I'll conclude this discussion with an example of the use of *GD::Text::Align* and *GD::Text::Wrap* that generates figure 11.5.

---

[8] This has actually happened. Just after this book reached the stage where it became too much to change the version of *Image::Magick* used in it, the methods QueryFont() and QueryFontMetrics() were added to the API. With the help of these functions it should be possible to replicate the functionality of the *GD::Text* utilities for *Image::Magick*.

Figure 11.5
Text rendered with *GD::Text::Align*, demonstrating rotation and bottom-centered alignment, and *GD::Text::Wrap*, demonstrating the automatic wrapping of text in a small box.

```perl
use GD;
use GD::Text::Align;
use GD::Text::Wrap;
use constant PI => 4 * atan2(1, 1);          ● Set the
                                               class-wide
GD::Text->font_path('/fonts:/usr/share/fonts/ttfonts');  ● font path

my $gd    = GD::Image->new(300, 150);
my $white = $gd->colorAllocate(255, 255, 255);    ● Create a canvas and
my $black = $gd->colorAllocate(  0, 0, 0);          allocate some colors
my $red   = $gd->colorAllocate(255, 0, 0);

my $gdta = GD::Text::Align->new($gd,
    color => $black,                          ● Create a
    valign => 'bottom',                          GD:Text::Align
    halign => 'center')                          object
        or die GD::Text::Align->error;
$gdta->set_font(
    ['verdanab', 'arialbd', gdMediumBoldFont], 24)
        or die $gdta->error;
$gdta->set_text("GD::Text::Align");
                                              ● Draw the text,
$gdta->draw(149, 74, PI/12) or die $gdta->error;  at an angle

$gdta->set(color => $red);                    ● draw it at a different
$gdta->draw(149, 74, 13 * PI/12)                 angle, in red
    or die $gdta->error;

my $gdtw = GD::Text::Wrap->new($gd,
    color => $black,                          ● Create a
    align => 'left',                             GD::Text::Wrap
    width => 80,                                 object
    text  => "Here is some text in a tiny font, wrapped")
        or die GD::Text::Wrap->error;
$gdtw->set_font(['verdana', 'arial', gdMediumBoldFont], 8)
  or die $gdtw->error;

$gdtw->draw(10, 5) or die $gdtw->error;
```

These modules clearly make dealing with strings and aligning them a lot easier. No more calculations of bounding boxes, translations, rotations and such, or at least a lot less. You simply come up with the coordinate that you want the string to align to, specify how you want it aligned, and the modules do the rest. You don't even really have to worry any more whether a certain font is available, or whether you're using a built-in or a TrueType font from disk. All you do need to be aware of is that, even with these modules, the built-in *GD* fonts do not rotate. They are rendered horizontally, or at 90 degrees only.

11.4   *SUMMARY*

We have concentrated in this chapter on how to properly align text if the drawing package doesn't do it for you. While most of the code in this chapter dealt with the *GD* module, it can be easily translated to any drawing package that provides enough information about the width and height of the text bounding box, relative to the handle where it will draw the characters. With more recent versions of *Image::Magick* this should now be possible.

Manipulating pixels and transparency

There may be times when you need to manipulate each pixel of an image individually, according to a set of rules; or something needs to be done with an image that cannot be achieved by using functionality provided by any of the modules that are available for Perl. In order to do this, it is essential that you know how to read the values of the individual pixels, and how to set their values to something else. Both *GD* and *Image::Magick* provide methods for this.

Before we have a look at this, a word of caution is needed: image manipulation is a very CPU-intensive process. The number of pixels in an image grows quadratically with its height or width,[1] so you may quickly find that you have to do the same operation thousands or even millions of times. Perl is not always the best choice for this sort of operation. There is a good reason that both *GD* and *Image::Magick* are implemented in C, and that there are no pure Perl modules for image manipulation. Perl should only be used for pixel-by-pixel image manipulation for jobs wherein the vast quantity of memory and CPU cycles needed are not going to present a problem.

---

[1] ...linearly with its area

That said, in this chapter we'll look at how to gain the information pertaining to individual image pixels, and how to change these values. We'll start the slow way, by using the Perl interfaces of standard modules. Once we've established how to do that, we will look at how it can be done much more quickly than with Perl alone.

12.1   *GD* AND *PIXELS*

GD offers the getPixel(x,y) and setPixel(x,y,index) methods to access the color properties of individual pixels. The getPixel() method returns the color palette index of the pixel at the given coordinate, after which the rgb() method can be used to get a list of the red, green, and blue components of that color. The setPixel() method is available to set the color palette index of the pixel at the given coordinates to a certain value. You use one of the colorAllocate(), colorClosest(), colorExact() or colorResolve() to actually put a certain color in the palette.

Table 12.1   Methods to manipulate individual pixels and color palette entries for *GD*. The top part of the table shows the methods that can be used to work with individual pixels, and the bottom part shows the methods that can be used to work with color palette entries.

getPixel(x,y)	Get the color index of the pixel at coordinates x,y
setPixel(x,y,index)	Set the color of the pixel at coordinates x,y to the color specified by index
rgb(index)	Get the RGB values of the color at the specified index as a list
colorAllocate(r,g,b)	Allocate an index entry for the color specified
colorDeallocate(index)	Remove the specified color from the index
colorClosest(r,g,b)	Find the color in the index that most closely matches the specification
colorExact(r,g,b)	Find this exact color in the index
colorResolve(r,g,b)	First try a colorExact(), and if that fails, a colorAllocate()
colorsTotal()	Get the number of colors allocated

12.1.1   Example: rotating RGB values

The following code rotates the red, green, and blue components of the colors of each pixel:

```
use GD;
# Read in the image
open(PNG, 'logo.png') or die "<logo.png: $!";
my $gd =  GD::Image->newFromPng(\*PNG) or die "newFromPNG";
close PNG;
# Get the dimensions
my ($width, $height) = $gd->getBounds();
# Loop over the individual pixels
for (my $y = 0; $y < $height; $y++)
{
    for (my $x = 0; $x < $width; $x++)
    {
        my $index = $gd->getPixel($x, $y);
```

```
            my ($r, $g, $b) = $gd->rgb($index);
            $index = $gd->colorResolve($b, $r, $g);
            $gd->setPixel($x, $y, $index);
        }
    }
    # Save the image
    open(PNG, '>logo-rgbrot.png') or die ">logo-rgbrot.png: $!";
    binmode PNG;
    print PNG $gd->png;
    close PNG;
```

The above example is quite useless as is, in that it doesn't actually do anything that you'll likely need, but it does show how to get the color value of each pixel and how to change it. If you don't want to rotate the color components, but wish to do something else, then all you need is to change the code in the innermost loop to do what you want. For example, to change each pixel to a grayscale value with a brightness that is the average of the values of the three color components, the code in the innermost loop could be changed to something like the following:

```
            my $index = $gd->getPixel($x, $y);
            my ($r, $g, $b) = $gd->rgb($index);
            my $grey = int(($r + $g + $b)/3);
            $index = $gd->colorResolve($grey, $grey, $grey);
            $gd->setPixel($x, $y, $index);
```

12.1.2   Removing duplicate color palette entries

Because the number of colors in a *GD::Image* object is limited to 256,[2] we need to make sure we never try to allocate more than that. To minimize the number of entries in the color table it is possible to clean up any colors that are no longer in use and to consolidate duplicates:

```
my (%seen, @indexes);
my ($width, $height) = $gd->getBounds();

for (my $y = 0; $y < $height; $y++)
{
    for (my $x = 0; $x < $width; $x++)
    {
        my $index = $gd->getPixel($x, $y);
        my $key = join '-', $gd->rgb($index);
        if (exists $seen{$key})
        {
            next if $index == $seen{$key};
            $gd->setPixel($x, $y, $seen{$key});
        }
        else
        {
```

---

[2] ...something that will change in the (hopefully near) future now that *GD* is no longer tied to the GIF format, which traditionally has been limited to 256 colors.

```
            $seen{$key} = $index;
            $indexes[$index] = 1;
        }
    }
}

foreach my $index (0 .. 255)
{
    $gd->colorDeallocate($index) unless $indexes[$index];
}
```

The %seen hash is used to store the RGB values of the colors that have already been seen. For each pixel we first check whether its color has already been seen, and whether that color is set by the same index number. If not, we reset the current pixel's color index to the already seen value. This way we are able to rid the color table of duplicate entries.

When we notice a color that has been seen before, we store the RGB value as a key in %seen and set the index value in @indexes to a true value. Once we have looked at all pixels, we check for each possible index value (0 to 255) to determine whether there was at least one pixel that referred to it. If not, we deallocate the color.

Even though this can be used to postprocess a *GD* image in which we have just changed many colors, it doesn't solve the problem that in both examples in the previous section we will likely need twice as many colors to work with as were initially in the image. It is, after all, very unlikely that the new colors we allocate are already in existence in the image. One way to ensure that this will work is to use *Image::Magick*'s Quantize() method, which allows you to limit the number of colors in an image to 128, thereby leaving 128 more to be allocated during the process.

It might be easier to just use *Image::Magick* for the whole process, and not worry about limitations in the numbers of colors.

12.2   IMAGE::MAGICK AND PIXELS

When using *Image::Magick*, the individual pixels are accessible with the Get() and Set() methods, using the attribute pixel[x,y], where *x* and *y* are the coordinates of the point you are interested in. The Get() method returns a string, with a comma-separated list of the red, green, and blue values, as well as the opacity of the pixel, and the Set() method takes any of the valid color strings discussed in section A.6, "Common method arguments" on page 276.[3]

```
($x, $y) = (120, 240);
$im->Set("pixel[$x,$y]"), "#7f3ca200";
($red, $green, $blue, $opacity) = split /,/, $im->Get("pixel[$x,$y]");
```

---

[3] Note that if you compile ImageMagick with 16-bit color support, this code will actually set the color to #7f7f3c3ca2a20000. I, personally, consider this to be a bad behavior.

Since these manipulations require a lot of stringification of pixel coordinates and splitting and joining of color triplets or quadruplets, this can be quite costly in CPU load. That's not to say avoid it at all costs, but it is something to keep in mind when you decide to loop over all the pixels of an *Image::Magick* object.

12.2.1 Rotating RGB values

The following code does the same thing as the example on page 211, but with *Image::Magick* instead of *GD*.

```
use Image::Magick;
my $rc;

# Read in the image
my $im = Image::Magick->new();
$rc = $im->Read('logo.png');
die $rc if $rc;

# Get the dimensions
my ($width, $height) = $im->Get('width', 'height');
# Loop over the individual pixels
for (my $y = 0; $y < $height; $y++)
{
    for (my $x = 0; $x < $width; $x++)
    {
        my ($r, $g, $b, $o) =
            split /,/, $im->Get("pixel[$x,$y]");
        $im->Set("pixel[$x,$y]" =>
            sprintf "%d,%d,%d,%d", $b, $r, $g, $o);
    }
}

# Save the image
$rc = $im->Write("png:logo-im-rgbrot.png");
die $rc if $rc;
```

There are a few differences from the equivalent *GD* code, apart from the function calls, and they're related to the way color manipulation works.

The first difference is that here we have four elements in a color instead of three: the red, green and blue values, and the opacity. The opacity is, like the RGB values, an integer between 0 and 255 (65536 for 16-bit ImageMagick) and expresses how opaque (or transparent) this particular pixel is.

The second difference is the way color specifications are handled by *Image::Magick* (also see the discussion on *Image::Magick* color specification on "Colors" on page 278). The $im->Get("pixel[$x,$y]") call returns the color as a single string containing the above-mentioned values separated by commas. The value of that same argument in the Set() method can be formatted in various ways, but for this example the format is the same as that which came out of Get(). This introduces the necessity to manipulate strings inside a tight loop, which is CPU-intensive.

Versions of *Image::Magick* before 5.2.4 could also return a color name as the result of $im->Get("pixel[$x,$y]"). This introduces the need to resolve the color name to a comma-separated string with QueryColor(). If you still have an older version around, you might like to use this subroutine instead of the direct call to split() in the above code:

```
sub IMget_color
{
    my $im = shift;
    my ($x, $y) = @_;
    my $color = $im->Get("pixel[$x,$y]");
    $color = Image::Magick->QueryColor($color)
        unless $color =~ /\d+,\d+,\d+/;
    return split /,/, $color;
}
```

and call it this way:

```
my $im = Image::Magick->new();
# Time passes ...
my ($r, $g, $b, $o) = IMget_color($im, $x, $y);
```

All in all, *Image::Magick* is not the best tool to use when you require access to each individual pixel of an image. The manipulation of strings for both the coordinates and the color values is just too expensive in a loop that is going to be executed so often. However, if you need to have more than 256 colors in an image, you won't be able to fall back on *GD*. In section 12.5 we'll see a way around this problem.

12.3 CONVOLUTION

One of the standard operations in image manipulation is the application of a convolution filter. Convolution is a mathematical technique that expresses the amount of overlap between two functions as one is being shifted; in a way this blends the two functions. This mathematical technique can be used in a discrete form (using sums instead of integrals) to work with the data in an image.

When convolution is applied to images, a window of a certain size is scanned across the image (see figure 12.1). The input to the operation are all the pixels that are covered by the window. The output value is the weighted sum of the input pixels, in which the weights are the values of each cell in the window. This window, together with its weights, can be expressed as a matrix, and is called the *convolution kernel*.

0	1	2	1	0
1	2	3	2	1
2	3	10	3	2
1	2	3	2	1
0	1	2	1	0

Figure 12.1
The convolution kernel. The current pixel is at the center of the matrix, and gets a weight of 10. The pixels immediately surrounding it, horizontally and vertically get a weight of 3, the ones diagonally closest get a weight of 2, etc. The current pixel gets the value of the sum of all weighted cells.

One issue that arises when you consider this for a while is: what happens at the edges of the image? Parts of the window will jut out over the edge, and there will be no input for the kernel there. There is no single correct answer to this question, but several alternative solutions are in use (see figure 12.2):

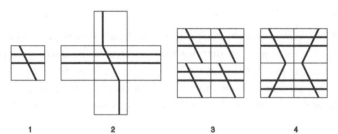

Figure 12.2
The four ways in which images can be extended beyond their border: 1. assume a constant value, 2. assume the same value as the edge, 3. tile the image, 4. mirror the image.

1 Every value outside the image is a constant, most frequently zero or some average value.

2 The edge values of the picture extend infinitely. Any "virtual" pixel outside the image is assigned the same value as the pixel at the edge closest to it.

3 The image is extended periodically or tiled. The values wrap around the edges of the image.

4 The image is mirrored at its boundaries.

Another question that might arise is: what happens if the convolution kernel has an even number of rows or columns? In this case there is no exact center cell for the window, which means that it cannot be centered on a certain pixel. Solutions to this problem can be provided by using interpolation between the cells of the kernel, or by allowing the output image to have different dimensions than the input image. In the following, however, we will assume that a convolution kernel has an odd number of rows and columns, so that there is always a clearly defined center.

12.3.1 Convolution with Image::Magick

We will now have a look at a program that implements a convolution filter algorithm using *Image::Magick*. The program provides a command-line interface to set the appropriate parameters. Since this is a full program, we'll start by declaring all the things we need:

```perl
#!/usr/bin/perl -w
use strict;
use Image::Magick;
use Getopt::Long;

my ($width, $height);
my (@kernel, $divider, $bias);
my ($x_offset, $y_offset);
$bias = 0;                              ❶ Declare and initialize
my $kernel_file;                           variables and options
my $output_type;
my $preserve_matte = 0;

GetOptions(
    "kernel-file=s"     => \$kernel_file,
    "output-type=s"     => \$output_type,
    "divider=i"         => \$divider,
    "bias=i"            => \$bias,
    "preserve-matte!"   => \$preserve_matte,
);
```

At the top of the program all the needed modules are imported; *Image::Magick* to do the graphics manipulation, and the standard *Getopt::Long* module to process command-line arguments.

❶ We declare all global variables we will need in the program. The width and height of the image operated on are stored in $width and $height. The matrix that makes up the convolution kernel will be stored in the array @kernel, and the command-line parameter --kernel-file, can be used to tell the program where to find it. The variable $preserve_matte controls whether the alpha channel of the original image will be copied, and can be set with the command-line option of --preserve-matte.

The variables $divider and $bias merit more explanation. In most cases you will want the output image to be, on average, as light or dark as the input image. To achieve this you should normalize the convolution kernel, i.e., the sum of the cells of the matrix should be exactly 1. In practice it is a lot easier to just write a matrix, and let the program worry about normalization. The variable $divider will contain the sum of the matrix cells, and will be used to normalize the output. For even greater flexibility, you can override this with a command-line option --divider. The bias is simply a number that gets added to the output after the convolution kernel has been applied. This allows you to make the image as a whole lighter or darker.

The variables `$x_offset` and `$y_offset` are used to center the window on each pixel. They express the number of cells to the left and above the center of the kernel.

```
read_kernel($kernel_file);        ❷ Read the convolution kernel
die "Divider cannot be zero\n" unless $divider;

my ($in_file, $out_file) = @ARGV;          ❸ Initialize input and output
$in_file  = '-' unless $in_file;              file names
$out_file = '-' unless $out_file;
```

❷ The first action of the program is to read in the kernel by calling the `read_kernel()` function, which we will see later. This subroutine also sets up `$divider`, `$x_offset` and `$y_offset`, and it makes sure the kernel is well-formed.

❸ Next, the input and output file names are set up. The special *Image::Magick* file name `'-'` is used, which signifies reading from STDIN or writing to STDOUT.[4] If there are no input files or output files given on the command line, this program will act as a filter; it will take its input from the standard input stream, and write its output to the standard output stream. This allows one to use it as part of a set of commands linked with pipes.

```
my $im_in = Image::Magick->new();
my $rc = $im_in->Read($in_file);               ❹ Read the input
die $rc if $rc;                                   image
($width, $height) = $im_in->Get('width', 'height');

my $im_out = Image::Magick->new(
    size => "${width}x$height");               ❺ Set up the
$rc = $im_out->Read('xc:white');                  output image
die $rc if $rc;
$im_out->Set('magick' => $im_in->Get('magick'));
```

❹ Two *Image::Magick* images are created, one for input and one for output. The input image is read in, and its width and height are extracted.

❺ The output image is initialized as a blank white canvas, the same size as the input image. This is necessary to make sure that the *Image::Magick* object contains at least one frame. The image format (the `magick` attribute) of the output image is initialized to be the same as that of the input image. Later, on output, this will be overridden by the value of `$output_type`, provided it was set.

The image can now be processed, pixel by pixel:

```
for (my $y = 0; $y < $height; $y++)
{
    for (my $x = 0; $x < $width; $x++)
    {
```

---

[4] Note that binmode has not been called on either STDIN or STDOUT. *Image::Magick* will make sure that any file handles that are used will be in the correct state.

```
            my @rgb = average_color($im_in, $x, $y);
            $im_out->Set("pixel[$x,$y]" => color_hex(@rgb));
    }
}
```

❻ Apply the convolution kernel to each pixel

❻ A loop is set up over all the pixels in the source image. For each pixel, the subroutine `average_color()` is called with the current image and the *x* and *y* coordinates as arguments. This subroutine returns a list of the red, green, and blue components after application of the weighted kernel.[5] The color of the corresponding pixel in the output image is then set to the calculated values.

After all pixels have been processed, the output image is almost ready to save. But prior to that, we need to make sure we copy back the alpha channel if that was requested:[6]

```
if ($preserve_matte)        ● Restore the alpha channel
{
    $im_in->Layer(layer => 'Matte');
    $rc = $im_out->Composite(compose => 'ReplaceMatte',
                             image   => $im_in);
    die $rc if $rc;
}

$out_file = "$output_type:$out_file" if $output_type;
$rc = $im_out->Write($out_file);        ❼ Write the output image
die $rc if $rc;
```

❼ Now that the transparency is set to what it should be, the image can be written. If an output type was specified on the command line, it is prepended here. If an output type was not specifically set, the output format of the image will be deduced from the extension of the output file name. If that is not possible, because, for example, we are writing to standard output, the value of the `magick` attribute determines the image format, which we earlier initialized to be the same as that of the input image.

This concludes the main outline of the program, and it is time to look deeper into the components that we skipped before: we need to define the subroutines that were used in the program.

First, we will have a look at the subroutine used to read in the kernel. It expects the name of a file that contains the rows of a matrix on each line, with the columns separated by whitespace. The kernel has to have an odd number of rows and an odd

---

[5] The opacity component of the source image is discarded (see the `get_color_safe()` subroutine later in the program). It is not customary to apply convolution filters to alpha channels at the same time they are applied to the color layers. It isn't difficult to adapt the program so that it works on the opacity component as well.

[6] If you have an *Image::Magick* version between 5.2.2 and 5.2.4, you will need to `Negate()` the alpha mask before applying it. Also see section 12.3.2.

number of columns,[7] but the number of rows and columns can be different. If no input file has been given, the special Perl file handle DATA will be used, which will read from the input source file, starting at the token __DATA__. The source file contains this at the end:

```
__DATA__
# This is the default kernel for this program
# The number of rows and columns should be odd

1    1    1
1    12   1
1    1    1
```

which also illustrates the format a kernel data file can take. The code to read this file is:

```
sub read_kernel
{
    my $file = shift;
    local(*DATA)                              if $file;
    open(DATA, $file) or die "$file: $!\n"  if $file;

    while(<DATA>)
    {
        chomp;
        next if /^#/ || /^\s*$/;
        push @kernel, [split];          ❽ Split and store the current row
    }

    for my $row (1 .. $#kernel)          ❾ Check that the
    {                                         kernel is well-formed
        die "Kernel row $row has wrong size\n"
            if @{$kernel[$row]} != @{$kernel[0]};
    }
    die "Kernel must be odd-sized\n"
        unless @kernel % 2 && @{$kernel[0]} % 2;

    unless ($divider)
    {
        foreach my $row (@kernel)
        {
            foreach my $col (@{$row})
            {
                $divider += $col;        ❿ Initialize divider to
            }                               sum of the kernel
        }                                   elements
    }

    $x_offset = $#kernel / 2;
    $y_offset = $#{$kernel[0]} / 2;
}
```

---

[7] Remember that the current pixel has to be placed at the center of the kernel. Only a matrix with an odd number of rows and columns will have a center element.

This subroutine checks whether a file name has been passed in, and if so, it localizes the *DATA glob (to make sure the file handle gets closed on exiting the subroutine) and reopens the DATA file handle to the file name passed in. If no file name was passed in, DATA is left in its original state, which will cause it to be opened to the source file, just after the __DATA__ token.

❽ The file is read in, line by line, skipping any lines that are empty or that start with a hash mark. This allows the file to contain comments and to be more "human readable." The elements of the matrix are stored in a global array (@kernel) of array references, in which each element in the array constitutes a row.

❾ Once the file has been read, the resulting matrix is checked to make sure that all the rows are of the same length, and that the number of rows and the number of columns are odd. This last check will also fail when a matrix is empty.

❿ If the divider hasn't been set as a command-line option, it is initialized here to the sum of all the kernel elements. Finally, the *x* and *y* offset are set.

The average_color() subroutine is defined as follows:

```
sub average_color
{
    my ($im, $x, $y) = @_;

    my @sum_rgb;

    for my $row_i (0 .. $#kernel)
    {
        for my $col_i (0 .. $#{$kernel[0]})
        {
            my @rgb = get_color_safe($im,
                $x + $row_i - $x_offset,
                $y + $col_i - $y_offset);

            for my $ci (0 .. $#rgb)
            {
                $sum_rgb[$ci] +=
                    $kernel[$row_i][$col_i] * $rgb[$ci];
            }
        }
    }

    return map {
            $_ = int($_/$divider) + $bias;
            $_ = 0 if $_ < 0;
            $_ = 255 if $_ > 255;
            $_
        } @sum_rgb;
}
```

This is where all the real work is carried out. This subroutine accepts an *Image::Magick* object and the coordinates of the pixel which is at the center of the window. It then iterates over all the elements of the kernel, calculating the appropriate *x* and *y* coordinates of the pixel that are covered by that particular cell, and getting the values for the three color components. We can't merely use the calculated *x* and *y* coordinates directly, because of edge effects. The `get_color_safe()` function is used to implement one of the methods discussed earlier (see figure 12.2).

For each color component, we add the value of the current pixel, multiplied by the value of the kernel element, to the relevant element of `@sum_rgb`. Thus, at the end of the outermost loop, the array `@sum_rgb` contains three elements, each representing one color component, and each value will be the sum of the respective color components of the pixels covered by the kernel, multiplied by the numbers in the corresponding elements of the kernel.

Before these values are returned, they are first checked to make sure they fall in the valid range between 0 and 255, and then divided by `$divider` and increased with `$bias`.

We will now return to the edge effects. When calculating the weighted average of one of the pixels close to the edge of the image, the kernel sticks out over the edge. There are several ways to deal with that (see figure 12.2). This program implements only one of them: it is assumed that pixels outside the boundaries of the image have the same value as the edge pixels.

```
sub get_color_safe
{
    my ($im, $x, $y) = @_;

    $x = 0 if $x < 0;                                    ● Edge conditions
    $y = 0 if $y < 0;
    $x = $width  - 1 if $x >= $width;
    $y = $height - 1 if $y >= $height;                     Discard
                                                           opacity
    return (split /,/, $im->Get("pixel[$x,$y]"))[0, 1, 2]; ● component (3)
}
```

This subroutine will simply return the red, green, and blue values of the pixel at the given coordinates, except when those coordinates fall outside the boundaries of the image, in which case it will return the RGB values for the pixel on the closest edge of the image.

This leaves only the definition of the `color_hex()` method, which is used only to translate a triplet of red, green, and blue values to a string of the shape #3a3a2b. This might be a familiar notation to anyone who has ever worked with colors in HTML. Each pair of hexadecimal digits after the hash mark encodes one of the red, green or blue color values, respectively.

```
sub color_hex
{
    return sprintf("#%02x%02x%02x", @_);
}
```

Table 12.2 Some results of applying convolution filters. The top row of the table shows the input images, the following rows show the result of a kernel and divider:bias combination (see the text for their meaning and the related command line options to the programs presented). A divider value of *sum* means that the sum of the kernel has been used, which is the default.

Originals						

Smooth	1 1 1 1 12 1 1 1 1	*sum:* 0	
Blur	1 1 1 1 1 1 0 0 0 1 1 0 0 0 1 1 0 0 0 1 1 1 1 1 1	sum: 0	
Edge Detect	−1 −1 −1 −1 −8 −1 −1 −1 −1	1:255	
Sharpen	−2 −2 −2 −2 48 −2 −2 −2 −2	*sum:* 0	
Emboss	0 −1 −2 1 0 −1 2 1 0	1;127	
Shadow	4 3 0 3 1 −3 0 −3 −4	*sum:* 255	

There are several ways in which this program could be improved. First, you could accept an option that controls which of the three color components the filter acts on. A second improvement could be to implement more ways of dealing with edge conditions, and allowing the user to select which of these he wants to use. Another improvement could be to preserve the transparency mask of the image, either by copying the original image's mask, or by applying the filter (separately) to an extracted mask, and inserting that into the output image.

One disadvantage of the program presented is that it is slow, terribly slow. There is little we can do about the algorithm to speed things up, but we can affect the way it is implemented. To avoid the need for checking the coordinates for each single pixel that we look at (in the `get_color_safe()` subroutine), we could make sure that there is always a value. Before doing any work, we'd increase the size of the image on the left and right by `$x_offset` pixels, and on the top and bottom by `$y_offset` pixels. The convolution would now run over only the pixels that were part of the original image, but wherever the window emerges over the edges of the *old* image, there are now the new pixels we put there. We would not have to call that subroutine for each single pixel, but we'd have to do the preparation work (allocating a new image, copying the current image to the correct spot in that new image, filling the pixels on the outside), and some new calculations. The speed improvement would be largest for larger images. For smaller images the situation could actually turn out to be worse.

12.3.2   Using Image::Magick's Convolve() method

There is, for newer versions of *Image::Magick,* a faster way to apply convolution filters to images. As of version 5.2.0, *Image::Magick* includes a `Convolve()` method. The program presented in the previous section should probably never be used in a real production sense, but it can be valuable as an illustration to demonstrate how the individual pixels of an image can be manipulated with this module. Also, there are some limitations to the `Convolve()` method that do not exist in the preceding code, that might necessitate the use of a slower explicit method. I will discuss these later.

A program using the `Convolve()` method doesn't have to do nearly as much work as the code presented earlier in this section, and can therefore be a lot simpler:

```
#!/usr/bin/perl -w
use strict;
use Getopt::Long;
use Image::Magick;

my $matrix_file;
my $output_type;
my $bias;
GetOptions(
    "matrix-file=s" => \$matrix_file,
    "output-type=s" => \$output_type,
    "bias=i"        => \$bias,
);

my $kernel = read_kernel($matrix_file);        ● Read the kernel image

my ($in_file, $out_file) = @ARGV;
$in_file  = '-' unless $in_file;
$out_file = '-' unless $out_file;
```

```perl
my $im = Image::Magick->new();
my $rc = $im->Read($in_file);          ● Read the
die $rc if $rc;                           source image

$rc = $im->Convolve(coefficients => $kernel);    ● Apply the convolution
die $rc if $rc;

if ($bias)          ● Apply the requested bias
{
    my $mask = $im->Clone();
    my $color = sprintf("#%02x%02x%02x", ($bias) x 3);
    $rc = $mask->Colorize(fill => $color, opacity => 100);
    warn $rc if $rc;
    $rc = $im->Composite(image => $mask, compose => 'Plus');
    warn $rc if $rc;
}

$out_file = "$output_type:$out_file" if $output_type;
$rc = $im->Write($out_file);
die $rc if $rc;

sub read_kernel
{
    my $file = shift;
    local(*DATA)                       if $file;
    open(DATA, $file) or die "$file: $!\n"  if $file;
    my @kernel;
    my $cols;

    while(<DATA>)
    {
        chomp;
        next if /^#/ || /^\s*$/;
        push @kernel, split;
        $cols = scalar @kernel unless $cols;
        die "Illegal row length\n" if @kernel % $cols;
    }
    die "Not a square matrix\n"
        unless @kernel == $cols * $cols;
    return \@kernel;
}

__DATA__
1   1   1
1   12  1
1   1   1
```

If you compare this program to the previous one, you'll notice immediately that the command line option --divider is not present. The reason for this is that the Convolve() method performs its own normalization on the kernel that you provide. Any divisions or multiplications on the cells of the kernel will result in no effect at all.

Another absentee is the --preserve-matte command-line option. By default, this program will preserve the matte channel, so no extra work needs to be performed.

If you want to add this option to the program, then all that's needed is to set the `matte` attribute of $im to a false value when the alpha channel should not be preserved.

The `read_kernel` method is responsible for reading a matrix of the same shape as accepted by the previous programs, and transforming it into a flat array of coefficients, which is what the `Convolve()` method expects (see page 256). Reading this subroutine also shows another limitation of the `Convolve()` method: the kernel must be square instead of rectangular.

12.3.3   Convolution with PDL

If you are really looking for speed, and are willing to spend some time learning new techniques and data structures, you could consider doing most of the work with the Perl Data Language, *PDL*. We will duplicate the functionality of the program discussed before as much as possible, but this time using the *PDL* modules.

Again, we start by declaring all the modules and variables we will need in the program, and process the options:

```
#!/usr/local/bin/perl -w
use strict;
use Getopt::Long;
use PDL;
use PDL::IO::Pic;
use PDL::Image2D;
my ($divider, $bias);

my $matrix_file;
my $output_type;
GetOptions(
    "matrix-file=s" => \$matrix_file,
    "output-type=s" => \$output_type,
    "divider=i"     => \$divider,
    "bias=i"        => \$bias,
);

die "Usage: $0 [options] --matrix-file file src dest\n"
    unless @ARGV >= 2;

my $kernel = read_kernel($matrix_file);
```

Getopt::Long is used again to process any command-line options, and we include those parts of the PDL libraries that we need: *PDL* itself, of course, *PDL::IO::Pic* to read and write images, with the help of the NetPBM package, and *PDL::Image2d* for some image manipulation functions. For a discussion of the variables, please see page 217.

Unfortunately, the *PDL::IO::Pic* interface is somewhat limited, and, unless we're willing to do a lot of work with temporary files, we cannot use the same sort of functionality as was available with *Image::Magick* in the programs in the previous sections. Since that would only serve to make this listing more difficult to follow, no attempt will be made to fully duplicate the interface. Instead, this program will simply require two file names as its last arguments.

Another argument that is mandatory for this simple program is the name of a matrix file. Why this is so will be explained when the `read_kernel()` subroutine is discussed later in this section.

```
my $im = rpic($ARGV[0]);
$im = $im->convert(double);
my @dims = $im->dims;
```

The source image is read from disk with the help of the `rpic()` subroutine from *PDL::IO::Pic*, and the values of the pixels are converted to a *double* type. This is a precaution to avoid rounding errors and overflow problems while performing the convolution calculations.

The *piddle* (PDL object) returned by `rpic()` is of a different dimensionality depending on whether the image read is a monochrome, grayscale, or RGB image.[8] For monochrome or grayscale images, the piddle will have the dimensions (*width, height*), and for RGB images (*3, width, height*). The `dims()` method returns a list of dimension sizes of a piddle. The number of elements in @dims can be used to distinguish between these two cases:

```
if(@dims == 2)         ❶ Monochrome or
{                         grayscale image
    $im = $im->conv2d($kernel, {Boundary => 'Reflect'});
    $im += $bias if $bias;
}
else       ❷ RGB image
{
    for my $i (0 .. 2)
    {
        my $channel = $im->slice("($i),:,:");
        $channel .= $channel->conv2d($kernel, {Boundary => 'Reflect'});
        $channel += $bias if $bias;
    }
}
```

❶ If the image is a grayscale image, we can simply apply the convolution kernel to the image, using the `conv2d()` function from *PDL::Image2d*. This function accepts an option[9] named *Boundary* with the possible values of (see also figure 12.2)

- *Default.* Assume periodic boundary conditions
- *Reflect.* Reflect the image at the boundaries
- *Truncate.* Truncate the image at the boundaries.

---

[8] The documentation is not explicit about this, but since all I/O through *PDL::IO::Pic* uses the PNM family of file formats, the only possibilities are grayscale, monochrome and RGB. Alpha channels are not supported at this time.

[9] The standard method in which options are passed to *PDL* functions is through a reference to a hash, with the keys being the option names, and the values being the corresponding option parameters.

After the convolution, the $bias parameter is added to the final result, as in the earlier program.

❷ If the source is an RGB image, the three color channels will have to be processed separately. *PDL* provides, among other indexing functions, the generic slice() method. This can be used to create a new *piddle* which contains part of the dimensions of the original, or, as in this case, part of the dimensionality.

The parameter to slice() is "($i),:,:", which means: for the first dimension, only give me element $i, but don't include it in the output. The second and third dimensions should be included in the output as a whole.[10] This neatly gives us a piddle with the dimensions (*width, height*), one for each color channel in turn, which can be used with the conv2d() function.

Note that there is no code to put the values of the $channel piddle back into $im; nor is it necessary. The slice() method, as with most *PDL* indexing functions, does not make an actual copy of the original data, but rather provides a window onto it. Changing the values in $channel actually changes the values in the original corresponding elements of $im.[11]

```
$im = $im->clip(0, 255)->convert(byte);
$im->wpic($ARGV[1]);
```

To ensure that the calculated values fit in the allowed range, we clip() them (setting all values below 0 to 0, and all values above 255 to 255) and convert the resulting piddle back to a *byte* type before saving the image.

All that is left now is the definition of the subroutine that reads the convolution kernel:

```
sub read_kernel
{
    my $file = shift || die "Need a matrix file name\n";
    local(*KERNEL);
    open(KERNEL, $file) or die "$file: $!\n";

    my @cols = rcols *KERNEL, {EXCLUDE => '/(^#)|(^\s*$)/'};
    die "Matrix file has no values" unless @cols;
    my $kernel = cat(@cols)->xchg(0,1);

    $divider = $kernel->sum        unless $divider;
    die "Divider cannot be zero\n" unless $divider;
    $kernel /= $divider;

    return $kernel;
}
```

❸ **Normalize the kernel**

The reading of the matrix that makes up the convolution kernel is accomplished with the help of the rcols() function. This function will read space-separated columns

---

[10] See the *PDL::Indexing* documentation for more explanation.

[11] If you don't want that, you can use the sever() or copy() methods on the resulting piddle.

from a file (or file handle) and return a list of piddles, one for each column. Unfortunately, it isn't possible to make `rcols` read from the internal DATA file handle as we did in the `read_matrix()` subroutine in the previous section, so we will have to be satisfied without a default matrix for this program.

To create a kernel matrix out of the separate columns, they are concatenated together with `cat()`. However, the resulting matrix has its rows and columns swapped, which can be remedied by using `xchg()` to exchange the first and second dimensions.

❸ The variable `$divider` is computed as the sum of all the kernel elements, unless it was given as a command-line option, and the kernel is adapted by dividing its elements by this number. Of course, care is taken not to divide by zero.

Apart from providing the `conv2d()` method, *PDL* can be tremendously useful in other areas of image manipulation. It can be difficult to understand, partly because of the data structures with which it deals, and partly because the documentation is still rudimentary. If you plan on doing a lot of image manipulation that falls outside of the application domain of *GD* or *Image::Magick*, you would be well advised to give the Perl Data Language a chance.

12.4 ALPHA CHANNELS AND TRANSPARENCY

Many image formats support some form of transparency, but only a few support full alpha channels. An alpha channel is an extra layer in your image that defines the amount of transparency or opacity for each pixel. Typically this is expressed as an integer value between 0 and 255, although floating point values between 0 and 1 are also fairly common (see, for example, the SVG format). Alpha channels normally express the amount of opacity, with a value of 0 denoting a fully transparent pixel, and a value of 255 (or 1) a fully opaque one.

Transparency can also be specified without a full alpha channel, for image formats that use a color palette. For example, the GIF format allows you to mark one of the colors in the palette as fully transparent, and the PNG format allows associating an opacity value with each palette entry separately.

Both of the main image manipulation packages for Perl, *Image::Magick* and *GD*, support transparency, but in very different ways. *GD* only allows you to mark a single color in its palette as transparent, while *Image::Magick* supports a full alpha channel model. Thus, if you want to do any serious transparency work, your only real option is *Image::Magick*.

12.4.1 Transparency and the GD module

As stated, the *GD* module only supports transparency in a very limited manner. This is due to the fact that all colors in *GD* are stored in an index, and only one of those index entries can be marked as transparent. This in turn is most likely inherited from the GIF format, wherein transparency is implemented in much the same way.

`transparent()` is the method to call for making a color transparent, and is used in the following manner:

```
use GD;

my $gd = GD::Image->new(200, 100);
my $white = $gd->colorAllocate(255, 255, 255);
my $black = $gd->colorAllocate(  0,   0,   0);

# Draw a black ellipse, centered
$gd->arc(99, 49, 150, 75, 0, 360, $black);

# Make the ellipse transparent
$gd->transparent($black);
# I changed my mind. Make the background transparent
$gd->transparent($white);
```

That's all there is to it. Note that this transparency will only be stored in image formats that can support it. If you save your *GD* object as a JPEG image, the transparency is lost.[12]

12.4.2 Transparency and Image::Magick

Image::Magick supports a full alpha channel, but it also supports simple palette-based transparency as described in the section on GD. The choice between them depends on whether you're working with an indexed image or a full color image, and in which format you are saving your results. In *Image::Magick,* the alpha channel is called the matte layer,[13] and the opacity is generally referred to as the matte value. A matte value of 0 indicates that a pixel is fully transparent, while a matte value of 255 indicates full opacity. Whenever an image has an active matte channel, the `matte` attribute for the image object should have a true value. If you want to add transparency to an image, you need to set `matte` to a true value.

Methods that can be used to directly influence the matte value of pixels are `Matte-FloodFill()`, `Draw()` with the `matte` primitive, `Transparent()`, and `Set()` with the `pixel[$x,$y]` attribute. The matte layer as a whole can be inspected using the `Layer()` method with the argument `'Matte'`, and the value of individual pixels can be read with `Get()` and the `pixel[$x,$y]` argument See appendix A for an in-depth discussion of these methods.

Replacing the whole alpha channel

The most flexible and easy way to add an alpha channel to your image is by directly inserting a grayscale image as the matte layer. The lighter the pixels in the grayscale

---

[12] *GD* also has trouble reading PNG images that contain more transparency information than it can handle internally. When you attempt to read a PNG image with a full alpha channel, an error message will be printed, and the alpha channel will be ignored.

[13] Although the terminology in the latest versions of *Image::Magick* is slowly changing towards channels, as opposed to layers.

Figure 12.3 Using a mask to insert an alpha channel into an image. The grayscale image in the middle was inserted into the alpha channel of the image on the left, producing the image on the right.

mask, the more transparent the image will become; white becomes fully transparent, and black fully opaque.

You can insert a grayscale image mask as the alpha channel (or indeed, any other channel) with the Composite() method:

```perl
#!/usr/local/bin/perl -w
use strict;
use Image::Magick;

die "Usage: $0 mask_image in_image out_image\n"
    unless @ARGV > 2;
my ($mask_file, $in_file, $out_file) = @ARGV;

my $rc;
my $mask = Image::Magick->new();
$rc = $mask->Read($mask_file);
die $rc if $rc;
my $im = Image::Magick->new();
$rc = $im->Read($in_file);
die $rc if $rc;

$rc = $mask->Quantize(colorspace => 'Gray');
die $rc if $rc;

$rc = $im->Composite(compose => 'ReplaceMatte',
                     image   => $mask,
                     tile    => 1);
die $rc if $rc;

$rc = $im->Write($out_file);
die $rc if $rc;
```

This program requires three file names, one of an image to use as a transparency mask, one of an image to which to apply the mask, and one to write the result. It transforms the $mask image into a grayscale map, which is then tiled and inserted as the matte layer into $im with the Composite() method. Since the images aren't necessarily the same size, the mask is tiled under the original image. Of course, you are free to choose any other alignment of the two images.

The method described above can be used to create any arbitrary alpha channel, even if you don't have an image with the mask you want. You can simply create a gray-scale image with the desired characteristics. By replacing the ReplaceMatte in the code with one of the other replacement operations, this can be done for each individual color channel, which can generate some really interesting effects.

Replacing the alpha value per pixel

But, suppose you have good reasons to work directly with each pixel's matte value, perhaps because you would like to create a new value based on the old value and some other parameters, or because you are very short on RAM, and can only afford to keep one image in memory at a time. The following program shows how this can be done:

```perl
#!/usr/local/bin/perl -w
use strict;
use Image::Magick;
my ($width, $height);

die "Usage: $0 in_image out_image\n" unless @ARGV > 1;
my ($in_file, $out_file) = @ARGV;

my $rc;
my $im = Image::Magick->new();
$rc = $im->Read($in_file);
die $rc if $rc;

($width, $height) = $im->Get('width', 'height');
$rc = $im->Set(matte => 1);
die $rc if $rc;

for my $x (0 .. $width)
{
    for my $y (0 .. $height)
    {
        my ($r, $g, $b, $o) =
            split /,/, $im->Get("pixel[$x,$y]");
        $o = new_opacity($x, $y, $o);
        $im->Set("pixel[$x,$y]" =>
            sprintf("#%02x%02x%02x%02x", $r, $g, $b, $o));
    }
}

$rc = $im->Write($out_file);
die $rc if $rc;

sub new_opacity
{
    my ($x, $y, $old_o) = @_;
    my $o = (abs($x/$width  - 0.5) +
            abs($y/$height - 0.5))**3 * 255;
```

```
    $o = 255 if $o > 255;
    return $o;
}
```

This program is only marginally more complex than the one in section 12.2, and shouldn't be surprising. All you need to do is replace the `new_opacity()` subroutine with one that does exactly what you want it to do, and pass it all the information it needs.

12.4.3 How to view partially transparent images

X11 displays can work only with fully transparent or fully opaque pixels. It isn't always easy to preview your image and see the transparency correctly with the `Display()` method, or even using the `display` command line tool that ImageMagick provides. Unless you have another graphics viewer that renders transparency correctly, you might just have to guess what the end result will look like while you are developing a program. Luckily, *Image::Magick* can solve the problem. You just combine the image that has an alpha channel with a background (I tend to choose a plain yellow for most applications), and view it:

```
sub show_trans
{
    my $im = shift;
    my $background = shift || "yellow";
    my ($w, $h) = $im->Get('width', 'height');
    my $bg = Image::Magick->new(size => "${w}x$h");
    $bg->Read("xc:$background");
    $bg->Composite(image => $im);
    $bg->Display;
    return $bg;
}
```

Inclusion of this little subroutine in your code while you are debugging can shorten your development cycle quite a bit. It eliminates the need to switch between your code editor, your command line, and your graphics viewer. The subroutine accepts two arguments: an *Image::Magick* object, and a background color to use wherever the image is transparent. The background color defaults to yellow, because that is a color that contrasts nicely with the majority of images with which I work. It also returns the newly created *Image::Magick* object, so that the caller can do anything he wishes with it.

12.5 *FAST MANIPULATION OF IMAGE PIXELS*

Perl is fast for the type of language it is. However, image manipulation is one of the areas in computer programming in which fast is just not fast enough; it needs to be as fast as possible. The fastest way of working with image data is to write the code that deals with the pixels in a language that can be compiled into machine code. As mentioned in the introduction to this chapter: there is a good reason that most image manipulation code is implemented in C, and not in Perl.

Perl has several facilities for extending Perl with C code, the two major ones being XS (eXternal Subroutines) and SWIG (Simplified Wrapper and Interface Generator). Both of these are difficult to learn,[14] even if you are proficient in both Perl and C. Recently, however, a new way of integrating Perl and C code has become available, through Brian Ingerson's *Inline* module. This module allows Perl programmers to integrate other programming languages directly into their own programs and modules. One can now have the speed of C in a Perl program without too much effort, and just when it is needed.

12.5.1 Using Inline::C

Let's see how we can use *Inline::C* together with *Image::Magick* to work directly with image pixels, and to do so almost as fast as if we'd written everything in C. We'll write a basic program that uses *Image::Magick* to read an image from disk, *Inline::C* to do the actual pixel manipulation, and *Image::Magick* again to save the image.

The *Inline* modules can, if instructed to do so, read their code from Perl's special DATA file handle, which starts input just after the current source file's __END__ or __DATA__ token. We will use this mechanism to include the C code that rotates the red, green, and blue channels of an image. The actual C code will be discussed later in this section, but we'll look at the Perl aspect first.

```
#!/usr/local/bin/perl -w
use strict;
use Image::Magick;
use Inline C => 'DATA';

die "Usage: $0 src_image dest_image\n" unless @ARGV >= 2;
my ($in_file, $out_file) = @ARGV;
```

The program takes a source and destination image file on the command line. The destination image will get the source image's red, green and blue channels as its green, blue and red channels, respectively, ignoring the alpha channel. The specified source image is read from disk by *Image::Magick* and the RGB data is extracted as a string from this image:

```
my $im = Image::Magick->new();
my $rc = $im->Read($in_file);
die $rc if $rc;
my ($width, $height) = $im->Get('width', 'height');

$im->Set(magick => "RGB", depth => 8);        ❶ Get the Image data as
my $rgb = $im->ImageToBlob();                       raw RGB pixels
```

❶ The RGB data that *Image::Magick* exports is a sequence of bytes. Each byte has a value between 0 and 255, because we force the image's color depth to 8 bits per

---

[14] The writing of XS has become significantly easier recently, but the changes have not been documented yet, so only very few people know how easy it actually is, and how to do things.

channel, per pixel. If you want to work with 16-bit pixels, you'll have to change that, and make sure that the C code later in the program can deal with this correctly.

The order of the bytes is straightforward: the red, green, and blue bytes are grouped together in sets of three. The groups of bytes are ordered by rows first, then by columns. The first row of the image appears in the first three times the image width bytes of the string, the second row in the second three times the image width bytes, and so forth. Later, when we cover the C part of this program, we'll discuss this to a greater extent.

Now that we have the image's raw information, we pass this off to the `rotate_rgb()` subroutine, which is actually a C function that we will soon define.

```
$rgb = rotate_rgb($width, $height, $rgb);        ❷ Rotate the RGB channels
die "Couldn't do it" unless $rgb;

$im = Image::Magick->new(
        size   => "${width}x$height",
        magick => 'RGB',
        depth  => 8);                            ❸ Create the output
$rc = $im->BlobToImage($rgb);                       image, and save it
die $rc if $rc;
$rc = $im->Write($out_file);
die $rc if $rc;
```

❷ The return value of that subroutine is another string of raw RGB information of the same size, so we create a new *Image::Magick* object, pass it the returned data, and save it with the specified file name. You'll notice that the variables `$rgb` and `$im` are reused in the program as soon as they are no longer needed. Normally I'd advocate against that, but in this particular case there is a good reason to do this: images are often large, and require a good deal of memory. If we didn't reuse the variables, then we would have four copies of the image in our program: the image object that was read in, its raw RGB data, the output of `rotate_rgb()`, and the image object created from that. Reusing these variable will, hopefully, reduce that number to two instead of four.

❸ We need to presize the `$im` object, because the raw RGB stream does not contain size information. To make sure that this code works when *Image::Magick* is compiled for 16-bit pixels, the `depth` attribute is explicitly set to 8.

This concludes the Perl part of the program. We'll now have a look at the C code that does the actual work behind the `rotate_rgb()` subroutine. As mentioned before, the C code is given, in this particular program, after the `__DATA__` token, where the *Inline* module will pick it up, compile it, and save the result.[15]

---

[15] See the documentation for *Inline* to read more about how and where your compiled C code gets cached.

The C code in this program has been written with an eye to future extensions. Presently, the task at hand is quite trivial: rotate the input red, green, and blue channels for the output image; but in the future we might want to extend this to take the alpha channel into account, so that we would work with four channels instead of three, and we might like to add other functions that work in similar ways. We might even consider making this into a separate module, once the number of functions has become large enough to start reusing them in other programs.

We'll start by defining some macros. The NCHANNELS macro defines how many channels we expect from the Perl code. In more mature code this probably would be a global variable or an argument to the defined functions. For the sake of simplicity, it is a simple macro here. The OFFSET macro calculates the offset for a byte in the RGB string, given the current x and y coordinates, the width of the image, and the channel we're interested in. The typedef defines the type of function that we will use as a callback for the main function that actually loops over the image's pixels: do_pixels().

```
__DATA__
__C__
#define NCHANNELS 3
#define OFFSET(x,y,w,c) \
    (y * w * NCHANNELS + x * NCHANNELS + c)

typedef char (*pixel_func)
    (int, int, int, int, int, char *, void *);

static SV *
do_pixels(int width, int height, char *rgba,
    pixel_func fn, void *data)
{
    char *buf;
    int bufsiz = width * height * NCHANNELS;
    int x, y, chan;

    if (!(buf = malloc(bufsiz + 1)))
        return &PL_sv_undef;
    buf[bufsiz] = '\0';

    for (chan = 0; chan < NCHANNELS; chan++)
      for (x = 0; x < width; x++)
        for (y = 0; y < height; y++)
          buf[OFFSET(x,y,width,chan)] =
              fn(x, y, chan, width, height, rgba, data);

    return newSVpv(buf, bufsiz);
}
```

The function do_pixels() accepts as arguments the image's width, height and pixel data as raw red, green, and blue bytes, and a callback function to invoke to create the individual bytes for the destination buffer. It allocates enough space to create this buffer, and then loops over each channel, each row and each column of this output buffer, and calls the specified callback for each of these coordinates.

The callback is responsible for calculating the value for the specified channel for the specified pixel. To do this it gets the current coordinates and channel, the original image's width, height and content, as well as a pointer to some data that can be anything the programmer wants it to be. The only restriction that this particular scheme imposes is that the destination image and source image need to be the same size. This function is not meant to be called from Perl; instead, wrapper functions should be written that do any extra work, such as setting up the data to pass around, initializing variables, preprocessing the image data, post-processing the image data, or anything else that is specific to that function, before calling do_pixels. The functions that this program uses are defined as follows:

```
static char
rotate_rgb_pixel(int x, int y, int chan,
    int width, int height, char *src)
{
    int src_chan = (chan == 3) ? 3 : (chan + 1) % 3;
    return src[OFFSET(x,y,width,src_chan)];
}

SV *
rotate_rgb(int width, int height, char *rgba)
{
    return do_pixels(width, height, rgba,
        &rotate_rgb_pixel, NULL);
}
```

As you can see, they are fairly trivial. The rotate_rgb() function directly calls the do_pixels() function, specifying rotate_rgb_pixel() as the callback with no user data. The work performed in rotate_rgb_pixel() is also quite minimal. It calculates the channel one higher than the current channel, and returns the value of the current byte in that channel. To make sure that the resulting channel number is valid (0, 1 or 2), the result is taken modulus three. If the current channel is the alpha channel (number 3), it is used directly. One notable fact is that this function already takes into account that there might be four channels in an image, in which case it leaves the alpha channel unchanged. If you want to use this code, or something similar to it, it would be wise to adopt the same strategy when you write your callbacks. It will save you a lot of time when you change that NCHANNELS macro at the top of the C code, and the magick attribute for the source image to RGBA.

All of the glue work that we'd normally have to provide with XS or SWIG has been taken care of by the *Inline* module. The C code that is included in the presented program is almost entirely standard C, apart from a few macros which are part of the Perl API.

SEE ALSO Even *Inline* can't do all the work for you, and if you get serious about writing plug-in C code for Perl, you will have to read up on the Perl API and understand how Perl's internals work. The documentation contained in the `perlguts`, `perlxs`, and `perlxstut` manual pages should move you a long way in the right direction. The new and upcoming book about using Perl and C [33] promises to be a valuable source of information for programmers interested in this area.

The strategic implementation of time-critical code as C, with the help of *Inline::C*, can allow a programmer to have all the power of Perl and its modules available, and at the same time be able to achieve the speed and performance that can make the difference between a failed and successful project.

12.6   SUMMARY

In this chapter we have seen how we can access and manipulate the values of individual pixels in an image. We've discussed some techniques for which this can be useful, and noticed that Perl is, by itself, not always fast enough to implement algorithms that require modification of individual pixels. However, with a smattering of C knowledge and the *Inline* modules, this problem can be solved.

## PART 4

Appendices

As is often the case with technical books such as this, the appendices contain various bits and pieces that wouldn't easily fit into any chapters without being in the way of textual flow, or in some cases simply don't belong in any specific part of the book. This is not to say that the material covered herein isn't useful; it is expected that many programmers will find the first appendix to be a very valuable resource.

Appendix A contains a fairly complete reference for the *Image::Magick* module. This includes a summary of all the image attributes and all the methods available to the user of the module, as well as deeper explanations of some of the more esoteric features of *Image::Magick*.

Appendix B contains some Perl implementations of algorithms to convert between RGB, HSV and HLS color spaces.

The last appendix includes code for a few more modules in the *Canvas::Polar* namespace, as introduced in chapter 10.

Image::Magick introduction & reference

Image::Magick, aka PerlMagick, doesn't actually come with sufficient online documentation that can be accessed with `perldoc`. Instead you are referred to the ImageMagick documentation on the web at http://www.wizards.dupont.com/cristy/www/perl.html or http://www.imagemagick.org/www/perl.html. These same HTML pages arrive bundled with the ImageMagick distribution, and I advise anyone who is going to use *Image::Magick* on a regular basis to keep it handy, because it will be needed. Even the complete documentation for *Image::Magick* does not always make everything perfectly clear, and often you'll find yourself reading the manual pages for the command line utilities `convert`, `mogrify` and `combine` to glean information which is missing from the *Image::Magick* pages. Plus, you will still have to experiment a bit, now and again, to determine the exact behavior of certain functions. The main reason for the incompleteness of the documentation is that ImageMagick is a work in progress. Many of the features are implemented with no documentation written for them. The Perl interface, *Image::Magick* is not always precisely synchronized with the command-line tools or the C API, and it needs some separate work, which often occurs at a later stage or not at all.

In addition to the examples scattered throughout this book, this appendix strives to provide a reference to get you started with *Image::Magick*, and hopefully summarizes the options and methods sufficiently. This appendix covers *Image::Magick* up to version 5.4.4. The API of *Image::Magick* hasn't always been entirely stable because of major changes to functionality, and name changes to reflect the actual intent or operations better than before. Most of the code in the book was written for *Image::Magick* version 5.2.6, and should run fine against that version. Between versions 5.2.6 and 5.4.4 some API changes were introduced that broke some of the code in this book. Where possible the text in this book has been adapted to reflect those changes.

The ImageMagick developers have agreed to provide as much backward compatibility with the code in this book as possible, and have in fact, reversed some API changes in version 5.4.4 to make that work, but they can, of course, guarantee nothing. This means that you should be able to trust the code in this book and the documentation in this appendix up to a certain point, but that you should consult the *Image::Magick* documentation when things don't seem to work as described herein.

In short, you should make sure that you have *Image::Magick* version 5.4.4–5 or later to ensure that the code and documentation in this book match the actual implementation best.

A.1   BASIC IMAGE::MAGICK OPERATIONS

To create an *Image::Magick* object, use the new() constructor, which takes any of the arguments that the Set() method accepts (see the *Image::Magick* documentation, and later sections in this appendix).

```
use Image::Magick;
$im  = Image::Magick->new();
$im2 = Image::Magick->new(size       => '200x400',
                          background => 'PeachPuff');
```

or, if you prefer the indirect syntax (which I do not):

```
$im3 = new Image::Magick;
```

Image::Magick objects are implemented as a blessed reference to an array. This means that any standard Perl array operations can be used to work with the object. The elements of the array are the individual images, and every method can be called on each image separately. You remove an image from an *Image::Magick* array by undefining it (or by using the Perl built-in splice). To wipe out all images, assign an empty list to the array to which it refers.

```
# Create a new object, and read two image files
$im1 = Image::Magick->new();
$im1->Read($file1);
$im1->Read('*.png');

# Get rid of the third image (but keep the slot)
$im1->[2] = undef;
```

```
# Clone only the fifth image in $im1 into $im2
$im2 = $im1->[4]->Clone();

# Add the first image from $im1 as the last of $im2
push @{$im2}, $im1->[0];

# Add all the images of $im2 to $im1
push @$im1, @$im2;

# Get rid of the first and last image in $im1
shift @$im1;
pop @$im1;

# Remove all images from $im1
@{$im1} = ();

# The following does the same, but is semantically unattracive.
@{$im1} = undef;
```

Initially, an *Image::Magick* object is empty, i.e., it contains no images. To create an image in the array, use the `Read()` method:

```
$im->Read('logo.png');
$im->Read('logo.png', 'foo.jpeg');
$im->Read(@filenames, '*.png');
$im->Read('xc:white');
$im->Read('label:Just some text');
$im->Read('gradation:lavender-chartreuse');
$im->Read('graphics/vr/*.jpg');
```

The arguments to `Read()` consist of an optional format specification and, in most instances, a file name. If the format specification has not been included, *Image::Magick* will try to determine the format from the file headers. For a partial list of supported file formats see table 2.1 on page 24, and for a list of the special internal formats see table 2.2 on page 25.

If you have already read an image in, or you have image data from, for example, *GD* that you would like to transfer to an *Image::Magick* object, you can use the `BlobToImage()` method:

```
# $gd is a GD::Image object
$im->BlobToImage($gd->png);

# $jpg contains JPEG data read from a file
$im->BlobToImage($jpg);
```

A.2 ERROR HANDLING

From the perspective of error handling, there are two sorts of *Image::Magick* operations: Those that return an object, and those that don't. In case of a failure, the returned value is a string containing the error, with an error number embedded in it. In the case of success, the returned scalar is either the reference to an object, or it is undefined.

The methods that return an object, such as `new()`, `Clone()` and `Montage()`, should be checked by making sure that the returned value is indeed a reference to an object:

```
my $im = Image::Magick->new();
die "Image::Magick->new failed: $im" unless ref $im;

my $copy = $im->Clone();
die "Cannot clone: $copy" unless ref $copy;

# Other code omitted ...

my $montage = $im->Montage();
if (ref $montage)
{
    # do what is necessary with the montage
}
else
{
    warn "Couldn't create montage: $montage";
}
```

It's a good practice to check for errors on any of the read-and-write operations, and you do yourself a great service if you also check for errors on all the other calls. It will be a big help in identifying typos in attributes:

```
$rc = $im->Read($filename);
die "Cannot read $filename: $rc\n" if $rc;

$rc = $im->Set(attribute => 'value');
warn $rc if $rc;

$rc = $im->Solarize();
warn "Cannot Solarize image ($rc), continuing\n" if $rc;

# Note the 'and', instead of a more customary 'or'
$rc = $im->Frame(geometry => '20x20+13+7') and
    warn "Frame: $rc";
```

Error numbers below 400 indicate a warning, meaning that the requested command did not succeed, but that no damage has been done. Conversely, an error above 400 means that something internal in the *Image::Magick* object is irreversibly wrong, due to acute memory shortage or other serious errors. Hence, an error code of 400 and above means that you should probably give up trying to do anything more with the object. Note that a failure to read an image because the file doesn't exist results in an error code of 330, which in *Image::Magick*'s view is not fatal. It might, however, be regarded as fatal from the perspective of the application, if all it does is read.

```
$rc = $im->Read('file.jpg');
if ($rc)
{
    my ($errno) = $rc =~ /(\d+)/;
    ($errno >= 400) ? die "Fatal error: $rc" :warn "Error: $rc";
}
```

Once you have some images in the array, the *Image::Magick* methods can be applied to all images in the array or to a single image:

```
# Set the color space for all images
$im->Quantize(colorspace => 'Gray');

# Annotate the 3rd image
$im->[2]->Annotate(text => 'Annotation', x => 10, y => 20);
```

To write an image to disk, the `Write()` method is available. `ImageToBlob()` can be used to get the image data directly, for example to print it to an already open file handle, or to store it in a database.

```
# Write all the images to a MNG file
$rc = $im->Write('mng:file.mng') and warn $rc;

# Write the second image to a PNG file
$rc = $im->[1]->Write('png:file.png') and warn $rc;

# Print the image data for the third file to STDOUT
binmode STDOUT;
print STDOUT $im->[3]->ImageToBlob();
```

It should never be necessary, in well-written, modularized, correctly scoped programs, to explicitly destroy an *Image::Magick* object. That will automatically happen when the last reference to it goes out of scope. However, in real life we almost never have code that is so squeaky clean that every reference to each object and variable goes out of scope exactly when you want it to, freeing up the memory that is associated with it. If you are working with *Image::Magick* objects that contain images of 8,000 by 24,000 pixels, then you might very well want to reclaim the memory as soon as you can. In cases such as this, simply undefine the reference to the object:

```
my $im = Image::Magick->new();
# Do things with $im
undef $im;
```

A.3   DEALING WITH API CHANGES BETWEEN VERSIONS

One problematic aspect about the PerlMagick interface to ImageMagick is that it is very changeable. Commands appear and disappear, options change or disappear, and calling conventions evolve. You can't protect your source code from all these changes, but you can (after you discover a method name is no longer the same) do something about some problems.

One example of a changed method name is the evolution of `Layer()` to `Channel()` in version 5.2.9, although the `Layer()` method returned in version 5.4.4. Suppose that you have an elaborate program that calls `Layer()` several times, and that has to run on versions after and before the change. You could put something such as this at the start of your program:[1]

---

[1] Warnings are temporarily disabled in this block, because otherwise Perl will complain about either the name Layer or the name Channel being used only once.

```
use Image::Magick;

BEGIN
{
    no warnings;
    *Image::Magick::Layer = *Image::Magick::Channel
        if ($Image::Magick::VERSION ge "5.29" and
            $Image::Magick::VERSION lt "5.44")
}
```

This will insert an entry with the name Layer in the symbol table for the *Image::Magick* package that is identical to the entry for the `Channel()` method. So, what you have just done is create an alias with the old function name for the new function name, effectively giving you back access via the old name. Then, when you have been able to change all calls to `Layer()` in your program to `Channel()`, you can change the BEGIN block above to:

```
BEGIN
{
    no warnings;
    *Image::Magick::Channel = *Image::Magick::Layer
        if ($Image::Magick::VERSION lt "5.29")
}
```

and hopefully, some time in the future, you can remove that code altogether.

Of course, if the interface changes, or arguments disappear, there is not a lot that can be easily done. One possibility would be to write wrapper functions that conduct translations between the calling conventions for the various versions. This can quickly get out of hand.

A.4   IMAGE ATTRIBUTES

Image::Magick images have many attributes that can be set or altered with the `Set()` method, and even more that can be read with the `Get()` method. Many of these attributes can be overridden in method calls.

A.4.1   Read-write attributes

The following list shows the *Image::Magick* image attributes that can be set as well as read, and the type value for each attribute.

- `adjoin` *true/false*.   Join images into a single multi-image file. If this is set to a false value, a multi-image object will be saved as multiple files. The default behavior depends on the file format in which you are saving the object.

- `antialias` *true/false*.   Remove pixel aliasing. This will remove the ragged edges when you work with, for example, `Draw()` or `Annotate()`.

- `background` *color spec*.   The image background color. This color is used for any operation that creates background space. It also can influence how transparency ends up in certain file formats.

- `blue_primary` *x-value, y-value.* Chromaticity blue primary point. Don't worry about it if you are unfamiliar with it.

- `bordercolor` *color spec.* Set the border color of the image.

- `cache_threshold` *integer.* *Image::Magick* will use memory to store and manipulate images up to this value (default 80 MB). If it needs more memory, it will use the disk. Specify the size as an integer number of Megabytes.

- `colormap[i]` *color spec.* The color in the palette at position i.

- `colors` *integer.* The number of unique colors in the image. If this is set, the actual number of colors in the image will be no greater than this number. It takes effect only when `Quantize()` is called.

- `colorspace`. The color space to work in when reducing colors. Valid values are GRAY, OHTA, RGB, Transparent, XYZ, YCbCr, YIQ, YPbPr, YUV and CMYK. The Transparent color space is also known as RGBA, i.e., RGB with an alpha channel. This option is only useful when the `Quantize()` method is called on the image.

- `compress`. The type of image compression to use. This has an effect only if the image format you are using supports the compression method requested. Valid values are None, BZip, Fax, Group4, JPEG, LZW, RunLengthEncoded and Zip.

- `delay` integer. This parameter specifies the delay between frames in an animation in hundredths of a second.

- `depth` integer. The bit depth of the image, one of 8 or 16.

- `dispose` *integer.* The GIF disposal method. Valid values are

0	Unspecified.
1	Don't dispose between frames.
2	Restore the background color.
3	Restore the previous frame.

- `display`. The X server to contact.

- `dither` *true/false.* Apply Floyd/Steinberg error diffusion for colors that don't exactly match those in the color palette. Note that this attribute requires a call to `Quantize()` to take effect.

- `file` *filehandle.* Set the file handle to use for the `Read()` and `Write()` methods.

- `filename` *string.* The file name of the image. The default is the name of the file from which the image was read in.

- `fill` *color.* The fill color to use.

- font *font spec*. The font to use for text operations, such as `Annotate()` (also see the `pointsize` attribute). A full description of valid font specifications can be found on page 278.

- fuzz *integer*. For algorithms that search for a target color, all colors within this distance (in RGB space) will be considered equal.

- green_primary. See `blue_primary`.

- interlace. The type of interlacing to use. Valid values are None, Line, Plane or Partition. Not every image format supports any or all of these interlacing schemes.

- iterations *integer*. See `loop`.

- loop *integer*. Add the Netscape loop extension to a GIF animation. A value of 0 means loop forever, any other value indicates the number of repeats.

- magick *string*. Set the image format. Valid values are any of the supported formats (see table 2.1 on page 24).

- matte *true/false*. This is true if the image has transparency.

- mattecolor *color spec*. The color that should be made transparent for this image.

- monochrome *true/false*. The image is black and white.

- page. The preferred canvas size and location. Valid values are Letter, Tabloid, Ledger, Legal, Statement, Executive, A3, A4, A5, B4, B5, Folio, Quarto, 10x14 or a *geometry* specification. You also use this to position individual scenes in an animation at different offsets.

- pen *color spec*. The foreground color, or pen color to be used when drawing objects or text. This is deprecated in favor of the `fill` and `stroke` attributes.

- pixel[x,y] *color spec*. The color of the pixel at coordinates (*x, y*). The `Get()` method with this attribute returns the Red, Green, Blue, and Alpha values as a string of four comma-separated decimal numbers, e.g., 73,23,128,255. The `Set()` method with this attribute expects any of the color specifications described on page 278.

- pointsize *integer*. The point size of a TrueType or PostScript font (also see the `font` attribute).

- preview. The type of preview for an image. One of Rotate, Shear, Roll, Hue, Saturation, Brightness, Gamma, Spiff, Dull, Grayscale, Quantize, Despeckle, ReduceNoise, AddNoise, Sharpen, Blur, Threshold, Edge Detect, Spread, Shade, Raise, Segment, Solarize, Swirl, Implode, Wave, OilPaint, CharcoalDrawing or JPEG. The default is JPEG. This takes effect only when an image is written in preview mode, e.g., `$im->Write('preview:view.jpg')`.

- quality *integer*. The compression level. This is valid only for certain image types, such as JPEG, PNG and MIFF.

- red_primary. See blue_primary.

- rendering_intent. The type of rendering intent. Valid values are Undefined, Saturation, Perceptual, Absolute and Relative.

- scene *integer*. The number of the image as a scene in a sequence.

- server. See display.

- size *geometry*. The width and height of an image.

- stroke *color*. The stroke color to use when drawing.

- subimage *integer*. The number of the image as a subimage.

- subrange *integer*. The number of images relative to the base image.

- tile *string*. The name of the tile.

- texture *filename*. The name of the image file used as a texture tile for the background of the image.

- units. The units of image resolution (also see the density attribute). Valid values are Undefined, PixelsPerInch and PixelsPerCentimeter.

- verbose *true/false*. Print detailed information about the image.

- view *string*. FlashPix viewing parameters.

- white_point. Chromaticity white point (see also blue_primary).

A.1.2   Read-only attributes

The following list shows the *Image::Magick* image attributes that are read-only, and the type value for each attribute.

- base_columns *integer*. The image width before any applied transformations.

- base_filename *filename*. The original file name of the image.

- base_rows *integer*. The image height before any applied transformations.

- class. The class of the image, one of Direct or Pseudo. An image of class Direct has its colors stored per pixel, while a Pseudo class image uses a color palette.

- columns *integer*. The number of columns, i.e., width, in an image.

- comment *string*. The image comment. While this is a read-only attribute, the image comment can be set with the Comment() method.

- density *geometry*. The vertical and horizontal resolution of an image in ppi (pixels per inch), but also see the units attribute. The default is 72×72.

- filesize *integer*. The size of the image on disk, in bytes.

- filter *filter type*. The filter used by methods that require one, such as `Transform()`. Should be one of Point, Box, Triangle, Hermite, Hanning, Hamming, Blackman, Gaussian, Quadratic, Cubic, Catrom, Mitchell, Lanczos, Bessel, or Sinc.

- format *integer*. A string describing the image format (also see the `magick` attribute).

- gamma *double*. The gamma level of the image.

- height *integer*. The height of the image in pixels.

- label *string*. The image label.

- mean *double*. The mean error per pixel that was introduced by a color reduction. This is set on a call to `Quantize()` with *measure_error* set to a true value (see page 268).

- normalized_max *double*. The normalized maximum error per pixel that was introduced by a color reduction. This is set on a call to `Quantize()` with measure_error set to a true value (see page 268).

- normalized_mean *double*. The normalized mean error per pixel that was introduced by a color reduction. This is set on a call to `Quantize()` with measure_error set to a true value (see page 268).

- pipe *integer*. True when the image was read from a pipe as opposed to a file.

- rows *integer*. The number of rows, i.e. height, in an image.

- signature *string*. The signature associated with the image. For older versions of *Image::Magick* this is an MD5 sum, in more recent versions, a SHA1-256 signature. Also see the `Signature()` method.

- tainted *true/false*. True if the image has been modified, false if not.

- type. The image type, one of Bilevel, Grayscale, Palette, TrueColor, Matte or ColorSeparation.

- width *integer*. The width of the image in pixels.

- x_resolution *integer*. The resolution of the image in the *X* direction (also see density and units).

- y_resolution *integer*. The resolution of the image in the *Y* direction (also see density and units).

A.5 METHODS

Image::Magick provides many methods for manipulating, enhancing or otherwise working with images. This section provides an overview and short description of the methods. Almost all methods[2] can be called by the name specified here, as well as by that name with Image appended. Thus, `Read()` can also be called as `ReadImage()`, `Annotate()` as `AnnotateImage()` and `Quantize()` as `QuantizeImage()`. Some methods can be called by even more names; in those cases I have added the aliases to the description of its preferred name.

Many methods can be called with a single argument, instead of the name-value pairs specified in this chapter. It is normally a good idea to use the longer version to specify arguments, because that documents exactly what it is you're doing, instead of relying on the reader of the code to know what that particular single argument does. In less complicated cases, such as `Scale()` or `Blur()` the chances of confusion are slight. However, for the more complex methods that allow shortcuts, such as `Modulate()`, I would strongly advise getting in the habit of using the longer form.

Some arguments that are common to many methods are discussed in section A.6, to prevent repetition of their explanation in the following. The *radius* argument to many methods has been available since version 5.2.4. Before that version, this attribute was called *order*.

AddNoise()

Add noise to an image.

```
$im->AddNoise(noise => noise)
```

This method adds some random noise to an image. The parameter noise can be one of Uniform, Gaussian, Multiplicative, Impulse, Laplacian, or Poisson.

  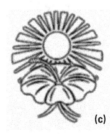

Figure A.1
The AddNoise (a), Blur (b) and Charcoal (c) filters.

Animate()

Animate an image sequence to a display.

```
$im->Animate(arguments)
```

`Animate()` can take any argument that is a settable attribute. Can also be called with the aliases `animate()` and `animateimage()`. This only works for X11 displays.

---

[2] Exceptions are `BlobToImage()`, `ImageToBlob()`, `Mogrify()`, `MogrifyRegion()`, and `QueryColor()`.

Annotate()

Annotate an image with text.

```
$im->Annotate(text      => string,
              font      => string,
              pointsize => integer,
              x         => integer,
              y         => integer,
              stroke    => color,
              fill      => color,
              density   => integer,
              box       => color,
              geometry  => geometry,
              gravity   => gravity,
              translate => "float,float",
              scale     => "float,float",
              rotate    => float,
              skewX     => float,
              skewY     => float)
```

This method can be used to place text on an image. If the value of the text argument starts with an @, the string will be read from the file with the filename following the @.[3] The font attribute is described on page 278, the gravity parameter on page 281, and the color values for stroke and fill on page 278. The geometry parameter can be used as a shortcut for the x and y arguments. If the box argument is given, a filled box of that color will be drawn with the text on top of it. The translate, scale, rotate, skewX and skewY arguments can be used to transform and warp the text. Also see Draw() on page 257.

Append()

Append a set of images.

```
$new_im = $im->Append(stack => boolean)
```

The sequence of images in $im will be joined together into a single image. All the images must have either the same height, in which case they will be joined horizontally, or the same width, which means they will be joined vertically. The stack attribute can be used to force a stacking order if, for example, all your images have the same height and the same width. A value of 'False' will force a horizontal stack, and a value of 'True' a vertical one. Append() returns a new image, and can also be called by the aliases append() and appendimage().

Average()

Take the average of a set of images.

```
$new_im = $im->Average()
```

---

[3] Make sure the file exists. Some versions of ImageMagick crash if it doesn't.

The `Average()` method will return a new image which is the average of all the images in `$im`. Other valid names for this method are `average()`, and `averageimage()`.

BlobToImage()
Read an image from a scalar.

```
$im->BlobToImage($Image_data)
```

This method reads image data from a Perl scalar variable. This allows the reading of images from sources with which *Image::Magick* cannot deal directly, e.g., database fields or images fetched directly from an HTTP server. Also see `ImageToBlob()`. Aliases for this method are `blobtoimage()`, and `blobto()`.

Blur()
Blur an image.

```
$im->Blur(radius => integer)
```

Blur an image by applying a convolution kernel. The parameter is the order of the convolution kernel: the larger the radius, the larger the kernel. The kernel must always be smaller than the image, so be sure to pick one that is low enough. Good values are odd numbers between 3 and 31. Also see `GaussianBlur()` and `Convolve()`.

Border()
Draw a border around an image.

```
$im->Border(geometry => geometry,
            fill     => color)
$im->Border(width    => integer,
            height   => integer,
            fill     => color)
```

Put a border around an image. The depth of the left and right border are specified by width, and the depth of the top and bottom one with height. The *geometry* parameter provides a shortcut notation for width × height. Also see `Frame()`.

Channel()
Extract a channel from an image. See the description of `Layer()`.

```
$im->Channel(channel => channel name)
```

This method is the new name for the `Layer()` method since version 5.2.9.

Charcoal()
Apply a charcoal filter.

```
$im->Charcoal(radius => integer)
```

This method makes an image look more or less as if it has been drawn with charcoal sticks. The larger *radius* is, the rougher the effect will look.

Chop()

Remove part of an image.

```
$im->Chop(geometry => geometry)
$im->Chop(x        => integer,
          y        => integer,
          width    => integer,
          height   => integer)
```

Removes the part of the image specified by the *geometry* parameter, or by the *x, y, width* and *height* parameters. Also see `Crop()`.

Coalesce()

Merge a sequence of images.

```
$new_im = $im->Coalesce()
```

This method can be used to apply the effects of an animation. This is useful when you have an animation in which all frames are not the same size or do not have the same offset. If you want to export this animation to another format, such as MPEG, which doesn't allow different frame sizes, you can use `Coalesce()` to ensure that all the frames are of the same size. In effect, this method runs the animation, and takes a snapshot of each resulting frame with the size of the first image.

Image::Magick 5.2.2 and before change the current image, later versions return a new image reference. In some versions of *Image::Magick*, the `Coalesce()` method doesn't work correctly.

ColorFloodfill()

Fill parts of an image with a color.

```
$im->ColorFloodfill(geometry    => geometry,
                    x           => integer,
                    y           => integer,
                    fill        => color,
                    bordercolor => color)
```

Change the color of all neighboring pixels that match the color of the pixel at coordinates (x, y) to the color specified by the *fill* argument. If the *bordercolor* argument is present, the color value is changed for any neighboring pixel that is not that border color. The image attribute *fuzz* influences which colors will be seen as the same as the specified colors. See also `MatteFloodfill()`.

Colorize()

Colorize an image.

```
$im->Colorize(fill    => color,
              opacity => string)
```

This method colorizes the image with the color specified by the *fill* argument. The *opacity* parameter expresses the amount of colorization as a percentage. If you want to apply separate colorization values to the individual channels of an image, provide a string with list of values for each channel, separated with slashes, e.g., `"10/50/25"`.

Comment()

Add a comment to your image.

```
$im->Comment(comment => string)
```

Use this method if you want to add a comment to your image. Most image formats support comments in files. See page 280 for the format of the string. Also see `Label()`.

Composite()

Combine one image with another.

```
$im->Composite(image    => image object,
               compose  => operator,
               geometry => geometry,
               x        => integer,
               y        => integer,
               gravity  => gravity,
               opacity  => percent,
               tile     => boolean)
```

The `Composite()` method combines the pixels of two images with the operator specified by the *compose* parameter. If it is not specified, the pixels in `$im` will be replaced by the pixels in the image specified by the *image* parameter. The values for *compose* can be `Over`, `In`, `Out`, `Atop`, `Xor`, `Plus`, `Minus`, `Add`, `Subtract`, `Difference`, `Bumpmap`, `Replace`, `ReplaceRed`, `ReplaceGreen`, `ReplaceBlue`, `ReplaceMatte`, `Blend`, `Displace`, `Annotate`, or `Modulate`.[4] For a description of what they do, see section 8.2.2, page 142. The *opacity* parameter is only used for Blend, and specifies how opaque the composite image should be. When *tile* is set to a true value, the composite image will be tiled repeatedly on the image.

Contrast()

Change the image contrast.

```
$im->Contrast(sharpen => boolean)
```

This method changes the contrast of an image. Use a true value for the *sharpen* attribute for contrast enhancement, and a false value for reduction.

---

[4] This is the list for *Image::Magick* 5.2.6. For later versions, Blend has disappeared, and the various Replace operators have been renamed to `Copy`. For a definitive list, see the current documentation for your installation.

Convolve()

Apply a convolution kernel to an image.

```
$im->Convolve(coefficients => array reference)
```

The array reference should refer to an array of n^2 elements, in which n is the order of the convolution kernel.[5] To specify a convolution kernel of order 3, with coefficients

$$\begin{pmatrix} 4 & 3 & 2 \\ 3 & 2 & 1 \\ 2 & 1 & 0 \end{pmatrix}$$

the following code can be used:

```
@kernel = (4, 3, 2,
           3, 2, 1,
           2, 1, 0);
$im->Convolve(coefficients => \@kernel);
```

Also see section 12.3, on page 215 for a more general discussion on convolution.

Copy() or Clone()

Make a copy of an image object.

```
$new_im = $im->Copy()
$new_im = $im->Clone()
```

Other names for this method are copy(), copyimage(), clone(), and cloneimage().

Crop()

Crop an image.

```
$im->Crop(geometry => geometry)
$im->Crop(x        => integer,
          y        => integer,
          width    => integer,
          height   => integer)
```

Removes the part of the image outside of the area specified by the *geometry* parameter, or by the *x, y, width* and *height* parameters. See also Chop() and Transform().

CycleColorMap()

Displace an image's color map.

```
$im->CycleColorMap(amount => integer)
```

This method changes the color map (palette) by moving each entry down by the number of places specified by the parameter, rotating the ones that fall off the end to the start.

---

[5] Convolution kernels for *Image::Magick* are always square.

Deconstruct()
Break up an image sequence.

```
$im->Deconstruct()
```

This method breaks down an image sequence into its constituent parts, and can be used for GIF or MNG animations.

Despeckle()
Reduce speckles and noise in an image.

```
$im->Despeckle()
```

This filter attempts to remove speckles and spots from your images. Also see `ReduceNoise()`.

Display()
Display an image on screen.

```
$im->Display(arguments)
```

Display takes any argument that is a settable image attribute. Aliases for this method are `display()` and `displayimage()`. This works only on X11 displays.

Draw()
Draw on an image.

```
$im->Draw(primitive   => shape identifier,
        points      => string,
        method      => method,
        stroke      => color,
        fill        => color,
        tile        => image object,
        linewidth   => float,
        bordercolor => color,
        translate   => float,
        scale       => "float,float",
        rotate      => float,
        x           => float,
        y           => float,
        skewX       => float,
        skewY       => float,
        gravity     => gravity)
```

This method allows you to draw on an image, using one of the drawing primitives *point, line, rectangle, roundRectangle, arc, ellipse, circle, polyline, polygon, bezier, path, color, matte, text,* or *image.*

The coordinates and dimensions of the points, angles and lines involved in the drawing are given as a single string to the *points* argument. The contents of the string are always a space-separated list of pairs of numbers, separated by an optional comma, e.g., `"12,56"` or `"34,56 67,23 45,0"`.

The *scale*, *rotate*, *skewX* and *skewY* attributes can be used to transform the element that you are drawing. The *stroke* and *fill* attributes give the stroke and fill color, respectively.

Not all combinations of attributes make sense. Some can be used with all primitives, some only with one. Some attributes provide a shorthand for others, or act differently in the presence of others. The possibility of combinations is so great, that I'll leave it to your inquiring nature to discover how to tweak each of them.

A more detailed description of each of the primitives follows:

point

Simply draw a point at the specified coordinate. To draw a single red pixel at coordinates (23,45):

```
$im->Draw(primitive => 'point',
          stroke    => 'red',
          points    => '23,45');
```

line

Draw a line between two points. To draw a green line from (12,34) to (23,45):

```
$im->Draw(primitive => 'line',
          stroke    => 'green',
          points    => '12,34 23,45');
```

rectangle

Draw a rectangle with the specified upper-left and bottom-right corners. Use *stroke* to draw the rectangle, and *fill* to fill it. To draw a green rectangle with red fill:

```
$im->Draw(primitive => 'rectangle',
          stroke    => 'green',
          fill      => 'red',
          points    => '12,34 23,45');
```

roundRectangle

Unfortunately, the coordinates for this primitive differ greatly from the ones for *rectangle*. The *roundRectangle* primitive requires three pairs of coordinates: the center of the rectangle, the width and height, and the horizontal and vertical number of pixels used to round the corners. To draw a rectangle of width 50 and height 30, centered around the point (65,75), with rounded corners that take 12 pixels from the horizontal edge, and 6 from the vertical:

```
$im->Draw(primitive => 'roundRectangle',
          stroke    => 'green',
          fill      => 'red',
          points    => '65,75 50,30 6,3');
```

The size of the rounded corners should be less than or equal to the height or width of the rectangle. If they are both equal to half, the resulting figure will be an ellipse. For example, the coordinate string "30,30 40,20 20,10" will result in an ellipse centered on the point (30,30), with a horizontal axis of 40, and a vertical axis of 20 pixels.

circle

`Circle` requires the coordinate of the center and a coordinate of a point on the edge. To draw a circle around (50,50) with a radius of 35:

```
$im->Draw(primitive => 'circle',
          stroke    => 'green',
          fill      => 'red',
          points    => '50,50 50,85');
```

ellipse

This can be used to draw an ellipse, or part of an ellipse. The coordinates required are the center of the ellipse, the width and height, and the start and end angle. To draw a full ellipse around (50,50) with a horizontal axis of 25, and a vertical axis of 40:

```
$im->Draw(primitive => 'ellipse',
          stroke    => 'green',
          fill      => 'red',
          points    => '50,50 25,40 0,360');
```

Note that angles go clockwise for this method, and start at the right side. Also note that using a fill with a partial ellipse does not likely net you the result you were seeking. Use *arc* instead.

arc

This primitive also describes a part of an ellipse, but requires a different set of coordinates. The first and second coordinates describe the *bounding box* of the ellipse, i.e., the upper-left and bottom-right corner of the rectangle that enclose the ellipse. The third coordinate expresses the start and end angles of the part of the ellipse. To draw the left half of an ellipse bounded by the rectangle with corners (0,0) and (100,50):

```
$im->Draw(primitive => 'arc',
          stroke    => 'green',
          fill      => 'red',
          points    => '0,0 100,50 90,270');
```

For *arc* angles are counted counter-clockwise, as they should be.

polyline and polygon

Define 3 or more points that will be joined by a line of color *stroke*. The area surrounded by that line will be filled with the color specified by *fill*. In the case of polygon, the last point will be connected with the first point, though for a polyline this will not be done. The fill will be the same for both. Draw a (less than perfect) star:

```
$im->Draw(primitive => 'polygon',
          stroke    => 'green',
          fill      => 'red',
          points    => '20,20 70,20 30,70 45,0 50,70');
```

bezier

Draw a bezier curve, defined by three or more points.

```
$im->Draw(primitive => 'bezier',
        stroke      => 'green',
        fill        => 'red',
        points      => '0,100 100,100 200,0 0,0');
```

Also see the discussion of bezier curves for the *path* primitive on page 282.

path

This primitive allows you to draw a generic shape which is defined by a set of movement operators. This is the only method that directly allows you to create shapes that have holes in them, as well as other complex multipart shapes. Paths are defined in the same way as they are in the Scalable Vector Graphics (SVG) format (also see page 19 and reference entries [22] and [16]). See page 281 for a description of the format of the *points* strings that this primitive takes.

color

This primitive can be used to perform a number of different functions, depending on the value of the method attribute.

point

The target pixel will receive the color set by stroke.

replace

Each pixel that matches the color of the target pixel will get the color set by stroke.

floodfill

All neighboring pixels matching the color of the target pixel are set to the color denoted by fill.

filltoborder

All neighboring pixels of the target pixel are set to the fill color, until pixels that have the border color are encountered (see bordercolor on page 246).

reset

All image pixels are reset to the stroke color.

```
# Set point (20,20) to green
$im->Draw(primitive => 'color',
        stroke      => 'green',
        method      => 'point',
        points      => '20,20');
# Fill all neighbors of (20,20) of the same color
$im->Draw(primitive => 'color',
```

```
fill      => 'red',
method    => 'floodfill',
points    => '20,20');
```

Also see `ColorFloodfill()` and the fuzz attribute on page 248.

matte

This primitive acts the same way as *color*, except that it sets each pixel's matte value to transparent. Also see `MatteFloodfill()`.

text

Put text on an image, using the current settings of the image attributes *font* and *point-size*, and the color specified by *fill*. One coordinate needs to be specified: the left side of the baseline of the string. The text to be drawn should be given as part of the *points* argument. To draw the text, *Some text*, in the current font and size, with the current fill color on the image:

```
$im->Draw(primitive => 'text',
       points    => '40,40 "Some text"');
```

See "String formatting" on page 280 for a description of special escapes in the string, and the `Annotate()` method for a more convenient way to do this.

image

Superimpose another image on this one. See `Composite()` for a much better way to accomplish this.

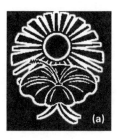  

Figure A.2
The Edge (a),
Emboss (b) and
Frame (c) filters.

Edge()

Detect edges in an image.

```
$im->Edge(radius => integer)
```

Apply a convolution kernel to detect edges in an image. Good values for radius are odd numbers between 3 and 31. See also `Convolve()`.

Emboss()

Emboss an image.

```
$im->Emboss(radius => integer)
```

Apply a convolution kernel to emboss an image. Good values for radii are odd numbers between 3 and 31. Also see `Convolve()` and `Shade()`.

Enhance()

Enhance an image.

```
$im->Enhance()
```

This filter reduces noise in an image by replacing each pixel with a weighted average of a 5 by 5 cell around it. Only pixels that are within a certain distance in the RGB color space are taken into account.

Equalize()

Apply histogram equalization to an image. Also see Normalize.

```
$im->Equalize()
```

Flip()

Mirror an image vertically.

```
$im->Flip()
```

Flop()

Mirror an image horizontally.

```
$im->Flop()
```

Frame()

Draw a frame around an image.

```
$im->Frame(geometry => geometry,
           fill     => color)
$im->Frame(width    => integer,
           height   => integer,
           inner    => integer,
           outer    => integer,
           fill     => color)
```

Draw a frame around an image of the specified width (left and right borders), height (top and bottom borders), with a three-dimensional inner and outer edge. The geometry specification is a shortcut notation for `'width x height + outer + inner'`. Also see `Border()`.

Gamma()

Gamma correction.

```
$im->Gamma(gamma => double)
$im->Gamma(red   => double,
           green => double,
           blue  => double)
```

Adjust the gamma for the whole image at once, or for each color channel separately. See the color space FAQ [6] for an explanation of gamma.

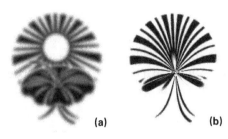

(a) (b)

Figure A.3
The GaussianBlur (a)
and Implode (b) filters.

GaussianBlur()

Apply a gaussian blur filter.

```
$im->GaussianBlur(width    => double,
                  sigma    => double)
$im->GaussianBlur(geometry => geometry)
```

This filter blurs an image by applying a gaussian blur with a width and standard deviation as specified by the parameters `width` and `sigma`. Alternatively, the *geometry* parameter might be used to specify these as a string of the form `"width x sigma"`. Also see `Blur()`.

Get()

Get image attribute values.

```
@values = $im->Get(attribute, attribute, ...)
```

Get the value of an image attribute or multiple attributes. Aliases for this method are: `GetAttribute()`, `GetAttributes()`, and the lowercase variants. See section A.4, on page 246, for a list of attributes and the `Set()` method.

ImageToBlob()

Write an image to a scalar.

```
$image_data = $im->ImageToBlob(arguments)
```

Write the image data to a Perl scalar variable. This can be used to write images to storage media that *Image::Magick* cannot deal with directly, e.g., database fields. Also see `BlobToImage()`. Valid arguments are any settable image attributes. Aliases for this method include: `ImageToBlob()`, `imagetoblob()`, `toblob()`, and `blob()`.

Implode()

Implode or explode an image.

```
$im->Implode(factor => percentage)
```

Implode (factor is positive) or explode (factor is negative) the image pixels toward or away from the center of the image.

Label()

Label an image.

```
$im->Label(label => string)
```

This method assigns a label to an image. Not all image formats will store this. If the first character of the string is @, the label will be read from the file specified by the rest of the string. See page 280 for more on the format of the string. Also see `Comment()`.

Layer()

Extract a layer from an image.

```
$im->Layer(layer => Red, Green, Blue, Matte)
```

This method replaces the current image with a grayscale image that contains the values of the specified channel. This method has been supplanted by `Channel()` in *Image::Magick* version 5.2.9.

Magnify()

Double the image size.

```
$im->Magnify()
```

Also see `Minify()`, `Sample()`, `Scale()`, `Resize()`, and `Transform()`.

Map()

Set the color map for an image.

```
$im->Map(image  => image object,
         dither => boolean)
```

Set the color map of an image to the color map of the image specified by the argument, optionally dithering the result. This can be used to specifically set the color palette of an image, or set of images, to a particular one; for example, the Netscape color palette in use for web browsers. Also see `Quantize()`.

MatteFloodfill()

Make parts of an image transparent.

```
$im->MatteFloodfill(geometry    => geometry,
                    x           => integer,
                    y           => integer,
                    matte       => integer,
                    bordercolor => color)
```

Change the matte value of all neighboring pixels that match the color of the pixel at coordinates (x, y) to the value specified by the matte argument. If the bordercolor argument is present, the color value is changed for any neighboring pixel that is not that border color. Also see `ColorFloodfill()`.

MedianFilter()

Apply a median filter to an image.

```
$im->MedianFilter(radius => integer)
```

Replace each pixel with the median value of the pixels around it. The argument specifies the order of a square convolution kernel.

Minify()

Halve the size of an image.

```
$im->Minify()
```

Also see `Magnify()`, `Sample()`, `Scale()`, `Resize()`, and `Transform()`.

Modulate()

Change HSV values of an image.

```
$im->Modulate(hue        => double,
              saturation => double,
              brightness => double)
$im->Modulate(string)
```

Change the hue, saturation and brightness of an image. Specify the amount you want each parameter changed as a percentage, larger than 100 for an increase, and between 0 and 100 for a decrease. The three parameters can also be specified as a single string. This string should contain the hue, saturation and brightness as comma-separated values in that order. To make an image 20 percent darker, and leave the hue and saturation unchanged, you specify '80,100,10' and to only change the saturation by 30 percent you use '100,100,130'.

Mogrify() and MogrifyRegion()

Apply any operation to an image.

```
$im->Mogrify(method, parameters)
$im->MogrifyRegion(geometry, method, parameters)
```

Apply any of the other discussed methods to an image, or part of an image. This method is really a wrapper that gets used internally by *Image::Magick* to invoke many of the other methods discussed in this section. You should never really need to call `Mogrify()` directly, but `MogrifyRegion()` can be used to achieve effects that cannot be attained otherwise. Suppose you only want to apply the charcoal filter to the left half of an image; for example, to see what the effect will be, you can try the following:

```
my ($w, $h) = $im->Get('width', 'height');
$w /= 2;
$im->MogrifyRegion("${w}x$h+0+0", 'Charcoal', radius => 11);
```

Methods that cannot be called through `Mogrify()` are generally the methods that return another image object, class methods, or methods that affect the number of images in the object: Append(), Average(), BlobToImage(), Coalesce(), Copy(), Display(), Get(), ImageToBlob(), Montage(), Morph(), Ping(), QueryColor(), Read(), Remote(), Set(), Transform(), Write().

Montage()

Create an image which is a composite of two images.

```
$new_image = $im->Montage(background  => color,
                          bordercolor => color,
                          borderwidth => integer,
                          compose     => operator,
                          filename    => file name,
                          fill        => color,
                          font        => font,
                          frame       => geometry,
                          geometry    => geometry,
                          gravity     => gravity,
                          label       => string,
                          mattecolor  => color,
                          mode        => frame option,
                          stroke      => color,
                          pointsize   => integer,
                          shadow      => boolean,
                          texture     => file name,
                          tile        => geometry,
                          title       => string,
                          transparent => color)
```

This is a powerful way to create thumbnail sheets of sets of images. To use it, you first read all the images into an *Image::Magick* object, after which you call the Montage() method with the attributes you wish to apply.

Most arguments are self-explanatory, or are explained in the discussions on the methods to which they apply. For example, for the *frame* attribute, read about Frame(), for *label*, check Label(); and for *compose*, see the section on Composite(). The *mode* attribute is a shortcut parameter for a few others. It specifies the framing mode for the tiles, and should be one of Frame, Unframe or Concatenate. The default is Unframe. The *tile* attribute should be set to a string that contains the number of rows and columns of images that is wanted, e.g., "4x5". The *geometry* parameter specifies the preferred tile size and border widths, for each tile on the sheet.

The images will automatically be scaled to fit the tiles, however, if you don't have a lot of memory, you might want to consider scaling the images to the appropriate size before invoking Montage(). If you have more images than will fit in the rows and columns specified, more than one sheet will be created and the object that is returned will contain multiple images.

Montage() can also be called by the aliases montage() and montageimage().

Morph()

Morph a set of images.

```
$im->Morph(frames => integer)
```

This method will create an animation sequence, filling in *frames* intermediate morphed images between each of the images in $im. Morph() can also be called by its name in lowercase.

 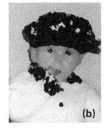 

(a)   (b)   (c)

Figure A.4
The Negate (a),
OilPaint (b) and
Raise (c) filters.

Negate()

Negate an image.

```
$im->Negate(gray => boolean)
```

Each pixel in the image will be replaced by its complementary color, changing an image to its negative. The filter will only apply to grayscale pixels if the argument has a true value.

Normalize()

Normalize an image.

```
$im->Normalize()
```

This filter enhances the appearance and contrast of an image by making sure that its colors span the full possible range of values. See also *Equalize()*.

OilPaint()

Apply an oil paint filter.

```
$im->OilPaint(radius => integer)
```

This filter changes the color of each pixel to the most frequent color inside the radius specified. Unless you have a large image, you probably want to keep the value of *radius* low.

Opaque()

Change a color.

```
$im->Opaque(color => color,
            fill  => color)
```

Change all pixels that have the color specified by *color* to the color specified by *fill*. Also see `ColorFloodfill()`.

Profile()

Manipulate an image profile.

```
$im->Profile(filename => file name,
             profile  => ICM, IPTC)
```

This method allows the addition or removal of an ICM or IPTC profile to an image, which will be loaded from the specified file.

Ping()

Get image information.

```
@img_info = Image::Magick->Ping(file name)
@img_info = Image::Magick->Ping(file => file handle glob)
@img_info = Image::Magick->Ping(blob => image data)
```

This method allows the retrieval of some basic information about an image without having to read in the complete image as an *Image::Magick* object. This information can be obtained from a file name, a file handle or from a blob of image data stored in a scalar. The returned list contains the width, height, size and image format, in that order. Aliases for this method are `ping()` and `pingimage()`.

In older versions of *Image::Magick*, `Ping()` returns a single comma-separated string with the above-mentioned information in the same order.

Quantize()

Set the number of colors in an image.

```
$im->Quantize(colors         => integer,
              colorspace     => color space,
              treedepth      => integer,
              dither         => boolean,
              measure_error  => boolean,
              global_colormap => boolean)
```

The `Quantize()` method sets the number of colors in an image to the number specified by the *colors* attribute. If that number is larger than the actual number, and the color space specified can contain all the current colors, no action is performed. If the number of colors specified is smaller than the current number of colors, the color map will be intelligently resized to the new number. The color space is one of RGB, Gray, Transparent, OHTA, XYZ, YCbCr, YIQ, YPbPr, YUV, or CMYK. If the argument *global_colormap* is set to a true value, then all images in the object will share the same color palette.

If *measure_error* is set to a true value, then the image's *mean*, *normalized_max* and *normalized_mean* attributes will be set to values that can be used to judge how much information was lost.

For a more detailed explanation of color quantization as done by *Image::Magick*, see the documentation.[6] Also see `Map()`.

QueryColor()

Get color information.

```
@colors = Image::Magick->QueryColor()
@color_info = Image::Magick->QueryColor(color specification)
```

This method returns a list of all known color names when called with no arguments, or a list of the red, green, blue and opacity values of the specified color when called with an argument. See the discussion on "Colors" on page 278 for more information.

QueryFont()

Get font information.

```
@fonts = Image::Magick->QueryFont()
@font_info = Image::Magick->QueryFont(font specification)
```

This method returns a list of all known fonts when called with no parameters, and a list of information about a font when called with a font name or specification. The returned list in this case contains the following elements: font name, description, family, style, stretch, weight, encoding, foundry, format, metrics, and glyphs values.

   `QueryFont()` first appeared in *Image::Magick* version 5.3.7.

QueryFontMetrics()

Get information on the size of a text string.

```
@text_info = Image::Magick->QueryFontMetrics(parameters)
```

This method accepts the same parameters as the `Annotate()` method, and can be used to obtain information on a string that you want to draw, without actually drawing it. This allows you to make more informed decisions on where to position the string. `QueryFontMetrics()` returns a list of the following information about the string and font used: character width, character height, ascender, descender, text width, text height and maximum horizontal advance.

   `QueryFontMetrics()` first appeared in *Image::Magick* version 5.2.6.

Raise()

Create a 3D button edge.

```
$im->Raise(geometry => geometry,
           raise    => boolean)
$im->Raise(width    => integer,
           height   => integer,
```

---

[6] ... if you're on Unix, the manual page *quantize(9)*; otherwise, refer to the HTML documentation.

```
x         => integer,
y         => integer,
raise     => boolean)
```

Create a three-dimensional border that makes the image look like it's a button. If *raise* is true, the image will look raised, otherwise it will look sunken. See Frame() for an explanation of the other parameters.

Read()

Read one or more images.

```
$im->Read(file specification)
```

See the discussion on page 242 for more information. This method is also available as read() or readimage().

ReduceNoise()

Reduce noise.

```
$im->ReduceNoise(radius => integer)
```

Reduce noise in an image with a noise peak elimination filter. Also see AddNoise(), Enhance() and Despeckle().

Resize()

Resize an image.

```
$im->Resize(geometry => geometry,
            filter   => filter,
            blur     => double)
$im->Resize(width    => integer,
            height   => integer,
            filter   => filter,
            blur     => double)
```

Resize an image to the size specified by *width* and *height*, or to the more flexible sizing parameters specified with the *geometry* parameter (see "Geometry" on page 277). Optionally apply a filter while doing this. The filter is one of Point, Box, Triangle, Hermite, Hanning, Hamming, Blackman, Gaussian, Quadratic, Cubic, Catrom, Mitchell, Lanczos, Bessel, or Sinc. The *blur* parameter can be larger than 1 for blur, and smaller than 1 for sharpening. Also see Sample(), Scale(), and Transform(). In older versions of *Image::Magick* (before version 5.2.3) this method was called Zoom().

Figure A.5
The Roll (a),
Rotate (b) and
Shade (c) filters.

Roll()

Roll an image.

```
$im->Roll(x          => integer,
          y          => integer)
$im->Roll(geometry => geometry)
```

Move the pixels of an image, wrapping them around the edge of the image. The image will be rolled horizontally by the number of pixels specified by *x* and vertically by the number of pixels specified by *y*. The *geometry* parameter can be used as a shortcut for *x* and *y*.

Rotate()

Rotate an image.

```
$im->Rotate(degrees => double,
            crop    => boolean,
            sharpen => boolean)
```

Rotate an image clockwise by the amount specified by the *degrees* argument, optionally sharpening the resulting image. If *crop* is true, the image will be cropped to its original size, otherwise the resulting size will be as large as is necessary to fit all of the rotated pixels. Any newly created area in the resulting image will be filled with the current background color of the image.

Sample()

Resize an image.

```
$im->Sample(width    => integer,
            height   => integer)
$im->Sample(geometry => geometry)
```

Resize an image, using pixel sampling. This method will not introduce any new colors into the resized image. See the discussion of the geometry parameter on page 277 for a description. Also see `Scale()`, `Resize()`, and `Transform()`.

Scale()

Resize an image.

```
$im->Scale(width   => integer,
           height  => integer)
$im->Scale(geometry => geometry)
```

The first version scales the image so that width and height become exactly the specified number of pixels. If either of the two is unspecified, the current size is used. The second form uses the full flexibility of the geometry parameter as discussed on page 277. Also see `Sample()`, `Resize()`, and `Transform()`.

Segment()

Segment an image.

```
$im->Segment(colorspace => color space,
             verbose    => boolean,
             cluster    => double,
             smooth     => double)
```

Segment an image by analyzing the histograms of the color channels and identifying units that are homogeneous.

The *cluster* threshold specifies the minimum number of pixels considered to be a valid cluster. The *smooth* parameter controls the amount of noise allowed to exist in the histogram's derivatives (default 1.5). The color space is one of RGB, Gray, Transparent, OHTA, XYZ, YCbCr, YCC, YIQ, YPbPr, YUV, or CMYK. For more information, please read the documentation for the command line tool *convert*, section *Image Segmentation*.

Set()

Set image attribute values.

```
$im->Set(attribute => value, attribute => value, ...)
```

Set the value of an image attribute or multiple attributes. Aliases for this method are: `SetAttribute()`, `SetAttributes()`, and the lowercase variants. See section A.4 for a list of attributes and `Get()`.

(a)

(b)

Figure A.6
The Shear (a) and
Solarize (b) filters.

Shade()

Apply a shading filter.

```
$im->Shade(geometry  => geometry,
           color     => boolean)
$im->Shade(azimuth   => double,
           elevation => double,
           color     => boolean)
```

The image will be taken as a relief map, and shaded as if a distant light were aimed at it. Under normal circumstances this will result in a grayscale image, but if the parameter *color* has a true value, the resulting image will preserve some of the original coloring. The *geometry* parameter can be used as a shortcut for *azimuth* and *elevation*. Also see `Emboss()`.

Sharpen()

Sharpen an image.

```
$im->Sharpen(radius => integer)
```

Apply a convolution kernel to sharpen an image. Also see `UnsharpMask()` and `Convolve()`.

Shear()

Shear an image.

```
$im->Shear(geometry => geometry,
           crop     => boolean)
$im->Shear(x        => double,
           y        => double,
           crop     => boolean)
```

Shear an image along the *x* or *y* axis, by the number of degrees specified. If *crop* is true, the image will be cropped to its original size; otherwise the resulting size will be as large as is necessary to fit all of the pixels. Any newly created area in the resulting image will be filled with the current background color of the image. The *geometry* parameter can be used as a shortcut for the *x* and *y* parameters.

Signature()

Generate a signature for an image.

```
$im->Signature()
```

This method generates a signature for an image which can be used to verify the data integrity of the image after it has been stored on disk or transported elsewhere. This signature is stored in the image file, whenever the format allows it. In older versions of *Image::Magick*, the signature was an MD5 sum, but in later versions an SHA1-256 signature is generated.

Solarize()

Solarize an image.

```
$im->Solarize(factor => percentage)
```

Apply a solarization filter to an image, which negates all pixels above the specified threshold. This produces a similar effect to exposing a photographic film to light during the development process.

**Figure A.7
The Spread (a),
Swirl (b) and
Wave (c) filters.**

Spread()

Spread pixels in an image.

```
$im->Spread(amount => integer)
```

Randomly displace pixels in an image by (up to) the specified *amount*.

Stereo()

Create a stereographic image from two images.

```
$im->Stereo(image => image object)
```

This method takes two images (the image operated on, and the one specified as the argument), and produces a single stereographic image (stereo anaglyph). The left side is saved as the red channel and the right side as the green channel. You'll need the proper type of stereo glasses to view the image.

Stegano()

Hide one image in another.

```
$im->Stegano(image  => image object,
             offset => integer)
```

This method invisibly hides (a grayscale version of) the image specified as the argument in the current image. See "Hiding information in an image" on page 150 for an example.

Swirl()

Swirl an image about the center.

```
$im->Swirl(degrees => double)
```

Swirls an image's pixels about the center by the number of degrees specified.

Texture()

Add a texture to an image.

```
$im->Texture(image => image object)
```

The image specified will be used as a tile on the background of the current image, instead of the background color.

Threshold()

Apply a threshold filter.

```
$im->Threshold(threshold => integer)
```

This method applies a threshold filter to the image, which results in an image with only two colors. Any pixel that falls above the threshold value will be set to the highest intensity value in the image, and the others will be set to the lowest.

Transform()

Scale or crop an image, applying a sharpening filter.

```
$new_im = $im->Transform(geometry => geometry,
                         crop     => geometry,
                         filter   => filter)
```

This method scales and crops the image according to the geometry specification (see page 277). The *filter* argument indicates an interpolation algorithm, and is one of Point, Box, Triangle, Hermite, Hanning, Hamming, Blackman, Gaussian, Quadratic, Cubic, Catrom, Mitchell, Lanczos, Bessel, or Sinc. If *filter* is unspecified, Lanczos will be used. Using `Transform()` instead of `Scale()` will often yield a better result, especially when scaling to a larger size. Also see `Crop()`, `Scale()`, and `Resize()`.

Transparent()

Make a color transparent in an image.

```
$im->Transparent(color => color)
```

This method marks all the pixels that have the specified color as fully transparent. Also see `MatteFloodfill()` and `Draw()` with the `matte` primitive.

Trim()

Trim edges from an image.

```
$im->Trim()
```

A call to this method will remove any background color pixels at the edges of the image.

UnsharpMask()

Sharpen an image.

```
$im->UnsharpMask(geometry  => geometry,
                 amount    => double,
                 threshold => double)

$im->UnsharpMask(radius    => double,
                 sigma     => double,
                 amount    => double,
                 threshold => double)
```

Sharpen an image using the unsharp mask algorithm. The geometry parameter is a shortcut for radius and sigma. Also see `Sharpen()`.

Wave()

Apply a sine wave filter to an image.

```
$im->Wave(amplitude  => double,
          wavelength => double)
$im->Wave(geometry   => geometry)
```

Displace the pixels in an image according to the sine specified by amplitude and wavelength. The parameter geometry can be specified as a shortcut for *amplitude* and *wavelength*.

Write()

Write an image to disk.

```
$im->Write(file specification)
```

`Write()` takes any arguments that are settable image attributes. See the discussion on page 244 for more information. `Write()` can also be called with its lowercase name.

Zoom()

This is an alias for `Resize()`

```
$im->Zoom(geometry => geometry,
          filter   => filter,
          blur     => double)
$im->Zoom(width    => integer,
          height   => integer,
          filter   => filter,
          blur     => double)
```

A.6 COMMON METHOD ARGUMENTS

Many *Image::Magick* methods take arguments with the same name, and often the same meaning. This section explains the arguments and values for these arguments, common to many of these methods.

Geometry

Many operations on *Image::Magick* objects take a geometry parameter. Depending on the operation you are performing, various parts of the geometry specification are important or useful. For many methods a geometry parameter can be specified that really has nothing to do with a geometry per se, but is merely a convenient shorthand for other parameters. We will not discuss that category elaborately here; instead, see the entries for the various methods for the possible interpretations of this argument.

The geometry specification for *Image::Magick* is derived from the standard X windows geometry specification, but has some extras beyond that. A full specification can be found in the documentation for the command-line tool *convert*:

```
<width>x<height>{+-}<x offset>{+-}<y offset>{%}{!}{<}{>}
```

The interpretation of these values specified depends partly on the operation in effect.

The width and height are normally maximum values, and the aspect ratio of the image will be maintained within these constraints. If only the width is specified, the height assumes the same value as the width. To scale an image to 300x300 pixels, the following are equivalent:

```
$im->Scale(geometry => '300');
$im->Scale(geometry => '300x300');
```

The *x* and *y* offsets should only be specified when needed. For example, to crop a 50 by 35 pixel area at horizontal and vertical offsets of 10 and 20:

```
$im->Crop(geometry => '50x35+10+20');
```

The offset parameters normally have the effect you would expect, but in some methods they take on a slightly different meaning. For example, in the `Frame()` method the offset parameters are used to specify the width of the inner and outer bevels on the border, and the width and height of the geometry string specify the width of the vertical and the height of the horizontal borders, respectively. To draw a border around an image, 12 pixels wide on the left and right, 10 pixels on top and bottom, and with a 3 pixel outer bevel and a 4 pixel inner bevel, the following specification should be used:

```
$im->Frame(geometry => "12x10+3+4");
```

If the current aspect ratio does not need to be preserved, but the size has to become exactly what is specified, an exclamation mark can be used in the specification:

```
$im->Scale(geometry => '300x300!');
```

You can also use relative sizes with the percent sign:

```
$im->Scale(geometry => '120%');
$im->Scale(geometry => '120%x150%'); # or 120x150%
```

The left and right angle brackets are conditional operators for the geometry specification. If the specification ends in a left angle bracket, the resizing will be done only if the current dimensions are less than the ones specified. The right angle bracket means that resizing only happens when the current dimensions are larger than the specified ones.

```
# resize only if smaller than 320x200
$im->Scale(geometry => '320x200<');

# resize only if larger than than 640x480
$im->Scale(geometry => '640x480>');

# resize to exactly 800x600, only if currently smaller
$im->Scale(geometry => '800x600<!');
```

Fonts

Image::Magick can work with various font sources:

- *An X font specification.* ("-*-times-medium-r-*-*-12-*-*-*-p-*-*-*") when working on a platform with an X server,

- *a path to a TrueType font file, preceded by @.* ("@/usr/share/fonts/Arial.ttf") if the FreeType library has been linked in, or

- *a PostScript font name ("Helvetica").* in the presence of Ghostscript.

In the latter two cases the attribute *pointsize* can be used to control the size of the characters. To specify a search path for TrueType font files in versions prior to 5.4.3, you can set the environment variable TTF_FONT_PATH to a colon-separated list of directories to search. In later versions you can specify a single search directory in the environment variable MAGICK_FONT_PATH (although this has not always been successful for me). In all versions you can specify a search path when compiling ImageMagick.

Colors

Colors in *Image::Magick* can be specified in several ways. The first is by using an X11 color name. There is a list of color names compiled in,[7] and the local X11 server will be consulted, or a database on disk will be read if there is no X server available. X11 color names are more or less standardized, and have names such as red, green, blue, orange, Blanched Almond, gray74, LavenderBlush2 or burlywood1. To see a full list of the colors your X server knows of, use the showrgb command. For the more exotic colors it is probably more convenient to use a numerical specification. The special color name *none* can be used to set a fully transparent color with RGB values of (0,0,0). To create a fully transparent canvas on which you may draw, use something akin to the following:

---

[7] There might be some variation in what *Image::Magick* thinks a color should look like, and what your X system thinks. For example, the color with the name *green* is different in version 5.2.6 (0,0.5,0) from the more common notion (0,1,0), which was also used in version 5.2.5 and before. From version 5.2.6 onwards, *Image::Magick* uses the color names as they are defined by the SVG and HTML specifications, instead of the X specification. To prevent these confusions, it is probably better to specify colors numerically.

```
$im = Image::Magick->new(size => '300x200');
$rc = $im->Read('xc:none');
die $rc if $rc;
$rc = $im->Set(matte => 1);
warn $rc if $rc;
```

The second way to assign a color is by using the same sort of color specification as is common in HTML: a hash mark followed by a set of hexadecimal numbers; one for each of the color components. *Image::Magick* is a bit more flexible than HTML in this regard. Whereas a color specification in HTML requires three color components to be specified as a two-character hexadecimal value between 00 and FF, *Image::Magick*'s colors can be given in the form of any of the following strings:

```
#RGB
#RRGGBB
#RRRGGGBBB
#RRRRGGGGBBBB
#RGBA
#RRGGBBAA
#RRRRGGGGBBBBAAAA
```

where R, G, and B are placeholders for the red, green and blue components of the color, given as a hexadecimal value, and A is a placeholder for the opacity (or alpha) value.[8] *Image::Magick* can be compiled to support 8-bit or 16-bit colors. Whichever you chose when you installed the package, the color specifications given above will all be scaled appropriately for the color precision in use.

NOTE   When ImageMagick (version 5.4.4) is compiled for 16-bit pixels, the color RGB values returned for a `Get("pixel[x,y]")` request are not always correct, or at least they can be unexpected. For example, if you set the color to `#3c7f2b`, you will read out the color `#3c3c7f7f2b2b`, instead of the more intuitive `#3c007f002b00`. However, if you set the color to the same value above, and then read that value from a pixel that is using 16-bit pixels (instead of the 8 assumed above), the color returned is the more intuitive one. This behavior is probably a bug, since it is inconsistent, and will hopefully be fixed in a future release.

A third way in which colors might be specified is with a string of the form `rgb(R,G,B)` or `rgb(R G B)` in which the R, G and B are decimal numbers denoting the components of the color. The first three characters (rgb) of the string are case insensitive.

Here are some examples of valid color specifications:

```
$im->Set(stroke      => 'red',
         bordercolor => '#3f4ce5',
         mattecolor  => 'rgb(127,12,213)',
         fill        => '#e3ff4ce5a34f',
         background  => 'RGB(255 255 127)',
```

---

[8]   Note the absence of the string #RRRGGGBBBAAA from the list.

As a special case, the `pixel[x,y]` argument to the `Set()` method accepts a string of four comma-separated decimal values, to match the output of the `Get()` method. This allows one to do the following:

```
$im1->Set("pixel[$x1,$y1]" => $im2->Get("pixel[$x2,$y2]"));
```

without having to convert from or to the different formats. A side effect of this is that you cannot use the `rgb(R,G,B)` specification as the value to a `pixel[x,y]` argument, although you still can use `rgb(R G B)`.

Versions of *Image::Magick* before 5.2.5 could also return a color name as the result of `$im->Get("pixel[$x,$y]")`. This introduces the need to resolve the color name to a comma-separated string with `QueryColor()`. If you still have an older version around, you might like to use this subroutine instead of the direct call to `split()` in the above code:

```
sub IMget_color
{
    my $im = shift;
    my ($x, $y) = @_;
    my $color = $im->Get("pixel[$x,$y]");
    $color = Image::Magick->QueryColor($color)
        unless $color =~ /\d+,\d+,\d+/;
    return split /,/, $color;
}
```

and call it this way:

```
my $im = Image::Magick->new();
# Time passes ...
my ($r, $g, $b, $o) = IMget_color($im, $x, $y);
```

String formatting

Some *Image::Magick* methods accept an argument that requires a string, which can contain escapes that will be replaced by information about the image before they are rendered (see, for example, `Comment()` and the text argument to `Annotate()`). The most important escapes are:

- `%b`—the file size in bytes
- `%d`—the directory that contains the image
- `%e`—the file name extension of the image
- `%f`—the file name of the image
- `%w`—the image width
- `%h`—the image height
- `%m`—the image format (the value of the *Magick* attribute)
- `%s`—the scene number of the image
- `%t`—the file name of the image, without extension.

See the *Image::Magick* HTML documentation or the manual page for the command line tool `convert` for a more complete list.

Gravity

The direction in which an object gravitates. One of NorthWest, North, NorthEast, West, Center, East, SouthWest, South, or SouthEast. The default is NorthWest.

A.7   THE PATH DRAWING PRIMITIVE

Versions of *Image::Magick* more recent than 5.2.4 can draw paths, as specified by the Scalable Vector Graphics format. This section provides a short description of what these paths are, and how to use them. For an in-depth discussion, please see the on-line documentation of the SVG format at http://www.w3c.org/Graphics/SVG/ or *Definitive SVG* by Kelvin Lawrence, et al. [16].

Paths are built up of a set of simple commands or instructions that draw the outline of a shape. This is done in the way that turtle programs often work: a pen is moved, drawing the outline of a shape.

Almost all of the other drawing primitives can be drawn with a path, but it's probably best to use the most fitting primitive when appropriate.

A path can be built up from multiple subpaths, each starting with a *moveto* command. All commands are expressed as a single character, followed by the coordinates and other data needed for the particular movement. The notation of a string of commands is fairly free-form, e.g., much of the spacing is optional, embedded new lines are allowed, and spaces between coordinates can be replaced by a comma. For many of the commands, multiple coordinate sets can be specified without repeating the command letter. The following are all valid and equivalent:

```
M 100,100 L 200,100 L 300,200
M 100 100 L 200 100 L 300 200
M 100 100 L 200 100 300 200
M100,100L200,100L300,200
```

The reason for this flexibility is that this notation is inherited from the SVG format, and for that format it is important to save space, and to end up with files as small as possible. When you specify paths in your *Image::Magick* programs, you probably should code for clarity rather than conciseness.

Each command has a version that works with absolute coordinates (expressed as an uppercase letter) and a version that works with coordinates relative to the current pen position (expressed as the same letter in lower case). If a relative command is used, the coordinates can be negative, to indicate a different direction. Positive relative coordinates move the pen right and downward, while negative coordinates move left and upward.

moveto

This starts a new subpath, and locates the pen at the given coordinates. No line will be drawn from the current point (if there is one) to the specified coordinates. A path always starts with a `moveto` command or an `arc` command.

M x,y moves to the coordinates specified by *x* and *y*; while *m x,y* moves *x* pixels to the right, and *y* down. If *m* is the first command, then it is treated as if *M* were specified.

lineto

Draw a straight line. The end point of the line becomes the new current point.

L x,y and *l x,y* draw a line from the current point to the point specified by *x* and *y*, or from the current point to the location, x pixels to the right, and y down.

H x and *h x* draw a horizontal line to the specified *x* coordinate, or horizontally *x* pixels away.

V y and *v y* draw a vertical line to the specified y coordinate, or vertically *y* pixels away.

closepath

Close the current path by drawing a line from the current point to the starting point of the current path. The commands to do this are *Z* or *z*, both with the same effect.

bezier curve

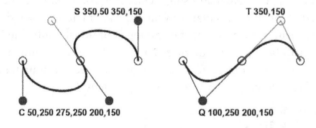

S 350,50 350,150

T 350,150

C 50,250 275,250 200,150

Q 100,250 200,150

Figure A.8
A cubic and a quadratic bezier curve, with their control points. Each curve consists of two parts, where the second part uses the mirrored control point of the previous curve.

Draw a bezier curve. It is possible to draw cubic and quadratic bezier curves in several ways.

C x1,y1 x2,y2 x,y and *c x1,y1 x2,y2 x,y* draw a cubic bezier curve from the current point to *x,y*. The coordinates *x1,y1* and *x2,y2* specify the control points at the current point and the end point, respectively.

S x2,y2 x,y and *s x2,y2 x,y* are shorthand for *C* and *c*. The coordinates of the first control point, *x1,y1*, are assumed to be the reflection of the second control point of the previous command. If the previous command had no control point, then it is assumed to be the current point.

Q x1,y1 x,y and *q x1,y1 x,y* draw a quadratic bezier curve from the current point to *x,y*. The control point is specified by *x1,y1*.

T x,y and *t x,y* are shorthand for *Q* and *q*. The control point of this curve is assumed to be the reflection of the control point of the previous command. Again, if there is no previous control point, it is assumed to coincide with the current point.

arc

Draw an arc, part of an ellipse or circle, with the commands *A* or *a*. Both these commands take a rather large list of arguments: *rx,ry x-axis-rotation large-arc-flag sweep-flag x,y*. The command will draw an arc through the current point and the point indicated by *x,y*. The center of the arc will be calculated from the other arguments given; *rx,ry* are the radii of the two axes of the ellipse.

x-axis-rotation expresses the number of degrees that the ellipse will be rotated.

large-arc-flag and sweep-flag are used to determine in which direction the arc should be drawn.

x,y is the second point through which to draw this arc. The first point is the current location.

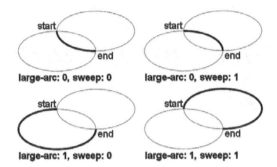

Figure A.9
The effect of the *large-arc* and *sweep* flags for the arc commands.

If only the current point, the radii and the destination point are given, there are still (generally) four possible ways to draw an arc. The *large-arc-flag* and *sweep-flag* arguments determine which of these four will be chosen. There are four different possibilities because two different ellipses can be drawn, and on these two ellipses, the short path around can be chosen, or the long one. When the *large-arc* flag is 1, the larger of two possible paths will be chosen, and when the *sweep* flag is 1, the arc is drawn in the clockwise direction. Figure A.9 shows the effect of these two flags.

Color space conversion algorithms

This appendix shows the implementation of various algorithms for the conversion of colors between some color spaces. For more information on color spaces and their relation, see section 1.3, "Color spaces and palettes," on page 7.

B.1   RGB TO HSV

The value component of HSV is defined as max(R,G,B), and saturation is simply [max(R,G,B) - min(R,G,B)]/max(R,G,B). Both are easy to compute. Where the conversion becomes nonlinear is the determination of the hue component. Its computation depends on which of the three RGB components is the largest:

```
sub max
{
    my $max = shift;
    for (@_) { $max = $_ if $max < $_ }
    return $max
}
sub min
```

```
{
    my $min = shift;
    for (@_) { $min = $_ if $min > $_ }
    return $min
}

sub rgb_to_hsv
{
    my ($r, $g, $b) = @_;
    my ($h, $s, $v);

    my $max = max($r, $g, $b);
    my $min = min($r, $g, $b);
    $v = $max;
    $s = ($max) ? ($max - $min)/$max : 0;

    return (0, $s, $v) if $s == 0;

    if ($r == $max)
    {
        $h = ($g - $b)/($max - $min);
    }
    elsif ($g == $max)
    {
        $h = 2 + ($b - $r)/($max - $min);
    }
    else # ($b == $max)
    {
        $h = 4 + ($r - $g)/($max - $min);
    }
    $h *= 60;
    $h += 360 if $h < 0;

    return ($h, $s, $v);
}
```

The last two statements adjust the hue to a value between 0 and 360, so that it is expressed as *degrees on the color circle* instead of a number between 0 and 6.

B.2 HSV TO RGB

Conversion back from HSV to RGB may look quite complex but isn't really that difficult to follow.

```
sub hsv_to_rgb
{
    my ($h, $s, $v) = @_;

    return ($v, $v, $v) if $s == 0;

    $h = 0 if $h == 360;
    $h /= 60;
    my $f = $h - int($h);
    my $p = $v * (1 - $s);
    my $q = $v * (1 - $s * $f);
```

```
my $t = $v * (1 - $s * (1 - $f));

for my $sw (int($h))
{
    ($sw == 0) && return ($v, $t, $p);
    ($sw == 1) && return ($q, $v, $p);
    ($sw == 2) && return ($p, $v, $t);
    ($sw == 3) && return ($p, $q, $v);
    ($sw == 4) && return ($t, $p, $v);
    ($sw == 5) && return ($v, $p, $q);
}
}
```

As a first shortcut, we can safely return a grayscale point if the saturation is 0. If it isn't, the hue is recalculated (from degrees) to indicate into which of the six 60 degree arcs of the color circle the color falls. Then $f (for fraction) is calculated, which expresses the position of the color *inside* this particular arc, and int($h) tells us which of the six arcs is involved. Three values are calculated that can be used to express parts of the coordinates in RGB space. To determine which part they represent, we need to know which of the six arcs the color falls in. The for statement takes care of that.

B.3 RGB TO HLS

Conversion of RGB to HLS is similar, but not entirely identical to conversion to HSV space.

```
sub rgb_to_hls
{
    my ($r, $g, $b) = @_;
    my ($h, $l, $s);

    my $max = max($r, $g, $b);
    my $min = min($r, $g, $b);
    $l = ($max + $min)/2;

    return (0, $l, 0) if ($max == $min);

    $s = ($l < 0.5) ?
            ($max - $min)/($max + $min) :
            ($max - $min)/(2 - $max - $min);

    if ($r == $max)
    {
        $h = ($g - $b)/($max - $min);
    }
    elsif ($g == $max)
    {
        $h = 2 + ($b - $r)/($max - $min);
    }
    else # ($b == $max)
    {
```

```
        $h = 4 + ($r - $g)/($max - $min);
    }
    $h *= 60;
    $h += 360 if $h < 0;

    return ($h, $l, $s);
}
```

Lightness is defined as $[\max(R,G,B) + \min(R,G,B)]/2$, and is calculated first, closely followed by the calculation of the saturation, which in this color model depends on the value of the lightness. The calculation of hue is identical to the RGB to HSV conversion method.

B.4 HLS TO RGB

The conversion back to RGB can be implemented with the following two subroutines:

```
sub hls_value
{
    my ($q1, $q2, $h) = @_;

    $h -= 360 if ($h > 360);
    $h += 360 if ($h < 0);

    ($h < 60)  && return $q1 + ($q2 - $q1) * $h/60;
    ($h < 180) && return $q2;
    ($h < 240) && return $q1 + ($q2 - $q1) * (240 - $h)/60;
    return $q1;
}

sub hls_to_rgb
{
    my ($h, $l, $s) = @_;
    my ($p1, $p2);

    return ($l, $l, $l) if $s == 0;

    $p2 = ($l < 0.5) ?
            $l * (1 + $s) :
            $l + $s - ($l * $s);
    $p1 = 2 * $l - $p2;

    return (hls_value($p1, $p2, $h + 120),
            hls_value($p1, $p2, $h),
            hls_value($p1, $p2, $h - 120));
}
```

APPENDIX C

Module code

This appendix contains example module code that was referred to, but not covered, in chapter 10.

C.1 CANVAS::POLAR::SVG

Canvas::Polar::SVG is a driver for the Scalable Vector Graphics format (SVG, see http://www.w3.org/Graphics/SVG/).

```
package Canvas::Polar::SVG;
use XML::Grove;
use XML::Grove::AsCanonXML;
use Coordinate;
use strict;

sub new
{
    my $proto = shift;
    my $class = ref($proto) || $proto;
    my ($width, $height, $bgcolor) = @_;

    my $self = {};
    $self->{canvas} = XML::Grove::Element->new(
        Name        => 'svg',
```

```perl
                    Attributes => {width => $width,
                                   height => $height});

        bless $self, $class;
}

sub line
{
        my $self = shift;
        my ($r1, $r2, $angle, $color, $width) = @_;
        my ($x1, $y1) = map int, polar2cart($r1, $angle);
        my ($x2, $y2) = map int, polar2cart($r2, $angle);

        my $style = "stroke:$color";
        $style .= "; stroke-width:$width" if $width;

        push @{$self->{canvas}->{Contents}},
            XML::Grove::Element->new(
                Name       => 'line',
                Attributes => {x1      => $x1, y1 => $y1,
                               x2      => $x2, y2 => $y2,
                               style => $style}
            );
}

sub fill_circle
{
        my $self = shift;
        my ($radius, $color) = @_;
        my ($cx, $cy) = get_origin();

        push @{$self->{canvas}->{Contents}},
            XML::Grove::Element->new(
                Name       => 'circle',
                Attributes => {r       => $radius,
                               cx      => $cx,
                               cy      => $cy,
                               style => "fill:$color;stroke:$color"}
            );
}

sub svg
{
        my $self = shift;
        $self->{canvas}->as_canon_xml;
}
1;
```

The module creates an SVG fragment that can either be used stand-alone, or as part of a larger SVG document. The program that produced figure C.1a is:

```perl
use Clock;
use Canvas::Polar::SVG;

my $canvas = Canvas::Polar::SVG->new(121, 121, '#ffffff');
```

```perl
my $clock = Clock->new(
    radius       => 60,
    hand_color   => '#000000',
    face_color   => '#dfdfdf',
    marker_color => '#00007f',
    center_color => '#ff0000',
);
$clock->draw($canvas, 60, 60);

open(OUT, ">SVGclock.svg") or die $!;
print OUT $canvas->svg;
close(OUT);
```

Now all you need to do is to find a good rendering engine for SVG, and you can enjoy the way it looks. The clock in figure C.1(a) was rendered by Image::Magick to an image. It would look a lot better if it was rendered at much higher resolution.

(a)   (b)

Figure C.1
The clock from section 10.2, drawn with the *Canvas::Polar::SVG* and *Canvas::Polar::PostScript* modules.

C.2   *CANVAS::POLAR::POSTSCRIPT*

This section shows a driver module for the clock examples of chapter 10.

```perl
package Canvas::Polar::PostScript;
use Coordinate;
use strict;

my $RES = 1.0;

sub new
{
    my $proto = shift;
    my $class = ref($proto) || $proto;
    my ($width, $height, $bgcolor) = @_;
    my $self = { res => $RES, canvas => "" };
    bless $self, $class;
}

sub set_resolution
{
    my $proto = shift;
    my $res   = shift or return;
    (ref $proto ? $proto->{res} : $RES) = $res;
}

sub _add_commands
{
```

APPENDIX C   MODULE CODE

```perl
    my $self = shift;
    local $" = "\n";
    $self->{canvas} .= "@_\n";
}

sub _ps_color
{
    my @rgb = map {hex($_)/255}
                unpack "x a2 a2 a2", shift;
    wantarray ? @rgb : join(' ', @rgb);
}

sub line
{
    my $self = shift;
    my ($r1, $r2, $angle, $color, $width) = @_;
    my ($x1, $y1) =
        map int, polar2cart($r1, 2 * PI - $angle);
    my ($x2, $y2) =
        map int, polar2cart($r2, 2 * PI - $angle);

    $self->_add_commands(
        "$x1 $y1 moveto",
        "$x2 $y2 lineto",
        "currentlinewidth",
        ($width ? "$width setlinewidth" : ()),
        _ps_color($color) . " setrgbcolor",
        "stroke",
        "setlinewidth",
    );
}

sub fill_circle
{
    my $self = shift;
    my ($radius, $color) = @_;
    my ($xc, $yc) = get_origin();

    $self->_add_commands(
        "$xc $yc $radius 0 360 arc",
        _ps_color($color) . " setrgbcolor",
        "fill",
    );
}

sub postscript
{
    my $self = shift;
    my $x = shift || 0;
    my $y = shift || 0;
    return <<EOPS;
gsave
$self->{res} $self->{res} scale
$x $y translate
```

```
$self->{canvas}
grestore
EOPS
}

1;
```

The module exports a PostScript fragment that should be included in another document, or encapsulated. The program that produced figure C.1b just creates an encapsulated PostScript file from the output of *Canvas::Polar::PostScript* by adding the appropriate header and trailer information:

```
use Clock;
use Canvas::Polar::PostScript;

my $canvas = Canvas::Polar::PostScript->new(121, 121, '#ffffff');

my $clock = Clock->new(
    radius        => 60,
    hand_color    => '#000000',
    face_color    => '#dfdfdf',
    marker_color  => '#00007f',
    center_color  => '#ff0000',
);
 $clock->draw($canvas, 60, 60);

my $c_date = localtime;

open(OUT, ">PSclock.eps") or die $!;
print OUT <<EOPSH;
%!PS-Adobe-3.0 EPSF-3.0
%%BoundingBox: 0 0 120 120
%%Creator: ($0)
%%Title: (PSclock.eps)
%%CreationDate: ($c_date)
%%LanguageLevel: 2
%%EndComments

@{ [$canvas->postscript] }

%%Trailer
%%EOF
EOPSH
close(OUT);
```

The PostScript output of this module is quite naive, and doesn't make use of the full functionality of PostScript. If this module were destined to be taken up in production, it would probably have a class method that would generate PostScript for the prologue defining a few named procedures that map exactly to the objects that you need to draw. Then, when the time comes to draw them, all you need to do is print the parameters, and the name of the defined procedure. This makes the module slightly easier to read, but more importantly, it makes your PostScript file much smaller.

references

[1]   Shawn P. Wallace. *Programming Web Graphics with Perl and GNU Software*. O'Reilly & Associates, Inc., first edition, March 1999.

[2]   Larry Wall, Tom Christiansen, and Jon Orwant. *Programming Perl*. O'Reilly & Associates, Inc., third edition, July 2000.

[3]   Andrew L. Johnson. *Elements of Programming with Perl*. Manning Publications Co., October 1999.

[4]   Randal L. Schwartz and Tom Christiansen. *Learning Perl*. O'Reilly & Associates, Inc., second edition, July 1997.

[5]   Ray Kurzweil. *The Age of Spiritual Machines*. Penguin USA, January 2000.

[6]   David Bourgin. The color space FAQ. http://www.neuro.sfc.keio.ac.jp/~aly/polygon/info/color-space-faq.html or news:comp.graphics.

[7]   Charles Poynton. The color FAQ. http://www.inforamp.net/~poynton/ColorFAQ.html.

[8]   CICA graphics list image file formats. http://www.cica.indiana.edu/graphics/image.formats.html.

[9]   NCSA FTP directory of graphics formats. ftp://ftp.ncsa.uiuc.edu/misc/file.formats/graphics.formats/.

[10] Computer graphics on the net. http://ls7-www.cs.uni-dortmund.de/html/englisch/servers.html/.

[11] James D. Murray. The graphics file format FAQ. http://www.dcs.ed.ac.uk/~mxr/gfx/faqs/FileFormats.faq.

[12] Martin Reddy. The graphics file format page. http://www.dcs.ed.ac.uk/~mxr/gfx/.

[13] Paul Oliver. The programmer's file format collection. http://www.wotsit.org/.

[14] Greg Roelofs. PNG (Portable Network Graphics) home site. http://www.cdrom.com/pub/png/.

[15] Greg Roelofs and Glenn Randers-Pehrson. MNG (Multi-image Network Graphics) home page. http://www.cdrom.com/pub/mng/.

[16] Kelvin Lawrence, Philip Mansfield and Darryl Fuller. *Definitive SVG*. Manning Publications Co., to be published Winter 2002.

[17] John Cristy. The ImageMagick home page. http://www.imagemagick.org/.

[18] The Gnuplot home page. http://www.cs.dartmouth.edu/gnuplot_info.html.

[19] Peter Mattis and Spencer Kimball. The GIMP home page. http://www.gimp.org/.

[20] Tim Pearson. Pgplot graphics subroutine library. http://astro.caltech.edu/~tjp/pgplot/.

[21] Adobe Systems Incorporated. *PostScript(R) Language Reference*. Addison-Wesley Publishing Company, third edition, February 1999.

[22] World Wide Web Consortium. W3C scalable vector graphics (SVG). http://www.w3.org/Graphics/SVG/.

[23] Carey Bunks. *Grokking the Gimp*. New Riders Publishing, first edition, February 2000. Also see http://gimp-savvy.com/.

[24] Mark Segal and Kurt Akeley. The OpenGL specification 1.2. ftp://ftp.sgi.com/opengl/doc/opengl1.2/opengl1.2.1.pdf.

[25] "The OpenGL API specifications." http://www.opengl.org/developers/documentation/specs.html.

[26] Mason Woo, Jackie Neider, Tom Davis, and Dave Shreiner. *OpenGL programming guide; The Official Guide to Learning OpenGL, Version 1.2*. Addison-Wesley Publishing Company, third edition, August 1999.

[27] Dave Shreiner(Editor) and Opengl Architecture Review Board. *OpenGL reference manual; The Official Reference Document to OpenGL, Version 1.2*. Addison-Wesley Publishing Company, third edition, December 1999.

[28] Steve Upstill. *The RenderMan Companion*. Addison-Wesley Publishing Company, July 1989.

[29] Anthony A. Apodaca and Larry Gritz. *Advanced RenderMan: Creating CGI for Motion Pictures*. Morgan Kaufmann Publishers, December 1999.

[30] "The RenderMan interface specification." http://www.pixar.com/products/renderman/toolkit/RISpec/.

[31] "The RenderMan FAQ." http://www.faqs.org/faqs/graphics/renderman-faq/.

[32] Damian Conway. *Object Oriented Perl*. Manning Publications Co., August 1999.

[33] Simon Cozens and Tim Jenness. *Extending and Embedding Perl*. Manning Publications Co., July 2002.

[34] Tom Christiansen and Nathan Torkington. *Perl Cookbook*. O'Reilly & Associates, Inc., first (minor corrections) edition, September 1998.

index

Colophon

This book was written with the use of LaTeX, vim, GNU make, Ghostscript, and other standard open source tools running on Linux and Solaris

All vector illustrations presented within the chapters of this book were created with tgif

All images were created with the Gimp, ImageMagick, BMRT and the Perl modules and programs presented

Final typesetting was done in Adobe FrameMaker